The culture industry

A leading member of the 'Frankfurt School' of social theory, Theodor W. Adorno is one of the towering intellectual figures of the twentieth century. His account of the modern mass culture industry is one of the cornerstones of his critical theory of society; and it has recently come back into prominence as one of the central theoretical targets of postmodernism.

This volume collects together for the first time Adorno's essential essays on the culture industry, both in general and on particular arts and media, especially music, film and television. Included are two previously untranslated pieces, 'Free Time' and 'The Schema of Mass Culture', one of Adorno's most challenging essays in this field. In the Introduction J.M. Bernstein explains the importance of Adorno's thinking for the postmodernist debate raging today and provides a defence of Adorno against his postmodernist critics.

An ideal introduction to Adorno's thought on culture, *The Culture Industry* is full of his dazzling and unparalleled insights. It will be essential reading for students of sociology, cultural studies and philosophy.

J.M. Bernstein is Reader and Head of the Department of Philosophy, University of Essex.

The culture industry
Selected essays on mass culture

Theodor W. Adorno

Edited with an Introduction by J.M. Bernstein

ROUTLEDGE

First published 1991
by Routledge
11 New Fetter Lane, London EC4P 4EE

Reprinted 1992, 1993, 1996

Routledge is an International Thomson Publishing company

Typeset in Times by NWL Editorial Services, Langport, Somerset
Printed and bound in Great Britain by
Mackays of Chatham PLC, Chatham, Kent

British Library Cataloguing in Publication Data
A catalogue record for this book is available from the British Library

ISBN 0-415-03896-0 (hbk)
ISBN 0-415-05831-7 (pbk)

Contents

Acknowledgements

The editor and publishers would like to thank the following for permission to reproduce the essays in this book: Chapter 1,'On the Fetish Character in Music and the Regression of Listening', in Andrew Arato and Eike Gebhardt (eds) *The Essential Frankfurt School Reader* (New York: The Continuum Publishing Company, 1982); Chapter 2, 'Das Schema der Massenkultur', in Adorno's *Gesammelte Schriften III. Dialektik der Aufklärung* (Frankfurt a. M.: Suhrkamp Verlag, 1981), pp. 299–335; Chapter 3, 'Culture Industry Reconsidered', translated by Anson G. Rabinbach, *New German Critique* 6, Fall 1975, pp. 12–19; Chapter 4, 'Culture and Administration', translated by Wes Blomster, *Telos* 37, Fall 1978, pp. 93–111; Chapter 5, 'Freudian Theory and the Pattern of Fascist Propaganda', in Andrew Arato and Eike Gebhardt (eds) *The Essential Frankfurt School Reader* (New York: The Continuum Publishing Company, 1982); Chapter 6, 'How to Look at Television', *The Quarterly of Film, Radio and Television* 8 (3), 1954, pp. 213–35, reprinted by permission of the Regents of the University of California; Chapter 7, 'Transparencies on Film', translated by Thomas Y. Levin in *New German Critique* 24–5, Fall–Winter 1981–2, pp. 199–205; Chapter 8, 'Freizeit', *Gesammelte Schriften* 10/2, *Kulturkritik und Gesellschaft* (Frankfurt a. M.: Suhrkamp Verlag, 1977), pp. 645–55; Chapter 9, 'Resignation', translated by Wes Blomster in *Telos* 35, Spring 1978, pp. 165–8.

I would also like to thank the following: Mr Gordon Finlayson and Mr Nicholas Walker for the translation of Chapter 8, 'Free Time'; Mr Nicholas Walker for the translation of Chapter 2, 'The Schema of Mass Culture'; Peter Dews for his careful reading of Chapter 2 and his many helpful suggestions and Gillian Rose for her comments on the Introduction.

Introduction

The contentious arguments surrounding the idea of an affirmative postmodernist culture have brought with them a persistent theoretical depreciation of the claims of high modernist art as well as a positive re-evaluation of the character and potentialities of popular (mass) culture. Both of these critical re-evaluations often take the form of a sustained criticism of the cultural theory of T.W. Adorno. Adorno's apparently uncompromising defence of modernist art and his apparently uncompromising critique of mass culture as a product of a 'culture industry' has served the proponents of postmodernism as a negative image against which their claims for a democratic transformation of culture may be secured. In their view Adorno is an elitist defending esoteric artistic modernism against a culture available to all. Equally, by calling for a continuation of the project of artistic modernism and perceiving only manipulation and reification in the products of the culture industry, Adorno's critical theory appears to proscribe the transformation of culture in an emancipatory direction.

While it is certainly true that the cultural landscape has altered substantially in the twenty years since Adorno's death, and perhaps in ways he had not anticipated, our current situation may be a great deal less sanguine than its proponents suppose. Even if some of the historical and sociological details of Adorno's analyses were composed to address a specific context, it does not follow that his critical diagnosis of the predicament of culture is not applicable to the present. In collecting together a broad selection of Adorno's writings on the culture industry the aim is to allow a wider appreciation of his achievement in this area, as well as, and more importantly, a more informed confrontation between Adorno's critical theory and the claims of postmodernist cultural theory. Since the essays collected in this volume represent only one side of Adorno's critical theory, his analysis of the culture industry, and since these essays are to a large extent self-explanatory, this Introduction will focus on setting these analyses in the wider theoretical context in which they belong, and on suggesting avenues of analysis through which the understanding of Adorno's critical theory may lead to a more nuanced evaluation of the claims of postmodernism.

Instrumental reason and the culture industry

No one statement of Adorno's concerning the great divide between artistic modernism and the culture industry is either more famous or better encapsulates his view than the one found in his letter to Walter Benjamin of 3 March 1936. There he states that both high art as well as industrially produced consumer art 'bear the stigmata of capitalism, both contain elements of change (but never, of course, the middle term between Schönberg and the American film). Both are torn halves of an integral freedom, to which, however, they do not add up.'[1]

In reading Adorno, especially his writings on the culture industry, it is important to keep firmly in mind the thought that he is not attempting an objective, sociological analysis of the phenomena in question. Rather, the *question* of the culture industry is raised from the perspective of its relation to the possibilities for social transformation. The culture industry is to be understood from the perspective of its potentialities for promoting or blocking 'integral freedom'. These positive or negative potentialities, however, are not naively or immediately available; and this because the terms through which we might gauge potentialities for change are themselves not naively or immediately available. According to Adorno the division of labour between disciplines such as sociology, philosophy, history and psychology is not contained in or dictated by their material, but has been forced on them from the outside. There is no discrete or unique object, for example, the mind or psyche, whose objective characteristics entail or directly correspond to the concepts and categories of psychology or psychoanalysis; nor is there a discrete object whose objective characteristics entail or correspond to the concepts and categories of sociology, history or philosophy. Rather, the same forces of fragmentation and reification which have produced the great divide between high art and the culture industry produced the division of labour among the various disciplines.

In the present context, this thought has the consequence of doubling the intransigent difficulty faced by the cultural critic: not only do high art and the products of the culture industry represent two halves of an integral freedom, to which, however, they do not add up, but the disciplines whose task it is to reckon the potentialities of culture for radical transformation are themselves divided, torn. Adorno's reckoning of 'what does not add up' is equivocal: he provides a philosophically informed sociology of the culture industry, and a sociologically informed philosophy of high modernist art. The 'integral freedom', from the vantage point of which the potentialities of divided culture are found wanting, also implies the overcoming of the division of labour among the theoretical disciplines that register cultural division in the first instance.

From the outset, Adorno's reflections on the culture industry were embedded in the wider context demanded by the collapse of the classical Marxist evolutionary schema for historical development. For Adorno, the Marxist belief that capitalist forces of production when unfettered from capitalist relations of production will generate a free society is illusory. Capital does not possess such immediately emancipatory forces or elements; the drift of capitalist development, even the underlying or implicit drift of such development, is not towards freedom but towards further integration and domination. Hence, the Marxist history that places capitalism into a naive narrative of the progress of freedom and reason becomes, through its attempt to unify and integrate history, complicit with its object. 'Universal history must be construed and denied. After the catastrophes that have happened, and in view of the catastrophes to come, it would be cynical to say that a plan for a better world is manifested in history and unites it.'[2] Classical Marxist theory unknowingly perpetuates such a cynicism. Adorno continues his thought thus: 'No universal history leads from savagery to humanitarianism, but there is one leading from the slingshot to the megaton bomb. It ends in the total menace which organized mankind poses to organized men, in the epitome of discontinuity.'

Not socialism but fascism represented the realization of Western rationality for Adorno since it continued reason's work of domination through integration and unification. While this view may not provide for a completely convincing analysis of fascism, it did allow Adorno to perceive early on that liberal capitalism was coming to be displaced by a more reified social order under the dictate of instrumental reason. The culture industry, which involves the production of works for reproduction and mass consumption, thereby organizing 'free' time, the remnant domain of freedom under capital in accordance with the same principles of exchange and equivalence that reign in the sphere of production outside leisure, presents culture as the realization of the right of all to the gratification of desire while in reality continuing the negative integration of society. While Adorno nowhere identifies the culture industry with the political triumph of fascism, he does imply, both directly and indirectly, that the culture industry's effective integration of society marks an equivalent triumph of repressive unification in liberal democratic states to that which was achieved politically under fascism. This analogical interpretation of the culture industry itself requires the terms of reference provided by the idea of 'integral freedom'.

While most of the central tenets of his theory of the culture industry were already formulated in 'On the Fetish Character in Music and the Regression of Listening' (1938), an essay best regarded as a polemic against Benjamin's 'The Work of Art in the Age of Mechanical Reproduction', Adorno's philosophical and historical placement of his culture industry theory makes its first perspicuous appearance in his and Horkheimer's *Dialectic of Enlightenment*. This work charts the self-destruction of Enlightenment. Its central claim is that the very same rationality which provides for humankind's emancipation from the bondage of mythic powers and allows for progressive domination over nature, engenders, through its intrinsic character, a return to myth and new, even more absolute forms of domination. The feature of enlightened reason which accounts for this reversal is its identification of rationality and understanding with the subsumption of the particular under the universal. Subsumptive or instrumental rationality disregards the intrinsic properties of things, those properties that give each thing its sensuous, social and historical particularity, for the sake of the goals and purposes of the subject – originally self-preservation itself. Thus, such a rationality must treat unlike (unequal) things as like (equal), and subsume objects under (the unreflective drives of) subjects. Subsumption, then, is domination in the conceptual realm. The purpose of subsumption is to allow for conceptual and technical mastery. When subsumptive rationality came to be considered the whole of reason, then the possibility of cognition of the particular in its own right and the ends for the sake of which the path of enlightened rationality was undertaken became occluded. Without the possibility of judging particulars and rationally considering ends and goals, the reason which was to be the means to satisfying human ends becomes its own end, and thereby turns against the true aims of Enlightenment: freedom and happiness.

The economic organization of modern capitalist society provides for this final realization of instrumental reason and self-destruction of Enlightenment. Under capitalism all production is for the market; goods are produced not in order to meet human needs and desires, but for the sake of profit, for the sake of acquiring further capital. While production for exchange rather than use is a feature of most economic forms, what uniquely characterizes capitalist economies is the tendential universality of production for exchange rather than use. This too is a procedure for making and treating unlike things as identical, for displacing the intrinsic properties of things for the sake of ends (capital accumulation) extrinsic to them. The domination of use value by exchange value thus realizes and duplicates the tendencies of enlightened reason: as enlightened rationality occludes ends-oriented rationality, so capitalist production occludes production for use; and as enlightened rationality subsumes particulars under universals indifferent and insensitive to sensuous particularity, so capitalist production subsumes the use value of things under exchange value. Enlightened rationality and capital production preclude reflection; Enlightenment's irresistible progress in the domination of nature and the securing of the means for the possible realization of happiness come, in fact, to entail an irresistible regression.

Throughout their genealogy of reason, Adorno and Horkheimer mark out the role of art and culture in the presumptive progress of Enlightenment. Odysseus' encounter with the Sirens figures in their account as an allegorical anticipation of the role of art in modernity. The song of the Sirens, which tells of all that has ever happened, promises happiness through relief from the relentless striving that is the meaning of the future under the aegis of the drive for self-preservation. Death, however, is the price the Sirens exact for their enchantment. Cunning Odysseus devises two strategies of escape: his men, who must row with all their strength through the danger, have their ears stopped with wax; Odysseus has himself bound firmly to the mast of the ship. The rowers, like modern labourers, must not be distracted from their work; while Odysseus, who can hear the beauty of the Sirens' song, is impotent to realize the happiness it promises.

...the greater the temptation the more he has his bonds tightened – just as later burghers would deny themselves happiness all the more doggedly as it drew closer to them with the growth of their own power. What Odysseus hears is without consequence for him; he is able only to nod his head as a sign to be set free from his bonds; but it is too late: his men, who do not listen, know only the song's danger but nothing of its beauty, and leave him at the mast in order to save him and themselves. They reproduce the oppressor's life together with their own, and the oppressor is no longer able to escape his social role. The bonds with which he has irremediably tied himself to practice, also keeps the Sirens away from practice: their temptation is neutralized and becomes a mere object of contemplation – becomes art.[3]

Art is the emphatic assertion of what is excluded from Enlightenment's instrumental rationality: the claim of sensuous particularity and rational ends. Art is the cognition of ends and of sensuous particularity cut off from practice. Pre-modern art hoped to alter reality, while autonomous art is the quintessence of the division between mental and manual labour in a class society.

High art is bought at the price of the exclusion of the lower classes – 'with whose cause, the real universality, art keeps faith precisely by its freedom from the ends of the false universality'.[4] Illusory universality is the universality of the art of the culture industry, it is the universality of the homogeneous same, an art which no longer even promises happiness but only provides easy amusement as relief from labour: 'Amusement under late capitalism is the prolongation of work. It is sought as an escape from the mechanized work process, and to recruit strength in order to be able to cope with it again'.[5] Because mechanization has such power over man's leisure, and 'so profoundly determines the manufacture of leisure goods', experiences of mass culture are 'inevitably after-images of the work process itself'.[6]

There is an evident strain involved in a thesis which claims autonomous, bourgeois art is what sustains the true universality of the claims of the oppressed, while the art produced for the masses, which is quite other than an art of the masses, is critiqued as the reproduction of the alienated needs of mass society. Rather than attempting to hide this strain, which after all only reflects the fact that the achievements of culture belong to society as a whole and not just the ruling classes, Adorno emphasizes the dialectical entwinement of high and low art, it is their broken unity, the illusory universality of mass art and the abstract, restricted particularity of autonomous art, and not just the always complicit 'progressive' aspects of high art alone, which is the true object of his concern: 'Light art has been the shadow of autonomous art. It is the social bad conscience of serious art. The truth which the latter necessarily lacked because of its social premises gives the other the semblance of legitimacy. The division itself is the truth: it does at least express the negativity of the culture which the different spheres constitute.'[7] The 'truth' which the division between high and low represents is neither an empirical nor a philosophical truth, at least as truth is usually understood. The division of high and low art as a division, reveals the fate of particular and universal in contemporary society. That division, which spells domination, is again, only perceivable from the perspective of 'integral freedom', the speculative unity of particular and universal, high and low. Because the 'truth' about culture is neither an empirical nor theoretical truth – both these forms of truth-stating have been taken over by instrumental rationality – because 'truth' itself is no longer true, there is a difficulty in revealing the 'truth' about culture.

In their 'Introduction' Adorno and Horkheimer state that since public opinion has become a commodity, and language the means for promoting that commodity, then established linguistic and conceptual conventions could not be trusted, relied upon, to chart the 'indefatigable self-destructiveness of enlightenment...[t]here is no longer any available form of linguistic expression which has not tended toward accommodation to dominant currents of thought; and what a devalued language does not do automatically is proficiently executed by societal mechanisms'.[8] *Dialectic of Enlightenment* is, as a consequence, a work of fragments and the chapter 'The Culture Industry: Enlightenment as Mass Deception' is 'even more fragmentary'[9] than the other parts of the book.

Fragmentary writing is premised upon the refusal of the operations that establish 'rational' connections between statements in theoretical discourse (inference, entailment, deduction) and their linguistic representatives ('therefore', 'because', etc.). For Adorno, these operations are the markers for domination in the conceptual realm. Equally fragmentary writing does not pretend to empirical accuracy (truth as correspondence). Fragmentary writing is modernist, its logical and syntactical dislocations the cognitive equivalent of dissonance in music. Fragmentary writing functions through the multiplication of logically distinct perspectives, each one of which is something of a theoretical caricature. Through the multiplication of diverse perspectives a complex portrait of the phenomenon in question is produced. This procedure stands somewhere between Nietzsche's call for many eyes, many perspectives, and the phenomenological procedure of eidetic variation wherein through the imaginative act of producing deformations of some phenomenon one discovers what is invariant or essential to it. Of course, Adorno is seeking after historical truth, not the ahistorical, rational essence of phenomena. Historical truth is 'shown' in fragmentary writing, which does not then explicitly aim to demonstrate or to explain. Explaining and demonstrating neutralize the phenomena in question; to explain is to explain away. When 'truth' is untrue, then only what is not true according to standing regimes of truth can make manifest the illusory character of society's claim to truth. Only by presenting society in terms of its extremes – 'the whole is false' and 'truth' is no longer true – can reveal the distortions that are less than what ironic statement must present them to be.

The 'Culture Industry' chapter opens with the claim that, while sociologically it would appear that with the decline of established religions, the growth of technological and social differentiation, and the dissolution of the last remnants of precapitalism that cultural chaos should reign, yet, this is not so. Never has culture been more unified or integrated: 'Culture now impresses the same stamp on everything. Films, radio and magazines make up a system which is uniform as a whole and in every part.'[10] Culture has become openly, and defiantly, an industry obeying the same rules of production as any other producer of commodities. Cultural production is an integrated component of the capitalist economy as a whole. Culture is no longer the repository of a reflective comprehension of the present in terms of a redeemed future; the culture industry forsakes the promise of happiness in the name of the degraded utopia of the present. This is the ironic presentation of the present.

Its degradation, since it does not appear as overt oppression or naked domination, can only be captured in conceptual terms as the 'false identity of the general and the particular'.[11] What makes the identity illusory is not that it does not occur, but that the moment of particularity itself is illusory. Hence, the governing leitmotif of the chapter is the reiterated demonstration that what appears as particularity and individuality is not so, and that what might emerge as a point of resistance to the all-embracing unity of the system is immediately integrated and repressed. Since we do not possess an independent account of true particularity and individuality, it is through the contrast between the typical productions of the culture industry and those of autonomous art that the culture industry's false identity of particular and universal is established.

For example, Adorno contrasts the fate of the detail in high and low art. In high art, the assertion of detail in opposition to the unified work, in the period from Romanticism to Expressionism, was, aesthetically, a protest against the ideal of organic unity; the extra-aesthetic sense of this protest was to reveal the illusory character of the unity portrayed in harmonious works. Dissonance in music, the stress on individual colours or brush strokes in painting, or particular words, images or psychological states in the novel negatively express the false unity of the whole. All this is done away with by the culture industry: 'Though concerned exclusively with effects, it crushes their insubordination and makes them subserve the formula, which replaces the work.'[12] Effects have become 'special effects', and pictorial dissonance the rule of television advertising.

Analogously, Adorno stresses the ersatz character of the pleasure the culture industry offers the consumer. Real pleasure is not even on offer; the promissory note, which is the plot and staging of the work, is in reality all that is on offer, thus making the original promise illusory: 'all it actually confirms is that real point will never be reached, that the diner must be satisfied with the menu'.[13] This is not to claim that autonomous works were sexual exhibitions; they engage with the difficulty of sensual happiness by representing 'deprivation as negative'. Thus: 'The secret of aesthetic sublimation is its representation of fulfillment as a broken promise. The culture industry does not sublimate; it represses... Works of art are ascetic and unashamed; the culture industry is pornographic and prudish.'[14]

In spite of his use of a contrastive method, Adorno does not intend thereby that autonomous art should be regarded as utterly innocent. As we have already seen, autonomous art arises fully only in a class society through the exclusion of the working classes. The purposelessness of pure works of art, which denies the utility and instrumentality that reign in the world outside art, is premised on commodity production. The 'autonomy', the freedom from external purposes, of pure works derives from their being produced 'privately' and not on demand for a particular consumer (church, state, patron). Works of art are commodities just the same, indeed pure commodities since they are valuable only to the extent that they can be exchanged. Works' non-utility, their 'unsaleability', is the hypocritical source of their value; the art market is pure because unconstrained by need. The culture industry's inversion of this is its offering of culture goods, exhibitions or concerts on the television or radio, free of charge, as a 'public service'; in truth, the price for them has been long-since paid for by the labouring masses.

The effectiveness of the culture industry depends not on its parading an ideology, on disguising the true nature of things, but in removing the thought that there is any alternative to the status quo. 'Pleasure always means not to think about anything, to forget suffering even where it is shown.' Hence, pleasure is always flight 'from the last remaining thought of resistance'; the liberation promised by amusement 'is freedom from thought and negation'.[15] This is why consideration of the culture industry is embedded in a fragmentary genealogy of reason: the *telos* of instrumental rationality, the rationality first licensed by the drive for self-preservation, is the silencing of reflection in the name of the illusory universality pervaded by the culture industry. Instrumental rationality in the form of the culture industry thus turns against reason and the reasoning subject. This silencing of reflection is the substantial irrationality of enlightened reason.

The culture industry is the societal realization of the defeat of reflection; it is the realization of subsumptive reason, the unification of the many under the one. This unification is equally the theme of the most difficult essay in this volume, 'The Schema of Mass Culture' – a continuation of the 'Culture Industry' chapter of *Dialectic of Enlightenment* not previously translated. The 'schema' of the title does not refer to Adorno's outline of the culture industry but rather to the culture industry's own schematizing (a Kantian term), patterning or pre-forming of experience. Hence, the essay opens with what I shall suggest later is the controlling movement of postmodernism: the collapse of the difference between culture and practical life, which here is the same as the false aestheticization of the empirical world, an aestheticization of empirical life that does not transform it in accordance with the ideals of sensuous happiness and freedom, but rather secures the illusion that empirical life realizes those ends to the degree to which such is possible. Since this false transformation is carried out through the self-same procedures of the culture industry, these ends are not realized at all, but the illusion of success suppresses the thinking that could claim that this is the case.

Adorno pursues his theme, again, through fragments, through a series of analyses and analogies that seek to reveal how the culture industry's schematization works and what its content is. So, we find discussions of: the fate of conflict in works of art, how variety-hall turns reveal the structure of temporality in mass culture, the significance of virtuosity in the art of the culture industry, the status of information, the likeness of culture to sport (sport as a schema for culture), and so forth. This is the darkest and most prescient of Adorno's writings on culture since in it even modernist art is shown to be infected by the schema of mass culture; here cultural negativity, what resists universality, is even more severely marginalized than it would be if it were merely a product of autonomous 'high' culture. At the end of the essay Adorno shows how the forms of behaviour the culture industry offers to people have the perverse character of making them practice on themselves the 'magic' that is already worked upon them. The human is now only a secret writing, a hieroglyph beneath the masks culture offers: 'In every peal of laughter we hear the menacing voice of extortion and the comic types are legible signs which represent the contorted bodies of revolutionaries. Participation in mass culture stands under the sign of terror.'

Seeing through and obeying

One might object to the analysis presented thus far on the grounds that no one is quite as manipulated or deceived by the claims of the culture industry as Adorno appears to suppose. Watching television or the latest Hollywood movie is not a sign that one has, after all, lost the capacity for reflection; that one cannot simultaneously see through the manipulation at work and sustain a critical distance from what is on offer. However, Adorno does not regard strict belief or naïveté as a condition for the culture industry to succeed. At the conclusion of the section on the culture industry in *Dialectic of*

Enlightenment he states: 'The triumph of advertising in the culture industry is that consumers feel compelled to buy and use its products even though they see through them.'[16] In the 'Schema of Mass Culture' he states: 'Mass culture is unadorned make-up.' Adorno works through this possibility of seeing through and obeying at the same time in his extended analysis of the astrology column of the *Los Angeles Times*, 'The Stars Down to Earth', which, alas, proved too lengthy for inclusion in this volume. While the overall aim of the study is to gain a better understanding of the nature and motivations of large-scale social phenomena that contain a distinctively irrational element, for the purposes to hand I want to focus on just the linkage of simultaneously seeing through and obeying, on not believing and believing at the same time.

Irrationality, Adorno contends, need not be regarded as adopting policies wholly disconnected from individual and collective ego aims. On the contrary, it is cases where rational self-interest as normally understood is pushed to extremes so as to become irrational, the historical fate of reason presented in *Dialectic of Enlightenment,* that are to be studied. The surface rationality of the common sense advice proffered by astrology columns corresponds to this premise. Such columns are far from esoteric in what they advise; for example, today is a good day to avoid family arguments, sort out one's financial situation, buy, sell, plan a holiday, begin a relationship, beware of involvements, etc.

The occult of astrology columns is a 'secondary superstition', that is, the occult here appears as 'institutionalized, objectified and, to a large extent, socialized'.[17] The type of readers who take cognizance of the advice offered do so without any personal basis for their belief, and without receiving, or requiring, justification for the general practice of astrological reasoning. In the astrology columns of large circulation newspapers and magazines the mechanics of the astrological system are never divulged.

Secondary occultism involves a certain lack of seriousness; unlike serious religious belief it trades in a common sense rationality, demands nothing from the believer, certainly nothing as demanding as faith, and often overtly concedes, in its advice, pride of place to its opposite; modern natural science. By screening its fundamental assumptions, taking up a modest posture with respect to natural science, keeping its actual advice pragmatic and psychologically well-grounded, and yet addressing the real anxieties and dislocations of its readers, providing them with strategies and compensations that appear as more than imaginary, astrology permits belief and obedience without demanding readers to *overtly* sacrifice the claims of rational evidence and reflection. Astrology survives through its

11

distance from seriousness: 'This alienation from experience, a certain abstractness enveloping the whole realm of the commercialized occult may well be concomitant with a substratum of disbelief and scepticism, the suspicion of phoniness so deeply associated with modern big time irrationality.'[18] No doubt occultism has been with us since time immemorial as a secondary superstition. However, contemporary occultism is transformed through institutionalization in the mass media, and by the fact that today the incompatibility between it and progress in natural science, between astrology and astrophysics, is vivid and undeniable. Hence, those who combine a 'belief' in both 'are forced to an intellectual retrogression which formerly was hardly required'.[19]

In the course of his content analysis of the column Adorno seeks to demonstrate how it tends to fulfil a conservative ideology of justifying the status quo by presenting a benign image of society requiring only conformity added by the 'insight' and limited individual effort recommended by the column for personal success. The image of social conformity is promoted by the column's implicit and ubiquitous rule that one must adjust oneself to the commands of the stars at given times. The column appeals to the narcissism of the reader by portraying her as someone in an unspecified position of power at work, who generally is able to alter circumstances through her activity. Adorno hazards that the column creates the image of its addressee as a 'vice-president', while in fact addressing an average lower-middle-class reader. Operating a 'bi-phasic' approach, the column carefully separates pleasure from work, making pleasure a reward for work, and prevents itself from falling into overt contradiction in offering conflicting advice by spacing the advice as appropriate at differing times. And while an atmosphere of pseudo-individuality and pseudo-activity is created in the column, it equally indicates the individual's powerlessness, and imaginatively compensates for it with suggestions of unexpected good fortune, assistance and the like.

While some of the details of Adorno's analysis and the general picture of oppressive conformism he draws are specific to the time being studied, his analysis remains striking. What is above all anomalous and requires explanation is the combination of rationality, in the form of advice which is either pragmatically or psychologically well-grounded, and the irrationality present in the source and structuring of this advice. As already noted, the irrationality is kept remote, and treated as impersonal and thing-like; there is an underlying philosophy of what might be called 'naturalist super-naturalism'.[20] Astrology, like the culture industry, blurs the distinction between fact and fiction, maintaining a content level of overrealism while giving that content an irrational metaphysical aura in terms of its source.

Astrology's dual structure replicates and legitimates the dual structure of everyday life, a life of mundane activities set within a system opaque to the understanding and inexorable in its operations.

In as much as the social system is the 'fate' of most individuals independent of their will and interest, it is projected upon the stars in order to thus obtain a higher degree of dignity and justification in which the individuals hope to participate themselves. At the same time, the idea that the stars, if only one reads them correctly, offer some advice mitigates the very same fear of the inexorability of social processes the stargazer himself creates.[21]

Because people feel that empirical life is set within a complicated, mechanical but nonetheless interlinked system whose rationale they fail to comprehend, and suspect as lacking a rationale conformable to their wants and needs, they are prepared to accept an analogous system of delusion which at least provides imaginary solace. Indeed, like the movies, astrology, while dwelling in an empirical world where nothing is valuable in its own right, provides a message that appears 'metaphysically' meaningful, somewhere the spontaneity of life is being restored, while actually reflecting the very same reified conditions which seem to be dispensed with through an appeal to the 'absolute'.[22]

What allows astrology to be accepted, believed and obeyed, by sceptical, disillusioned people is the way its opaqueness mirrors that of the empirical world, so as to require little, if any, transcendent faith. It survives by overtly cognitively and affectively demanding so little while apparently offering so much. Why refuse such an offer? Adorno typifies the intellectual attitude expressed here as one of 'disoriented agnosticism'.[23] The demand for strict belief *appears* as not required, agnosticism *appears* as legitimate. The reader is never asked to evaluate the claims being made. By bracketing its cognitive status, astrology keeps the reader cognitively disoriented.

Astrology is the linking between two otherwise factual domains; the movement of the stars and a disillusioned 'popular' psychology. The appeal of astrology is in its relating of these two unrelated domains. 'Astrology', Adorno contends, 'presents the bill for the neglect of interpretive thinking for the sake of fact-gathering.'[24] Astrology, we might say, is the 'social bad conscience' of critical theory; its blind synthesis of different domains responds to the same division of intellectual labour and opaqueness of the totality that animates critical reflection.

The tendency to occultism is a symptom of regression in consciousness. This has lost the power to think the unconditional and to endure the conditional. Instead of defining both, in their unity and difference, by conceptual labour, it mixes them indiscriminately. The unconditional becomes fact, the conditional an immediate essence.[25]

What holds for astrology exemplifies the culture industry generally from advertising to film and television.

The impossible practice of cultural criticism

'To think the unconditional and to endure the conditional', while perhaps sounding like an ascetic recipe for inaction, in fact inscribes a difficult critical stance. How difficult is made clear in Adorno's essay 'Cultural Criticism and Society'. In general, the position of a critic of culture is a dubious one; as critic he reveals a discontent with the very civilization to which he owes his discontent. His stance implies that he possesses the culture which culture lacks. Worst of all, by attending to culture with such seriousness, he confers a spurious dignity and autonomy on it. 'Where there is despair and measureless misery, he sees only spiritual phenomena, the state of man's consciousness, the decline in norms. By insisting on this, criticism is tempted to forget the unutterable, instead of striving, however impotently, so that man may be spared.'[26]

Adorno does not intend by this that criticism is inappropriate; on the contrary, culture is 'true only when implicitly critical';[27] as such, criticism is an integral and essential component of culture. Nonetheless, the critic doubles the objectification of culture by making it his object, while the very meaning of culture is the 'suspension of objectification'.[28] And this points to the real difficulty; the notion of culture itself. No authentic work of art or true philosophy, Adorno suggests, has been exhausted in its purity and isolation. According to their inner meaning, their insistence on their separation from the actual life-process of society, their 'very rejection of the guilt of a life which blindly and callously reproduces itself',[29] implies, however implicitly or unconsciously, the promise of happiness, the promise of a state where freedom would be realized. But this promise must remain equivocal so long as culture is purchased at the price of domination. Culture, as it is now conceived of, exists because freedom does not. Culture's power, which is co-extensive with its impotence, is its withdrawal from praxis; this renunciation was forced on culture by history.

Because of its impotence before the power of capital, and equally because its promises come increasingly to appear as an insult to those excluded from what is held out, culture is taken over by the very powers it had criticized. Consumer culture is the degradation of culture. By forgetting culture's complicity with what it criticizes, conservative cultural critics can see the entanglement of culture and commerce only as a disgraceful corruption caused by a materialist society. Hence, conservative cultural critics call for the return of culture to autonomous purity. Yet, Adorno states, 'all culture shares the guilt of society. It ekes out its existence only by virtue of injustice already perpetrated in the sphere of production.'[30]

Adorno regards the conservative defence of high art and culture as reflecting an unreflective hypostatization of culture that protects the economic status quo. He perceives the end of culture as the suspension of its reified status, its resubmersion in the actual life-process of society. And this final joining of culture and society would token the realignment of mental and manual labour, to whose radical separation culture owes its existence. Dialectical criticism, as opposed to conservative cultural criticism, aims to heighten 'cultural criticism until the notion of culture is itself negated, fulfilled and surmounted in one'.[31] Whatever the hyperbole involved in this statement of the procedures and goals of cultural criticism, its point is to reveal the gap between the claims of culture and the world it inhabits. High culture exists because what it promises does not. One can only defend culture by indicting the reasons for and not the fact of its existence.

It is worth noting at this juncture how deeply akin Adorno's criticisms of cultural conservativism are to some of the dominant elements of postmodernist thought. Both Adorno and postmodernist thought, taking their cue from the historical avant-garde, view the reification of culture as a critical gesture whose completion would be the fulfillment of high art's promise. Fulfilling that promise means demystifying the discourse of high art, overcoming the division between high and low, and reintegrating art with everyday life. Nonetheless, there is a difference between Adorno's stance and that of postmodernism, as we shall see more fully below. Adorno objects to a conservative approach to high culture; it should not be protected for its own sake. Tendentially, postmodernism assimilates high culture to its conservative appropriation, thus the fact and not the reasons for its existence becomes the enemy. In this way, postmodernism loses the ability to distinguish between the overcoming of the divide between high and low, and the fulfillment of the promise of high art.

Adorno perceives dialectical criticism as an uneasy combination of transcendent and immanent critique. Transcendent critique takes up a position outside society in order to condemn it as a whole. Such a position corresponds to the definition of ideology as socially necessary appearance. One sees through the appearances by seeing them as products of the interest structure of society and revealing their historical genesis. The validity of such a critique depends upon the epistemological self-righteousness of the critic, allowing him to distinguish between subjective and objective interests, and to separate the real evolutionary trends of society from its apparent history. What is correct in the procedure of transcendent criticism is its appreciation of the totality as reified; but this is also its weakness. Under liberal capitalism revealing the ideological status of cultural products had a significant role, the moment of falsehood and false consciousness could make a difference to social understanding; but as society has grown more one-dimensional 'critical theory must insist on the moment of truth of ideologies against technocratic reason'.[32] The more one-dimensional society becomes the more critique must pay attention to the internal structure and relatively autonomous logic of cultural objects. This transcendent critique fails to do; its critical position outside society is as fictitious as the most abstract utopias. By its lack of inwardness, sympathy and attention to particulars, transcendent criticism is at one with domination: 'In wishing to wipe away the whole as with a sponge, transcendent critique develop[s] an affinity to barbarism.'[33]

Immanent critique, which does take cultural particulars seriously, realizes that it is not ideology in itself which is untrue 'but rather its pretension to correspond to reality'.[34] As a consequence, the goal of immanent criticism, achieved through careful analysis of the meaning and structure of the object, is to reveal the contradiction between the objective idea offered by the work and its pretension. In the period of liberal capitalism, immanent critique involved the comparison of society's ideological claims about itself, for example, that justice was instantiated, with the social reality of exchange equivalence. In the present epoch, when such claims have been withdrawn, immanent criticism finds its proper home in culture. For immanent criticism, a successful work 'is not one which resolves objective contradictions in a spurious harmony, but one which expresses the idea of harmony negatively by embodying the contradictions, pure and uncompromised, in its inner-most structure. Confronted with this kind of work, the verdict 'mere ideology' loses its meaning.'[35]

While the moment of negativity in immanent critique is equally the critical moment for Adorno, he denies that immanent criticism is self-sufficient. Its activities are restricted to the efforts of the intellect, and, in discovering the mind's contradictions with itself, it remains locked in a world of reflection. Immanent critique does nothing to alter the existence to which it bears witness. Immanent critique must, then, step outside the object, it must 'relate the knowledge of society as a totality and of the mind's involvement in it to the claim inherent in the specific content of the object that it apprehended as such'.[36] This means, for example, that dialectical criticism must relate its literary critical encounter with a work to the social determinations that generate, without directly causing, the work's inner contradictions. Only by presenting society with the bill which the object, in itself hermetic, does not redeem, only, again, by bringing in an external perspective, can critique be saved from the temptation of a reversion to idealism, from the temptation of treating the mind and its products as self-sufficient – the original sin of autonomous culture.

The position of dialectical criticism is a non-position; it can neither immerse itself in the object in the manner of idealizing, redemptive criticism, nor take a stand outside culture by comparing it with a fictitious absolute. To take up the former stance would amount to acceding to the cult of the mind; while to take up the latter stance would be to reveal hatred of it. 'The dialectical critic of culture must both participate in culture and not participate. Only then does he do justice to his object and to himself.'[37]

Critical theory and postmodernism

Adorno states that the 'culture industry is the purposeful integration of its consumers from above. It also forces a reconciliation of high and low art, which have been separated for thousands of years, a reconciliation which damages them both. High art is deprived of its seriousness because its effect is programmed; low art is put in chains and deprived of the unruly resistance inherent in it when social control was not yet total.'[38] Adorno's characterization of the false reconciliation of high and low art through the engineering of the culture industry might well be regarded as Adorno's judgement in advance on postmodernist culture. While there are good reasons for acceding to Adorno's judgement here, it would be wrong to do so too quickly since the dynamics of the false overcoming of the great divide has not occurred through a simple intensification of the unifying trajectory of the culture industry of the 1940s and 50s. However, before attempting to diagnose what has occurred, let me briefly recount the standard objections to Adorno's theory, beginning with his view of the culture industry itself.

Adorno's critics have turned his version of the unifying and pacifying character of the culture industry back onto the theory itself: it is his theory that unifies and pacifies the culture industry which in reality is more dynamic, diverse and conflictual than the theory allows. Since mass media mediate social conflict and negotiate social change, they can be said to 'reflect, express, and articulate social reality in a mediated fashion'.[39] For the sake of gaining an audience and possessing credibility, mass media must reproduce social reality; the consequence of this is that they 'may deflate or undermine the ideological illusions of their own products and however unwittingly engage in social critique and ideological subversion'.[40] Analogously, the requirements of pleasing a mass audience, of providing something for everyone, may have the unintended consequence of revealing social alternatives and hence splintering 'the ideological hegemony which was once the fragile accomplishment of the culture industry'.[41] The culture industry is no longer the purveyor of a monolithic ideology but, however unwittingly or unintentionally, includes moments of conflict, rebellion, opposition and the drive for emancipation and utopia. While pop music, for example, may exhibit the features of commodification, reification and standardization, it can equally 'express emotions of pain, rage, joy, rebellion, sexuality, etc.'.[42] What is required, then, is a more complex and sensitive model of cultural interpretation, one that can pick up the symbolic dimension of mass media, respond to the progressive possibilities of technological innovation (video, cable television, etc.), and analyse the real political economy of mass media. Because Adorno's theory lacks these dimensions, it pictures the audience of the culture industry as the dupes of mass deception, denying thus the 'relative autonomy of consciousness'. This can but lead to a 'politics of resignation and despair and cannot account for struggles against advanced capitalism'.[43]

If Adorno's analyses of the culture industry overstates its power of manipulation, his critics contend that his theory of high art overstates its negativity, its power of refusal. Increasingly since the late 1950s, high modernist art has lost its critical status. If previously being esoteric, and hence available only to the elite few, was the price paid for sustaining a distance from commodification, modernist art now has become the most visible image of a sphere the value of whose items is determined wholly by a speculative market-place informed by a hermetic discourse of artistic progress. Adorno's defence of modernism relied upon an analysis that saw it exploiting the most advanced artistic materials. This notion of the most advanced state of artistic materials tended to prescribe the development of art as following a logical course implicit in those materials: colour, line, brush stroke and canvas in painting; word, image and meaning in literature, etc. Each apparently progressive movement in modernist art equally generated a growing canon of prohibitions: representation, figuration, narration, harmony, unity, etc. By its very nature, this logic was limited and defeatist. The postmodernist rebellion attempted to bring back into art all those elements that had been prohibited while simultaneously refusing the neat unilinear story demanded by a theory of the most advanced state of artistic materials. Since the excluded materials were just those that had come to be at home in the products of the culture industry, postmodernism's transgression of the modernist canon of prohibitions amounted to an overcoming of the separatist strategy of high modernism; postmodernism actively sought a (re-)unification of high and low art that was equally a democratic reaction to the elitism of high modernism. Further, the very success of modernism in calling into question the demands of traditional art through its negations of the constitutive elements of the autonomous and unified work deprived it of a foil against which those negations might function; dissonance, shock and incomprehension no longer result from modernist practices.

These criticisms provide a one-sided and inadequate picture of Adorno's position. His aesthetic theory was, almost from the outset, self-consciously delineating the ageing of modernism. Unlike the aesthetic theory of, say, Clement Greenberg, Adorno was not attempting to prescribe the future course of art; rather he was intent on revealing the truth content of high modernism, a truth content he knew to be fast disappearing. Nor was Adorno an essentialist who believed that the notion of advanced artistic materials represented an ahistorical logic of the different arts. The very idea of advanced artistic materials was a consequence of the exclusion from empirical reality of specific categorical possibilities of practice. Adorno's primary concern was not with the future of art but with salvaging those elements most under threat from enlightened reason: sensuous particularity, rational ends, a substantial notion of individuality, and authentic happiness. The logic of modernism, a logic determined as much from without as from within, was the historical inheritor of these categorial claims.[44] To Adorno this seemed worth documenting and elaborating, all the more so if high art was the only place within modern society where those categorial claims were emphatically realized. If this is no longer the case, it must not be construed as a criticism of Adorno but of culture.

There has been a dovetailing of the culture industry and high art; however both moments of this inward collapse, that is both alterations in the culture industry and in high art, can most plausibly be regarded as a false reconciliation of their difference, and hence a false reconciliation of universal and particular. A full defence of this claim is impossible here, but some indications can be provided.

There is a naive, Lukacsian optimism involved in the belief that mass media in reflecting, expressing and articulating social reality will, in so doing, deflate their own products, and, despite themselves, become vehicles for social critique and ideological subversion. As the claims for the market economy migrate ever more rapidly east, the widespread consensus is that there is no alternative to capitalism. Social conflicts are represented in the mass media, but these mostly represent claims against the ideologies of sexism and racism, which were always incompatible and regressive with respect to the egalitarian logic of legal persons in the market-place.

Diversity is more effectively present in mass media than previously, but this is not an obvious or unequivocal gain. By the late 1950s the homogenization of consciousness had become counter-productive for the purposes of capital expansion; new needs for new commodities had to be created, and this required the reintroduction of the minimal negativity that had been previously eliminated.[45] The cult of the new that had been the prerogative of art throughout the modernist epoch into the period of post-war unification and stabilization has returned to capital expansion from which it originally sprang. But this negativity is neither shocking nor emancipatory since it does not presage a transformation of the fundamental structures of everyday life. On the contrary, through the culture industry capital has co-opted the dynamics of negation both diachronically in its restless production of new and 'different' commodities and synchronically in its promotion of alternative 'life-styles'.

'Life-styles', the culture industry's recycling of style in art, represent the transformation of an aesthetic category, which once possessed a moment of negativity, into a quality of commodity consumption. The expansion of the role of competing life-styles, the permeation of these styles into the home, the pervasiveness of music, the way in which products have become a direct extension of their advertising image, all these phenomena token a closing of the gap between the culture industry and everyday life itself, and a consequent aestheticization of social reality.

> Just as art works become commodities and are enjoyed as such, the commodity itself in consumer society has become image, representation, spectacle. Use value has been replaced by a packaging and advertising. The commodification of art ends up in the aestheticization of the commodity. The siren song of the commodity has displaced the *promesse de bonheur* once held by bourgeois art, and consumer Odysseus blissfully plunges into the sea of commodities, hoping to find gratification but finding none.[46]

Odysseus, who is no longer significantly different from his men, can be unbound only because the Sirens have disappeared. The culture industry in its postmodernist phase has achieved what the avant-garde always wanted: the sublation of the difference between art and life. And this must signal a kind of 'end of art':

> One of the crucial antinomies of art today is that it wants to be and must be squarely Utopian, as social reality increasingly impedes Utopia, while at the same time it should not be Utopian so as not to be found guilty of administering comfort and illusion. If the Utopia of art were actualized, art would come to an end.[47]

The culture industry, which always sought to administer comfort and illusion, has benefited from the exhaustion of the modernist impulse. Without the ready rebuke of aesthetic modernism to contend with, without even the song of the Sirens or its stinging absence to counter it, the culture industry can entwine its version of aesthetic form with social form.

The disappearance of the Sirens, the disappearance of bourgeois art's (broken) promise of happiness, tokens the disappearance of the distinction between distracting pleasure and emphatic happiness, underlining Adorno's view that the culture industry is pornographic and prudish at once. With the loss of the idea of the unified work, even as counterpointed with a critical moment of dissonance, what has equally disappeared is the sublimation of desire for the sake of the production and enjoyment of a unique work. However, the culture industry's effort of desublimation does not correspond to the satisfaction of desire or a true overcoming of the repressions of the work ethic. Lacking an adequate conception of individuality, the new cultural matrix releases aggression in at least equal measure to its release of desire.

Without the constraint of form, which dictated the path of sublimation, desublimated desires find themselves set against the same illusory comforts and real obstacles to happiness as precipitated the need for desublimation in the first instance. The culture industry's response is the production of works, typified in the new architecture, that, through a mimesis of aestheticization, indict the spectator for failing to find gratification where there is none. The release from the rigours of form into the apparent utopian play of differences should have produced a sublime release from the repressions of everyday life under capital and the only illusory dynamic of high culture. Instead, the postmodern sublime (the sublime defeat of the a priori of closed forms), through its aggressive insistence on overcoming the divide between high and low, and integrating art and empirical life, perpetuates the sublime's violent repression of desire without the concomitant moment of release. By this route postmodernism's presumptive affirmation, by offering what is repression as satisfaction, makes the moment of self-negation permanent and thus an unintended celebration of death.[48] Because postmodernist practice alters the empirical world without transforming it, its abstract affirmations belie the despair that sustains it. That despair manifests itself in aggression and violence, a violence now represented, exploited and celebrated in the media. The violence perpetuated by instrumental reason on sensuous particularity, what Adorno terms the 'non-identical', is answered only with violence.

What makes this situation worse is that there is nothing, or so little, of high art to throw it into relief. If the critical energies of classical high modernism have been exhausted, postmodernism has only accidentally and haphazardly found the resources to produce an emphatic moment of negativity. It is this fact that has led to the erosion of the significance of aesthetic production today.[49] It was not just the existence of individual modernist works, but the project of artistic modernism that for a time was able to sustain its negative role in culture that made modernism culturally significant. Postmodernism by definition lacks this possibility. This does not portend a critique of postmodernism or a call for an instauration of the logic of modernism. It is not postmodernism's fault that history eclipsed modernism. The situation of postmodernism is more difficult and unstructured than that of modernism; artists can no longer rely on even the logic of their art and their materials to guide their productive activities. Postmodernism cannot be celebrated because the *drift* of its unifications of high and low art, of modernism and traditional art either aestheticizes empirical reality with the disastrous results already stated; or directly intends a unification which has forgotten or never knew what the division between high and low art critically signified – pop art being the most conspicuous example of this; or succeeds by deploying the 'method' of unification as a means for contriving negativity, hence continuing the project of modernism otherwise – magical realism is a pertinent example here. No matter how it is viewed, postmodernism has not succeeded in overcoming the great divide by producing a true integration of the two domains: it is either a false synthesis capitulating to the demands of capital, or a contingent procedure for continuing the project of modernism, the project of negation, by other means. The project of negation will continue to have point so long as the reconciliation of universal and particular remains illusory. The situation of postmodernism is an exacerbation rather than a diminuation of that illusory state. If the division between the culture industry and high art was the negative truth about society, where does that truth lie now? In asking this question one must not take up the stance of the cultural critic who bemoans the decline of culture and forgets the suffering and the unutterable devastations surrounding it.

Despite its overemphasis on the culture industry's goal of homogeneity, Adorno's theory and analyses continually call attention to the difference between pseudo-individuality and individuality, pleasure and happiness, consensus and freedom, pseudo-activity and activity, illusory otherness and non-identical otherness. These and kindred terms of analysis are the substantial core of Adorno's critical theory. The neutralizations and regressions the culture industry produces are, I would suggest, as Adorno portrays them. If the surface logic of the culture industry is significantly different from the time of Adorno's writing, its effects are uncannily the same. Adorno saw clearly the trajectory of the culture industry and the threat it posed. That his most pessimistic predictions have come to pass makes his writings on the culture industry uncomfortably timely.

Notes

1 Ernst Bloch *et al.* (1977) *Aesthetics and Politics,* translated and edited by Rodney Taylor, London: NLB, p. 123.
2 *Negative Dialectics* (1973) translated by E.B. Ashton, London: Routledge and Kegan Paul, p. 320. For a commentary on this passage see Gillian Rose (1978) *The Melancholy Science: An Introduction to the Thought of T.W. Adorno*, London: Macmillan, pp. 50–1. This work remains the best account of the issues broached in this section.
3 *Dialectic of Enlightenment* (1973) translated by John Cumming, London: Allen Lane, p. 34.
4 Ibid., p. 135.
5 Ibid., p. 137.
6 Ibid.
7 Ibid., p. 135. For a pointed extension of this thesis consider: 'The more they [works of art] sought to free themselves from external purposes, the more they became subject to self-posited principles of organizing the creative process. Thus they reflected and internalized the domination of society. If this is kept in mind, it becomes impossible to criticize the culture industry without criticizing art at the same time.' *Aesthetic Theory* (1984) translated by C. Lenhardt, London: Routledge and Kegan Paul, p. 26.
8 Ibid., p. xi, xii.
9 Ibid., p. xvi.
10 Ibid., p. 120.
11 Ibid., p. 121.
12 Ibid., p. 126.

13 Ibid., p. 139.
14 Ibid., p. 140.
15 Ibid., p. 144.
16 Ibid., p. 167
17 *Gesammelte Schriften* (1975) Band 9.2, Frankfurt am Main: Suhrkamp Verlag, p. 16. In English in original.
18 Ibid., p. 17.
19 Ibid., p. 18.
20 Ibid., p. 24.
21 Ibid., p. 25.
22 Ibid., p. 112–13.
23 Ibid., p. 111.
24 Ibid., p. 115.
25 *Minima Moralia: Reflections From Damaged Life* (1974) translated by E.F.N. Jephcott, London: NLB, p. 238.
26 *Prisms* (1967) translated by Samuel and Shierry Weber, London: Neville Spearman, p. 19.
27 Ibid., p. 22.
28 Ibid.
29 Ibid., p. 23.
30 Ibid., p. 26.
31 Ibid., p. 29.
32 Andrew Arato in Andrew Arato and Eike Gebhardt (eds and introductions) (1978) *The Essential Frankfurt School Reader*, Oxford: Basil Blackwell, p. 203. Arato's clear weighing of transcendent critique is worth quoting in full: '...only transcendent critique reproduces the image of the reified totality that all genuine critique must take into account, and only it has that total intransigence against all reification required by any future radical politics. And yet, the conceptual reproduction of the reified world on its own produces nothing worth saving; transcendent critique cannot ultimately suppress its affinity to barbarism' p. 203.
33 *Prisms*, op. cit., p. 32.
34 Ibid.
35 Ibid.
36 Ibid., p. 33.
37 Ibid.
38 'Culture Industry Reconsidered', Chapter 3 of this book.
39 Douglas Kellner (1984–5) 'Critical Theory and the Culture Industries: A Reassessment', *Telos* 62: 203.
40 Ibid.
41 Ibid.
42 Ibid., p. 204.
43 Ibid., p. 197.
44 For details of this claim see my *Beauty Bereaved: Aesthetic Alienation From Kant to Derrida and Adorno*, Oxford: Polity Press (forthcoming).
45 Moishe Gonzales (1984–5) 'Kellner's Critical Theory: A Reassessment', *Telos* 62: 208.

46 Andreas Huyssen (1986) *After the Great Divide: Modernism, Mass Culture and Postmodernism*, London: Macmillan Press, p. 21. This inflation of advertising and its homology with art for art's sake was seen clearly by Adorno, *Dialectic of Enlightenment*, op. cit., pp. 162–3.
47 *Aesthetic Theory*, op. cit., p. 47.
48 See Russell A. Berman (1984–5) 'Modern Art and Desublimation', *Telos* 62: 46. This seems to me the best single article on this topic, and represents a fully Adornoesque attempt to come to grips with the issues involved.
49 Ibid., p. 47.

Chapter one

On the fetish character in music and the regression of listening

Complaints about the decline of musical taste begin only a little later than mankind's twofold discovery, on the threshhold of historical time, that music represents at once the immediate manifestation of impulse and the locus of its taming. It stirs up the dance of the Maenads and sounds from Pan's bewitching flute, but it also rings out from the Orphic lyre, around which the visions of violence range themselves, pacified. Whenever their peace seems to be disturbed by bacchantic agitation, there is talk of the decline of taste. But if the disciplining function of music has been handed down since Greek philosophy as a major good, then certainly the pressure to be permitted to obey musically, as elsewhere, is today more general than ever. Just as the current musical consciousness of the masses can scarcely be called Dionysian, so its latest changes have nothing to do with taste. The concept of taste is itself outmoded. Responsible art adjusts itself to criteria which approximate judgements: the harmonious and the inharmonious, the correct and incorrect. But otherwise, no more choices are made; the question is no longer put, and no one demands the subjective justification of the conventions. The very existence of the subject who could verify such taste has become as questionable as has, at the opposite pole, the right to a freedom of choice which empirically, in any case, no one any longer exercises. If one seeks to find out who 'likes' a commercial piece, one cannot avoid the suspicion that liking and disliking are inappropriate to the situation, even if the person questioned clothes his reactions in those words. The familiarity of the piece is a surrogate for the quality ascribed to it. To like it is almost the same thing as to recognize it. An approach in terms of value judgements has become a fiction for the person who finds himself hemmed in by standardized musical goods. He can neither escape impotence nor decide between the offerings where everything is so completely identical that preference in fact depends merely on biographical details or on the situation in which things are heard. The categories of autonomously oriented art have no applicability to the contemporary reception of music; not even for that of the serious music, domesticated under the barbarous name of classical so as to enable one to turn away from it again in comfort. If it is objected that specifically light music and everything intended for consumption have in any case never been experienced in terms of those categories, that must certainly be conceded. Nevertheless, such music is also affected by the change in that the entertainment, the pleasure, the enjoyment it promises, is given only to be simultaneously denied. In one of his essays, Aldous Huxley has raised the question of who, in a place of amusement, is really being amused. With the same justice, it can be asked whom music for entertainment still entertains. Rather, it seems to complement the reduction of people to silence, the dying out of speech as expression, the inability to communicate at all. It inhabits the pockets of silence that develop between people moulded by anxiety, work and undemanding docility. Everywhere it takes over, unnoticed, the deadly sad role that fell to it in the time and the specific situation of the silent films. It is perceived purely as background. If nobody can any longer speak, then certainly nobody can any longer listen. An American specialist in radio advertising, who indeed prefers to make use of the musical medium, has expressed scepticism as to the value of this advertising, because people have learned to deny their attention to what they are hearing even while listening to it. His observation is questionable with respect to the advertising value of music. But it tends to be right in terms of the reception of the music itself.

In the conventional complaints about declining taste, certain motifs constantly recur. There is no lack of pouting and sentimental comments assessing the current musical condition of the masses as one of 'degeneration'. The most tenacious of these motifs is that of sensuality, which allegedly enfeebles and incapacitates heroic behaviour. This complaint can already be found in Book III of Plato's *Republic* in which he bans 'the harmonies expressive of sorrow' as well as the 'soft' harmonies 'suitable for drinking,' without its being clear to this day why the philosopher ascribes these characteristics to the mixed Lydian, Lydian, bass Lydian and Ionian modes. In the Platonic state, the major of later Western music, which corresponds to the Ionian, would have been tabooed. The flute and the 'panharmonic' stringed instruments also fall under the ban. The only modes to be left are 'warlike, to sound the note or accent which a brave man utters in the hour of danger and stern resolve, or when he faces injury, defeat or death, or any other misfortune, with the same steadfast endurance'. Plato's *Republic* is not the utopia it is called by the official history of philosophy. It disciplines its citizens in terms of its existence and will to exist even in music, where the distinction made be-

27

tween soft and strong modes was by Plato's time already little more than a residue of the mustiest superstition. The Platonic irony reveals itself mischievously in jeering at the flute-player Marsyas, flayed by the sober-sided Apollo. Plato's ethical-musical programme bears the character of an Attic purge in Spartan style. Other perennial themes of musical sermonizing are on the same level. Among the most prominent of these are the charge of superficiality and that of a 'cult of personality'. What is attacked is chiefly progress: social, essentially the specifically aesthetic. Intertwined with the forbidden allurements are sensual gaiety and differentiating consciousness. The predominance of the person over the collective compulsion in music marks the movement of subjective freedom which breaks through in later phases, while the profanation which frees it from its magic circle appears as superficiality. Thus, the lamented moments have entered into the great music of the West: sensory stimulation as the gate of entry into the harmonic and eventually the colouristic dimensions; the unbridled person as the bearer of expression and of the humanization of music itself; 'superficiality' as a critique of the mute objectivity of forms, in the sense of Haydn's choice of the 'gallant' in preference to the learned. Haydn's choice indeed, and not the recklessness of a singer with a golden throat or an instrumentalist of lip-smacking euphony. For those moments entered into great music and were transformed in it; but great music did not dissolve into them. In the multiplicity of stimulus and expression, its greatness is shown as a force for synthesis. Not only does the musical synthesis preserve the unity of appearance and protect it from falling apart into diffuse culinary moments, but in such unity, in the relation of particular moments to an evolving whole, there is also preserved the image of a social condition in which above those particular moments of happiness would be more than mere appearance. Until the end of prehistory, the musical balance between partial stimulus and totality, between expression and synthesis, between the surface and the underlying, remains as unstable as the moments of balance between supply and demand in the capitalist economy. *The Magic Flute*, in which the utopia of the Enlightenment and the pleasure of a light opera comic song precisely coincide, is a moment by itself. After *The Magic Flute* it was never again possible to force serious and light music together.

But what are emancipated from formal law are no longer the productive impulses which rebelled against conventions. Impulse, subjectivity and profanation, the old adversaries of materialistic alienation, now succumb to it. In capitalist times, the traditional anti-mythological ferments of music conspire against freedom, as whose allies they were once proscribed. The representatives of the opposition to the authoritarian schema become witnesses to the authority of commercial success. The delight in the moment and the gay façade becomes an excuse for absolving the listener from the thought of the whole, whose claim is comprised in proper listening. The listener is converted, along his line of least resistance, into the acquiescent purchaser. No longer do the partial moments serve as a critique of that whole; instead, they suspend the critique which the successful aesthetic totality exerts against the flawed one of society. The unitary synthesis is sacrificed to them; they no longer produce their own in place of the reified one, but show themselves complaisant to it. The isolated moments of enjoyment prove incompatible with the immanent constitution of the work of art, and whatever in the work goes beyond them to an essential perception is sacrificed to them. They are not bad in themselves but in their diversionary function. In the service of success they renounce that insubordinate character which was theirs. They conspire to come to terms with everything which the isolated moment can offer to an isolated individual who long ago ceased to be one. In isolation, the charms become dulled and furnish models of the familiar. Whoever devotes himself to them is as malicious as the Greek thinkers once were toward oriental sensuality. The seductive power of the charm survives only where the forces of denial are strongest: in the dissonance which rejects belief in the illusion of the existing harmony. The concept of the ascetic is itself dialectical in music. If asceticism once struck down the claims of the aesthetic in a reactionary way, it has today become the sign of an advanced art: not, to be sure, by an archaicizing parsimony of means in which deficiency and poverty are manifested, but by the strict exclusion of all culinary delights which seek to be consumed immediately for their own sake, as if in art the sensory were not the bearer of something intellectual which only shows itself in the whole rather than in isolated topical moments. Art records negatively just that possibility of happiness which the only partially positive anticipation of happiness ruinously confronts today. All 'light' and pleasant art has become illusory and mendacious. What makes its appearance aesthetically in the pleasure categories can no longer give pleasure, and the promise of happiness, once the definition of art, can no longer be found except where the mask has been torn from the countenance of false happiness. Enjoyment still retains a place only in the immediate bodily presence. Where it requires an aesthetic appearance, it is illusory by aesthetic standards and likewise cheats the pleasure-seeker out of itself. Only where its appearance is lacking is the faith in its possibility maintained.

The new phase of the musical consciousness of the masses is defined by displeasure in pleasure. It resembles the reaction to sport or advertising. The words 'enjoyment of art' sound funny. If in nothing else, Schonberg's music resembles popular songs in refusing to be enjoyed. Whoever still delights in the beautiful passages of a Schubert quartet or even in the provocatively healthy fare of a Handel concerto grosso, ranks as a would-be guardian of culture among the butterfly collectors. What condemns him as an epicure is not perhaps 'new'. The power of the street ballad, the catchy tune and all the swarming forms of the banal has made itself felt since the beginning of the bourgeois era. Formerly, it attacked the cultural privilege of the ruling class. But today, when that power of the banal extends over the entire society, its function has changed. This change of function affects all music, not only light music, in whose realm it could comfortably enough be made innocuous. The diverse spheres of music must be thought of together. Their static separation, which certain caretakers of culture have ardently sought – the totalitarian radio was assigned to the task, on the one hand, of providing good entertainment and diversion, and on the other, of fostering the so-called cultural goods, as if there could still be good entertainment and as if the cultural goods were not, by their administration, transformed into evils – the neat parcelling out of music's social field of force is illusionary.

Just as the history of serious music since Mozart as a flight from the banal reflects in reverse the outlines of light music, so today, in its key representatives, it gives an account of the ominous experiences which appear even in the unsuspecting innocence of light music. It would be just as easy to go in the other direction and conceal the break between the two spheres, assuming a continuum which permits a progressive education leading safely from commercial jazz and hit songs to cultural commodities. Cynical barbarism is no better than cultural dishonesty. What it accomplishes by disillusion on the higher level, it balances by the ideologies of primitivism and return to nature, with which it glorifies the musical underworld: an underworld which has long ceased to assist the opposition of those excluded from culture to find expression, and now only lives on what is handed down to it from above.

The illusion of a social preference for light music as against serious is based on that passivity of the masses which makes the consumption of light music contradict the objective interest of those who consume it. It is claimed that they actually like light music and listen to the higher type only for reasons of social prestige, when acquaintance with the text of a single hit song suffices to reveal the sole function this object of honest approbation can perform. The unity of the two spheres of music is thus that of an unresolved contradiction. They do not hang together in such a way that the lower could serve as a sort of popular introduction to the higher, or that higher could renew its lost collective strength by borrowing from the lower. The whole cannot be put together by adding the separated halves, but in both there appear, however distantly, the changes of the whole, which only moves in contradiction. If the flight from the banal becomes definitive, if the marketability of the serious product shrinks to nothing, in consequence of its objective demands, then on the lower level the effect of the standardization of successes means it is no longer possible to succeed in an old style, but only in imitation as such. Between incomprehensibility and inescapability, there is no third way; the situation has polarized itself into extremes which actually meet. There is no room between them for the 'individual'. The latter's claims, wherever they still occur, are illusory, being copied from the standards. The liquidation of the individual is the real signature of the new musical situation.

If the two spheres of music are stirred up in the unity of their contradiction, the demarcation line between them varies. The advanced product has renounced consumption. The rest of serious music is delivered over to consumption for the price of its wages. It succumbs to commodity listening. The differences in the reception of official 'classical' music and light music no longer have any real significance. They are only still manipulated for reasons of marketability. The hit song enthusiast must be reassured that his idols are not too elevated for him, just as the visitor to philharmonic concerts is confirmed in his status. The more industriously the trade erects wire fences between the musical provinces, the greater the suspicion that without these, the inhabitants could all too easily come to an understanding. Toscanini, like a second-rate orchestra leader, is called Maestro, if half ironically, and a hit song, 'Music, maestro, please', had its success immediately after Toscanini was promoted to Marshal of the Air with the aid of the radio.

The world of that musical life, the composition business which extends peacefully from Irving Berlin and Walter Donaldson – 'the world's best composer' – by way of Gershwin, Sibelius and Tchaikovsky to Schubert's B Minor Symphony, labelled *The Unfinished*, is one of fetishes. The star principle has become totalitarian. The reactions of the listeners appear to have no relation to the playing of the music. They have reference, rather, to the cumulative success which, for its part, cannot be thought of unalienated by the past spontaneities of listeners, but instead dates back to the command of publishers, sound film magnates and rulers of radio. Famous people are not the only stars. Works begin to take on the same role. A pantheon of best-sellers builds up. The programmes shrink, and the shrinking process not only removes the moderately good, but the accepted classics themselves undergo a selection that has nothing to do with quality. In America, Beethoven's Fourth Symphony is among the rarities. This selection reproduces itself in a fatal circle: the most familiar is the most successful and is therefore played again and again and made still more familiar. The choice of the standard works is itself in terms of their 'effectiveness' for programmatic fascination, in terms of the categories of success as determined by light music or permitted by the star conductors. The climaxes of Beethoven's Seventh Symphony are placed on the same level as the unspeakable horn melody from the slow movement of Tchaikovsky's Fifth. Melody comes to mean eight-beat symmetrical treble melody. This is catalogued as the composer's 'idea' which one thinks he can put in his pocket and take home, just as it is ascribed to the composer as his basic property. The concept of the idea is far from appropriate to established classical music. Its thematic material, mostly dissected triads, does not at all belong to the author in the same specific sense as in a romantic song. Beethoven's greatness shows itself in the complete subordination of the accidentally private melodic elements to the form as a whole. This does not prevent all music, even Bach, who borrowed one of the most important themes of *The Well-Tempered Clavier*, from being examined in terms of the category of ideas, with musical larceny being hunted down with all the zeal of the belief in property, so that finally one music commentator could pin his success to the title of tune detective.

At its most passionate, musical fetishism takes possession of the public valuation of singing voices. Their sensuous magic is traditional as is the close relation between success and the person endowed with 'material'. But today it is forgotten that it is material. For musical vulgar materialists, it is synonymous to have a voice and to be a singer. In earlier epochs, technical virtuosity, at least, was demanded of singing stars, the castrati and prima donnas. Today, the material as such, destitute of any function, is celebrated. One need not even ask about capacity for musical performance. Even mechanical control of the instrument is no longer really expected. To legitimate the fame of its owner, a voice need only be especially voluminous or especially high. If one dares even in conversation to question the decisive importance of the voice and to assert that it is just as possible to make beautiful music with a moderately good voice as it is on a moderately good piano, one will immediately find oneself faced with a situation of hostility and aversion whose emotional roots go far deeper than the occasion. Voices are holy properties like a national trademark. As if the voices wanted to revenge themselves for this, they begin to lose the sensuous magic in whose name they are merchandised. Most of them sound like imitations of those who have made it, even when they themselves have made it. All this reaches a climax of absurdity in the cult of the master violins. One promptly goes into raptures at the well-announced sound of a Stradivarius or Amati, which only the ear of a specialist can tell from that of a good modern violin, forgetting in the process to listen to the composition and the execution, from which there is still something to be had. The more modern technique of the violin bow progresses, the more it seems that the old instruments are treasured. If the moments of sensual pleasure in the idea, the voice, the instrument are made into fetishes and torn away from any functions which could give them meaning, they meet a response equally isolated, equally far from the meaning of the whole, and equally determined by success in the blind and irrational emotions which form the relationship to music into which those with no relationship enter. But these are the same relations as exist between the consumers of hit songs and the hit songs. Their only relation is to the completely alien, and the alien, as if cut off from the consciousness of the masses by a dense screen, is what seeks to speak for the silent. Where they react at all, it no longer makes any difference whether it is to Beethoven's Seventh Symphony or to a bikini.

The concept of musical fetishism cannot be psychologically derived. That 'values' are consumed and draw feelings to themselves, without their specific qualities being reached by the consciousness of the consumer, is a later expression of their commodity character. For all contemporary musical life is dominated by the commodity form; the last pre-capitalist residues have been eliminated. Music, with all the attributes of the ethereal and sublime which are generously accorded it, serves in America today as an advertisement for commodities which one must acquire in order to be able to hear music. If the advertising function is carefully dimmed in the case of serious music, it always breaks through in the case of light music. The whole jazz business, with its free distribution of scores to bands, has abandoned the idea that actual performance promotes the sale of piano scores and phonograph records. Countless hit song texts praise the hit songs themselves, repeating their titles in capital letters. What makes its appearance, like an idol, out of such masses of type is the exchange value in which the quantum of possible enjoyment has disappeared. Marx defines the fetish character of the commodity as the veneration of the thing made by oneself which, as exchange-value, simultaneously alienates itself from producer to consumer – 'human beings.' 'A commodity is therefore a mysterious thing, simply because in it the social character of men's labour appears to them as an objective character stamped upon the product of that labour; because the relation of the producers to the sum total of their own labour is presented to them as a social relation, existing not between themselves, but between the products of their labour.' This is the real secret of success. It is the mere reflection of what one pays in the market for the product. The consumer is really worshipping the money that he himself has paid for the ticket to the Toscanini concert. He has literally 'made' the success which he reifies and accepts as an objective criterion, without recognizing himself in it. But he has not 'made' it by liking the concert, but rather by buying the ticket. To be sure, exchange value exerts its power in a special way in the realm of cultural goods. For in the world of commodities this realm appears to be exempted from the power of exchange, to be in an immediate relationship with the goods, and it is this appearance in turn which alone gives cultural goods their exchange value. But they nevertheless simultaneously fall completely into the world of commodities, are produced for the market, and are aimed at the market. The appearance of immediacy is as strong as the compulsion of exchange value is inexorable. The social compact harmonizes the contradiction. The appearance of immediacy takes possession of the mediated, exchange value itself. If the commodity in general combines exchange value and use value, then the pure use value, whose illusion the cultural goods must preserve in a completely capitalist society, must be replaced by pure exchange value, which precisely in its capacity as exchange value deceptively takes over the function of use value. The specific fetish character of music lies in this *quid pro quo*. The feelings which go to the exchange value create the appearance of immediacy at the same time as the absence of a relation to the object belies it. It has its basis in the abstract character of exchange value. Every 'psychological' aspect, every ersatz satisfaction, depends on such social substitution.

The change in the function of music involves the basic conditions of the relation between art and society. The more inexorably the principle of exchange value destroys use values for human beings, the more deeply does exchange value disguise itself as the object of enjoyment. It has been asked what the cement is which still holds the world of commodities together. The answer is that this transfer of the use value of consumption goods to their exchange value contributes to a general order in which eventually every pleasure which emancipates itself from exchange values takes on subversive features. The appearance of exchange value in commodities has taken on a specific cohesive function. The woman who has money with which to buy is intoxicated by the act of buying. In American conventional speech, having a good time means being present at the enjoyment of others, which in its turn has as its only content being present. The auto religion makes all men brothers in the sacramental moment with the words: 'that is a Rolls Royce', and in moments of intimacy, women attach greater importance to the hairdressers and cosmeticians than to the situation for the sake of which the hairdressers and cosmeticians are employed. The relation to the irrelevant dutifully manifests its social essence. The couple out driving who spend their time identifying every passing car and being happy if they recognize the trademarks speeding by, the girl whose satisfaction consists solely in the fact that she and her boyfiend 'look good', the expertise of the jazz enthusiast who legitimizes himself by having knowledge about what is in any case inescapable: all this operates according to the same command. Before the theological caprices of commodities, the consumers become temple slaves. Those who sacrifice themselves nowhere else can do so here, and here they are fully betrayed.

In the commodity fetishists of the new model, in the 'sado-masochistic character', in those receptive to today's mass art, the same thing shows itself in many ways. The masochistic mass culture is the necessary manifestation of almighty production itself. When the feelings seize on exchange value it is no mystical transubstantiation. It corresponds to the behaviour of the prisoner who loves his cell because he has been left nothing else to love. The sacrifice of individuality, which accommodates itself to the regularity of the successful, the doing of what everybody does, follows from the basic fact that in broad areas the same thing is offered to everybody by the standardized production of consumption goods. But the commercial necessity of connecting this identity leads to the manipulation of taste and the official culture's pretence of individualism which necessarily increases in proportion to the liquidation of the individual. Even in the realm of the superstructure, the appearance is not merely the concealment of the essence, but proceeds of necessity from the essence itself. The identical character of the goods which everyone must buy hides itself behind the rigour of the universally compulsory style. The fiction of the relation between supply and demand survives in the fictitiously individual nuances.

If the value of taste in the present situation is questioned, it is necessary to understand what taste is composed of in this situation. Acquiescence is rationalized as modesty, opposition to caprice and anarchy; musical analysis has today decayed as fundamentally as musical charm, and has its parody in the stubborn counting of beats. The picture is completed by accidental differentiation within the strict confines of the prescribed. But if the liquidated individual really makes the complete superficiality of the conventions passionately his own, then the golden age of taste has dawned at the very moment in which taste no longer exists. The works which are the basis of the fetishization and become the cultural goods experience constitutional changes as a result. They become vulgarized. Irrelevant consumption destroys them. Not merely do the few things played again and again wear out, like the Sistine Madonna in the bedroom, but reification affects their internal structure. They are transformed into a conglomeration of irruptions which are impressed on the listeners by climax and repetition, while the organization of the whole makes no impression whatsoever.

The memorability of disconnected parts, thanks to climaxes and repetitions, has a precursor in great music itself, in the technique of late romantic compositions, especially those of Wagner. The more reified the music, the more romantic it sounds to alienated ears. Just in this way it becomes 'property'. A Beethoven symphony as a whole, spontaneously experienced, can never be appropriated. The man who in the subway triumphantly whistles loudly the theme of the finale of Brahms' First is already primarily involved with its debris. But since the disintegration of the fetishes puts these themselves in danger and virtually assimilates them to hit songs, it produces a counter tendency in order to preserve their fetish character. If the romanticizing of particulars eats away the body of the whole, the endangered substance is galvanically copper-plated. The climax which emphasizes the reified parts takes on the character of a magical ritual, in which all the mysteries of personality, inwardness, inspiration and spontaneity of reproduction, which have been eliminated from the work itself, are conjured up. Just because the disintegrating work renounces the moment of its spontaneity, this, just as stereotyped as the bits and pieces, is injected into it from the outside. In spite of all talk of new objectivity, the essential function of conformist performances is no longer the performance of the 'pure' work but the presentation of the vulgarized one with a gesture which emphatically but impotently tries to hold the vulgarization at a distance.

Vulgarization and enchantment, hostile sisters, dwell together in the arrangements which have colonized large areas of music. The practice of arrangement extends to the most diverse dimensions. Sometimes it seizes on the time. It blatantly snatches the reified bits and pieces out of their context and sets them up as a pot-pourri. It destroys the multilevel unity of the whole work and brings forward only isolated popular passages. The minuet from Mozart's E Flat Major Symphony, played without the other movement, loses its symphonic cohesion and is turned by the performance into an artisan-type genre piece that has more to do with the 'Stephanie Gavotte' than with the sort of classicism it is supposed to advertise.

Then there is the arrangement in colouristic terms. They arrange whatever they can get hold of, as long as the ukase of a famous interpreter does not forbid it. If in the field of light music the arrangers are the only trained musicians, they feel called upon to jump around all the more unrestrainedly with cultural goods. All sorts of reasons are offered by them for instrumental arrangements. In the case of great orchestral works, it will reduce the cost, or the composers are accused of lacking technique in instrumentation. These reasons are lamentable pretexts. The argument of cheapness, which aesthetically condemns itself, is disposed of by reference to the superfluity of orchestral means at the disposal of precisely those who most eagerly carry on the practice of arrangement, and by the fact that very often, as in instrumental arrangements of piano pieces, the arrangements turn out substantially dearer than performance in the original form. And finally, the belief that older music needs a colouristic freshening up presupposes an accidental character in the relation between colour and line, such as could be assumed only as a result of the crudest ignorance of Vienna classicism and the so-eagerly arranged Schubert. Even if the real discovery of the colouristic dimension first took place in the era of Berlioz and Wagner, the colouristic parsimony of Haydn or Beethoven is of a piece with the predominance of the principle of construction over the melodic particular springing in brilliant colours out of the dynamic unity. Precisely in the context of such parsimony do the bassoon thirds at the beginning of the third *Leonore Overture* or the oboe cadenza in the reprise of the first movement of the Fifth achieve a power which would be irretrievably lost in a multicoloured sonority.

One must therefore assume that the motives for the practice of arranging are *sui generis*. Above all, arranging seeks to make the great distant sound, which always has aspects of the public and unprivate, assimilable. The tired businessman can clap arranged classics on the shoulder and fondle the progeny of their muse. It is a compulsion similar to that which requires radio favourites to insinuate themselves into the families of their listeners as uncles and aunts and pretend to a human proximity. Radical reification produces its own pretence of immediacy and intimacy. Contrariwise, the intimate is inflated and coloured by arrangements precisely for being too spare. Because they were originally defined only as moments of the whole, the instants of sensory pleasure which emerge out of the decomposing unities are too weak even to produce the sensory stimulus demanded of them in fulfilment of their advertised role. The dressing up and puffing up of the individual erases the lineaments of protest, sketched out in the limitation of the individual to himself over and against the institution, just as in the reduction of the large-scale to the intimate, sight is lost of the totality in which bad individual immediacy was kept within bounds in great music. Instead of this, there develops a spurious balance which at every step betrays its falsity by its contradiction of the material. Schubert's *Serenade*, in the blown-up sound of the combination of strings and piano, with the silly excessive clarity of the imitative intermediate measures, is as nonsensical as if it has originated in a girls' school. But neither does the prize song from *Meistersinger* sound any more serious when played by a string orchestra alone. In monochrome, it objectively loses the articulation which makes it viable in Wagner's score. But at the same time, it becomes quite viable for the listener, who no longer has to put the body of the song together from different colours, but can confidently give himself over to the single and uninterrupted treble melody. Here one can put one's hands on the antagonism to the audience into which works regarded as classic fall today. But one may suspect that the darkest secret of arrangement is the compulsion not to leave anything as it is, but to lay hands on anything that crosses one's path, a compulsion that grows greater the less the fundamental characteristics of what exists lend themselves to being meddled with. The total social grasp confirms its power and mastery by the stamp which is impressed on anything that falls into its machinery. But this affirmation is likewise destructive. Contemporary listeners would always prefer to destroy what they hold in blind respect, and their pseudo-activity is already prepared and prescribed by the production.

The practice of arrangement comes from salon music. It is the practice of refined entertainment which borrows its pretensions from the *niveau* of cultural goods, but transforms these into entertainment material of the type of hit songs. Such entertainment, formerly reserved as an accompaniment to people's humming, today spreads over the whole of musical life, which is basically not taken seriously by anyone anymore and in all discussion of culture retreats further and further into the background. One has the choice of either dutifully going along with the business, if only furtively in front of the loudspeaker on Saturday afternoon, or at once stubbornly and impenitently acknowledging the trash served up for the ostensible or real needs of the masses. The uncompelling and superficial nature of the objects of refined entertainment inevitably leads to the inattentiveness of the listeners. One preserves a good conscience in the matter since one is offering the listeners first-class goods. To the objection that these are already a drug on the market, one is ready with the reply that this is what they wanted, an argument which can be finally invalidated by a diagnosis of the situation of the listeners, but only through insight into the whole process which unites producers and consumers in diabolical harmony.

But fetishism takes hold of even the ostensibly serious practice of music, which mobilizes the pathos of distance against refined entertainment. The purity of service to the cause, with which it presents the works, often turns out to be as inimical to them as vulgarization and arrangement. The official ideal of performance, which covers the earth as a result of Toscanini's extraordinary achievement, helps to sanction a condition which, in a phrase of Eduard Steuermann, may be called the barbarism of perfection. To be sure, the names of famous works are no longer made fetishes, although the lesser ones that break into the programmes almost make the limitation to the smaller repertoire seem desirable. To be sure, passages are not here inflated or climaxes overstressed for the sake of fascination. There is iron discipline. But precisely iron. The new fetish is the flawlessly functioning, metallically brilliant apparatus as such, in which all the cogwheels mesh so perfectly that not the slightest hole remains open for the meaning of the whole. Perfect, immaculate performance in the latest style preserves the work at the price of its definitive reification. It presents it as already complete from the very first note. The performance sounds like its own phonograph record. The dynamic is so predetermined that there are no longer any tensions at all. The contradictions of the music material are so inexorably resolved in the moment of sound that it never arrives at the synthesis, the self-production of the work, which reveals the meaning of every Beethoven symphony. What is the point of the symphonic effort when the material on which that effort was to be tested has already been ground up? The protective fixation of the works leads to its destruction, for its unity is realized in precisely that spontaneity which is sacrificed to the fixation. This last fetishism, which seizes on the substance itself, smothers it; the absolute adjustment of the appearance to the work denies the latter and makes it disappear unnoticed behind the apparatus, just as certain swamp-drainings by labour detachments take place not for their own sake but for that of the work. Not for nothing does the rule of the established conductor remind one of that of the totalitarian Führer. Like the latter, he reduces aura and organization to a common denominator. He is the real modern type of the virtuoso, as bandleader as well as in the Philharmonic. He has got to the point where he no longer has to do anything himself; he is even sometimes relieved of reading the score by the staff musical advisers. At one stroke he provides norm and individualization: the norm is identified with his person, and the individual tricks which he perpetrates furnish the general rules. The fetish character of the conductor is the most obvious and the most hidden. The standard works could probably be performed by the virtuosi of contemporary orchestras just as well without the conductor, and the public which cheers the conductor would be unable to tell that, in the concealment of the orchestra, the musical adviser was taking the place of the hero laid low by a cold.

39

The consciousness of the mass listeners is adequate to fetishized music. It listens according to formula, and indeed debasement itself would not be possible if resistance ensued, if the listeners still had the capacity to make demands beyond the limits of what was supplied. But if someone tried to 'verify' the fetish character of music by investigating the reactions of listeners with interviews and questionnaires, he might meet with unexpected puzzles. In music as elsewhere, the discrepancy between essence and appearance has grown to a point where no appearance is any longer valid, without mediation, as verification of the essence. The unconscious reactions of the listeners are so heavily veiled and their conscious assessment is so exclusively oriented to the dominant fetish categories that every answer one receives conforms in advance to the surface of that music business which is attacked by the theory being 'verified'. As soon as one presents the listener with the primitive question about liking or disliking, there comes into play the whole machinery which one had thought could be made transparent and eliminated by the reduction to this question. But if one tries to replace the most elementary investigative procedures with others which take account of the real dependence of the listener on the mechanism, this complication of the investigative procedure not merely makes the interpretation of the result more difficult, but it touches off the resistance of the respondents and drives them all the deeper into the conformist behaviour in which they think they can remain concealed from the danger of exposure. No causal nexus at all can properly be worked out between isolated 'impressions' of the hit song and its psychological effects on the listener. If indeed individuals today no longer belong to themselves, then that also means that they can no longer be 'influenced'. The opposing points of production and consumption are at any given time closely co-ordinated, but not dependent on each other in isolation. Their mediation itself does not in any case escape theoretical conjecture. It suffices to remember how many sorrows he is spared who no longer thinks too many thoughts, how much more 'in accordance with reality' a person behaves when he affirms that the real is right, how much more capacity to use the machinery falls to the person who integrates himself with it uncomplainingly, so that the correspondence between the listener's consciousness and the fetishized music would still remain comprehensible even if the former did not unequivocally reduce itself to the latter.

The counterpart to the fetishism of music is a regression of listening. This does not mean a relapse of the individual listener into an earlier phase of his own development, nor a decline in the collective general level, since the millions who are reached musically for the first time by today's mass communications cannot be compared with the audience of the past. Rather, it is contemporary listening which has regressed, arrested at the infantile stage. Not only do the listening subjects lose, along with the freedom of choice and responsibility, the capacity for conscious perception of music, which was from time immemorial confined to a narrow group, but they stubbornly reject the possibility of such perception. They fluctuate between comprehensive forgetting and sudden dives into recognition. They listen atomistically and dissociate what they hear, but precisely in this dissociation they develop certain capacities which accord less with the concepts of traditional aesthetics than with those of football and motoring. They are not childlike, as might be expected on the basis of an interpretation of the new type of listener in terms of the introduction to musical life of groups previously unacquainted with music. But they are childish; their primitivism is not that of the undeveloped, but that of the forcibly retarded. Whenever they have a chance, they display the pinched hatred of those who really sense the other but exclude it in order to live in peace, and who therefore would like best to root out the nagging possibility. The regression is really from this existent possibility, or more concretely, from the possibility of a different and oppositional music. Regressive, too, is the role which contemporary mass music plays in the psychological household of its victims. They are not merely turned away from more important music, but they are confirmed in their neurotic stupidity, quite irrespective of how their musical capacities are related to the specific musical culture of earlier social phases. The assent to hit songs and debased cultural goods belongs to the same complex of symptoms as do those faces of which one no longer knows whether the film has alienated them from reality or reality has alienated them from the film, as they wrench open a great formless mouth with shining teeth in a voracious smile, while the tired eyes are wretched and lost above. Together with sport and film, mass music and the new listening help to make escape from the whole infantile milieu impossible. The sickness has a preservative function. Even the listening habits of the contemporary masses are certainly in no way new, and one may readily concede that the reception of the pre-war hit song 'Puppchen' was not so very different from that of a synthetic jazz children's song. But the context in which such a children's song appears, the masochistic mocking of one's own wish for lost happiness, or the compromising of the desire for happiness itself by the reversion to a childhood whose unattainability bears witness to the unattainability of joy – this is the specific product of the new listening, and nothing which strikes the ear remains exempt from this system of assimilation. There are indeed social differences, but the new listening extends so far that the stultification of the oppressed affects the oppressors themselves, and they become victims of the superior power of self-propelled wheels who think they are determining their direction.

Regressive listening is tied to production by the machinery of distribution, and particularly by advertising. Regressive listening appears as soon as advertising turns into terror, as soon as nothing is left for the consciousness but to capitulate before the superior power of the advertised stuff and purchase spiritual peace by making the imposed goods literally its own thing. In regressive listening, advertising takes on a compulsory character. For a while, an English brewery used for propaganda purposes a billboard that bore a deceptive likeness to one of the whitewashed brick walls which are so numerous in the slums of London and the industrial cities of the North. Properly placed, the billboard was barely distinguishable from a real wall. On it, chalk-white, was a careful imitation of awkward writing. The words said: 'What we want is Watney's.' The brand of beer was presented like a political slogan. Not only does this billboard give an insight into the nature of up-to-date propaganda, which sells its slogans as well as its wares, just as here the wares masquerade as a slogan; the type of relationship suggested by the billboard, in which masses make a commodity recommended to them the object of their own action, is in fact found again as the pattern for the reception of light music. They need and demand what has been palmed off on them. They overcome the feeling of impotence that creeps over them in the face of monopolistic production by identifying themselves with the inescapable product. They thereby put an end to the strangeness of the musical brands which are at once distant from them and threateningly near, and in addition, achieve the satisfaction of feeling themselves involved in Mr Know-Nothing's enterprises, which confront them at every turn. This explains why individual expressions of preference – or, of course, dislike – converge in an area where object and subject alike make such reactions questionable. The fetish character of music produces its own camouflage through the identification of the listener with the fetish. This identification initially gives the hit songs power over their victims. It fulfils itself in the subsequent forgetting and remembering. Just as every advertisement is composed of the inconspicuous familiar and the unfamiliar conspicuous, so the hit song remains salutarily forgotten in the half-dusk of its familiarity, suddenly to become painfully over-clear through recollection, as if in the beam of a spotlight. One can almost equate the moment of this recollection with that in which the title or the words of the initial verse of his hit song confront the victim. Perhaps he identifies himself with this because he identifies it and thereby merges with his possession. This compulsion may well drive him to recall the title of the hit song at times. But the writing under the note, which makes the identification possible, is nothing else but the trademark of the hit song.

Deconcentration is the perceptual activity which prepares the way for the forgetting and sudden recognition of mass music. If the standardized products, hopelessly like one another except for conspicuous bits such as hit lines, do not permit concentrated listening without becoming unbearable to the listeners, the latter are in any case no longer capable of concentrated listening. They cannot stand the strain of concentrated listening and surrender themselves resignedly to what befalls them, with which they can come to terms only if they do not listen to it too closely. Benjamin's reference to the apperception of the cinema in a condition of distraction is just as valid for light music. The usual commercial jazz can only carry out its function because it is not attended to except during conversation and, above all, as an accompaniment to dancing. Again and again one encounters the judgement that it is fine for dancing but dreadful for listening. But if the film as a whole seems to be apprehended in a distracted manner, deconcentrated listening makes the perception of a whole impossible. All that is realized is what the spotlight falls on – striking melodic intervals, unsettling modulations, intentional or unintentional mistakes, or whatever condenses itself into a formula by an especially intimate merging of melody and text. Here, too, listeners and products fit together; they are not even offered the structure which they cannot follow. If atomized listening means progressive decomposition for the higher music, there is nothing more to decompose in the lower music. The forms of hit songs are so strictly standardized, down to the number of beats and the exact duration, that no specific form appears in any particular piece. The emancipation of the parts from their cohesion, and from all moments which extend beyond their immediate present, introduces the diversion of musical interest to the particular sensory pleasure. Typically, the listeners show a preference not merely for particular showpieces for instrumental acrobatics, but for the individual instrumental colours as such. This preference is promoted by the practice of American popular music whereby each variation, or 'chorus', is played with emphasis on a special instrumental colour, with the clarinet, the piano, or the trumpet as quasi-soloist. This often goes so far that the listener seems to care more about treatment and 'style' than about the otherwise indifferent material, but with the treatment validating itself only in particular enticing effects. Along with the attraction to colour as such, there is of course the veneration for the tool and the drive to imitate and join in the game; possibly also something of the great delight of children in bright colours, which returns under the pressure of contemporary musical experience.

The diversion of interest from the whole, perhaps indeed from the 'melody', to the charm of colour and to the individual trick, could be optimistically interpreted as a new rupture of the disciplining function. But this interpretation would be erroneous. Once the perceived charms remain unopposed in a rigid format, whoever yields to them will eventually rebel against it. But then they are themselves of the most limited kind. They all centre on an impressionistically softened tonality. It cannot be said that interest in the isolated colour or the isolated sonority awakens a taste for new colours and new sonorities. Rather, the atomistic listeners are the first to denounce such sonorities as 'intellectual' or absolutely dissonant. The charms which they enjoy must be of an approved type. To be sure, dissonances occur in jazz practice, and even techniques of intentional misplaying have developed. But an appearance of harmlessness accompanies all these customs; every extravagant sonority must be so produced that the listener can recognize it as a substitute for a 'normal' one. While he rejoices in the mistreatment the dissonance gives to the consonance whose place it takes, the virtual consonance simultaneously guarantees that one remains within the circle. In tests on the reception of hit songs, people have been found who ask how they should act if a passage simultaneously pleases and displeases them. One may well suspect that they report an experience which also occurs to those who give no account of it.

The reactions to isolated charms are ambivalent. A sensory pleasure turns into disgust as soon as it is seen how it only still serves to betray the consumer. The betrayal here consists in always offering the same thing. Even the most insensitive hit song enthusiast cannot always escape the feeling that the child with a sweet tooth comes to know in the candy store. If the charms wear off and turn into their opposite – the short life of most hit songs belongs in the same range of experience – then the cultural ideology which clothes the upper-level musical business finishes things off by causing the lower to be heard with a bad conscience. Nobody believes so completely in prescribed pleasure. But the listening nevertheless remains regressive in assenting to this situation despite all distrust and all ambivalence. As a result of the displacement of feelings into exchange value, no demands are really advanced in music any more. Substitutes satisfy their purpose as well, because the demand to which they adjust themselves has itself already been substituted. But ears which are still only able to hear what one demands of them in what is offered, and which register the abstract charm instead of synthesizing the moments of charm, are bad ears. Even in the 'isolated' phenomenon, key aspects will escape them, that is, those which transcend its own isolation. There is actually a neurotic mechanism of stupidity in listening, too;

the arrogantly ignorant rejection of everything unfamiliar is its sure sign. Regressive listeners behave like children. Again and again and with stubborn malice, they demand the one dish they have once been served.

A sort of musical children's language is prepared for them; it differs from the real thing in that its vocabulary consists exclusively of fragments and distortions of the artistic language of music. In the piano scores of hit songs, there are strange diagrams. They relate to guitar, ukelele and banjo, as well as the accordion – infantile instruments in comparison with the piano – and are intended for players who cannot read the notes. They depict graphically the fingering for the chords of the plucking instruments. The rationally comprehensible notes are replaced by visual directives, to some extent by musical traffic signals. These signs, of course, confine themselves to the three tonic major chords and exclude any meaningful harmonic progression. The regulated musical traffic is worthy of them. It cannot be compared with that in the streets. It swarms with mistakes in phrasing and harmony. There are wrong pitches, incorrect doublings of thirds, fifths and octave progressions, and all sorts of illogical treatments of voices, sometimes in the bass. One would like to blame them on the amateurs with whom most of the hit songs originate, while the real musical work is first done by the arrangers. But just as a publisher does not let a misspelled word go out into the world, so it is inconceivable that, well-advised by their experts, they publish amateur versions without checking them. The mistakes are either consciously produced by the experts or intentionally permitted to stand – for the sake of the listeners. One could attribute to the publishers and experts the wish to ingratiate themselves with the listeners, composing as nonchalantly and informally as a dilettante drums out a hit song after hearing it. Such intrigues would be of the same stripe, even if considered psychologically different, as the incorrect spelling in many advertising slogans. But even if one wanted to exclude their acceptance as too far-fetched, the typographical errors could be understood. On the one hand, the infantile hearing demands sensually rich and full sonority, sometimes represented by the luxuriant thirds, and it is precisely this demand in which the infantile musical language is in most brutal contradiction with the children's song. On the other hand, the infantile hearing always demands the most comfortable and fluent resolutions. The consequences of the 'rich' sonority, with correct treatment of voices, would be so far from the standardized harmonic relations that the listener would have to reject them as 'unnatural'. The mistakes would then be the bold strokes which reconcile the antagonisms of the infantile listener's consciousness.

No less characteristic of the regressive musical language is the quotation. Its use ranges from the conscious quotation of folk and children's songs, by way of ambiguous and half accidental allusions, to completely latent similarities and associations. The tendency triumphs in the adaptation of whole pieces from the classical stock or the operatic repertoire. The practice of quotation mirrors the ambivalence of the infantile listener's consciousness. The quotations are at once authoritarian and a parody. It is thus that a child imitates the teacher.

The ambivalence of the retarded listeners has its most extreme expression in the fact that individuals, not yet fully reified, want to extricate themselves from the mechanism of music reification to which they have been handed over, but that their revolts against fetishism only entangle them more deeply in it. Whenever they attempt to break away from the passive status of compulsory consumers and 'activate' themselves, they succumb to pseudo-activity. Types rise up from the masses of the retarded who differentiate themselves by pseudoactivity and nevertheless make the regression more strikingly visible. There are, first, the enthusiasts who write fan letters to radio stations and orchestras and, at well-managed jazz festivals, produce their own enthusiasm as an advertisement for the wares they consume. They call themselves jitterbugs, as if they simultaneously wanted to affirm and mock their loss of individuality, their transformation into beetles whirring around in fascination. Their only excuse is that the term jitterbugs, like all those in the unreal edifice of films and jazz, is hammered into them by the entrepreneurs to make them think that they are on the inside. Their ecstasy is without content. That it happens, that the music is listened to, this replaces the content itself. The ecstasy takes possession of its object by its own compulsive character. It is stylized like the ecstasies savages go into in beating the war-drums. It has convulsive aspects reminiscent of St Vitus's dance or the reflexes of mutilated animals. Passion itself seems to be produced by defects. But the ecstatic ritual betrays itself as pseudo-activity by the moment of mimicry. People do not dance or listen 'from sensuality' and sensuality is certainly not satisfied by listening, but the gestures of the sensual are imitated. An analogue is the representation of particular emotions in the film, where there are physiognomic patterns for anxiety, longing, the erotic look; for smiling; for the atomistic expressivo of debased music. The imitative assimilation to commodity models is intertwined with folkloristic customs of imitation. In jazz, the relation of such mimicry to the imitating individual himself is quite loose. Its medium is caricature. Dance and music copy stages of sexual excitement only to make fun of them. It is as if desire's surrogate itself simultaneously turned against it; the 'realistic' behaviour of the oppressed triumphs over his dream of happiness while being itself incorporated into the latter.

And as if to confirm the superficiality and treachery of every form of ecstasy, the feet are unable to fulfil what the ear pretends. The same jitterbugs who behave as if they were electrified by syncopation dance almost exclusively the good rhythmic parts. The weak flesh punishes the lies of the willing spirit; the gestural ecstasy of the infantile listener misfires in the face of the ecstatic gesture. The opposite type appears to be the eager person who leaves the factory and 'occupies' himself with the music in the quiet of his bedroom. He is shy and inhibited, perhaps has no luck with girls, and wants in any case to preserve his own special sphere. He seeks this as a radio ham. At twenty, he is still at the stage of a boy scout working on complicated knots just to please his parents. This type is held in high esteem in radio matters. He patiently builds sets whose most important parts he must buy ready-made, and scans the air for shortwave secrets, though there are none. As a reader of Indian stories and travel books, he once discovered unknown lands and cleared his path through the forest primeval. As radio ham he becomes the discoverer of just those industrial products which are interested in being discovered by him. He brings nothing home which would not be delivered to his house. The adventurers of pseudo-activity have already organized themselves on a large scale; the radio amateurs have printed verification cards sent them by the shortwave stations they have discovered, and hold contests in which the winner is the one who can produce the most such cards. All this is carefully fostered from above. Of all fetishistic listeners, the radio ham is perhaps the most complete. It is irrelevant to him what he hears or even how he hears; he is only interested in the fact that he hears and succeeds in inserting himself, with his private equipment, into the public mechanism, without exerting even the slightest influence on it. With the same attitude, countless radio listeners play with the feedback or the sound dial without themselves becoming hams. Others are more expert, or at least more aggressive. These smart chaps can be found everywhere and are able to do everything themselves: the advanced student who in every gathering is ready to play jazz with machine-like precision for dancing and entertainment; the gas station attendant who hums his syncopation ingenuously while filling up the tank; the listening expert who can identify every band and immerses himself in the history of jazz as if it were Holy Writ. He is nearest to the sportsman: if not to the football player himself, then to the swaggering fellow who dominates the stands. He shines by a capacity for rough improvisations, even if he must practise the piano for hours in secret in order to bring the refractory rhythms together. He pictures himself as the individualist who whistles at the world. But what he whistles is its melody, and his tricks are less inventions of the moment than stored-up experiences from acquaintance with sought-after technical things. His improvisations are always gestures of nimble subordination to what the instrument demands of him. The chauffeur is the model for the listening type of the clever fellow. His agreement with everything dominant goes so far that he no longer produces any resistance, but of his own accord always does what is asked of him for the sake of the responsible functionary. He lies to himself about the completeness of his subordination to the rule of the reified mechanism. Thus, the sovereign routine of the jazz amateur is nothing but the passive capacity for adaptation to models from which to avoid straying. He is the real jazz subject: his improvisations come from the pattern, and he navigates the pattern, cigarette in mouth, as nonchalantly as if he had invented it himself.

Regressive listeners have key points in common with the man who must kill time because he has nothing else on which to vent his aggression, and with the casual labourer. To make oneself a jazz expert or hang over the radio all day, one must have much free time and little freedom. The dexterity which comes to terms with the syncopation as well as with the basic rhythm is that of the auto mechanic who can also repair the loudspeaker and the electric light. The new listeners resemble the mechanics who are simultaneously specialized and capable of applying their special skills to unexpected places outside their skilled trades. But this despecialization only seems to help them out of the system. The more easily they meet the demands of the day, the more rigidly they are subordinated to that system. The research finding, that among radio listeners the friends of light music reveal themselves to be depoliticized, is not accidental. The possibility of individual shelter and of a security which is, as always, questionable, obstructs the view of a change in the situation in which one seeks shelter. Superficial experience contradicts this. The 'younger generation' – the concept itself is merely an ideological catch-all – seems to be in conflict with its elders and their plush culture precisely through the new way of listening. In America, it is just the so-called liberals and progressives whom one finds among the advocates of light popular music, most of whom want to classify their activity as democratic. But if regressive hearing is progressive as opposed to the 'individualistic' sort, it is only in the dialectical sense that it is better fitted to the advancing brutality than the latter. All possible mould has been rubbed off the baseness, and it is legitimate to criticize the aesthetic residue of an individuality that was long since wrested from individuals. But this criticism comes with little force from the sphere of popular music, since it is just this sphere that mummifies the vulgarized and decaying remnants of romantic individualism. Its innovations are inseparably coupled with these remnants.

Masochism in hearing is not only defined by self-surrender and pseudo-pleasure through identification with power. Underlying it is the knowledge that the security of shelter under the ruling conditions is a provisional one, that it is only a respite, and that eventually everything must collapse. Even in self-surrender one is not good in his own eyes; in his enjoyment one feels that he is simultaneously betraying the possible and being betrayed by the existent. Regressive listening is always ready to degenerate into rage. If one knows that he is basically marking time, the rage is directed primarily against everything which could disavow the modernity of being with-it and up-to-date and reveal how little has in fact changed. From photographs and movies, one knows the effect produced by the modern grown old, an effect originally used by the surrealists to shock and subsequently degraded to the cheap amusement of those whose fetishism fastens on the abstract present. For the regressive listener, this effect is fantastically foreshortened. They would like to ridicule and destroy what yesterday they were intoxicated with, as if in retrospect to revenge themselves for the fact that the ecstasy was not actually such. This effect has been given a name of its own and repeatedly been propagated in press and radio. But we should not think of the rhythmically simpler, light music of the pre-jazz era and its relics as corny; rather, the term applies to all those syncopated pieces which do not conform to the approved rhythmic formula of the present moment. A jazz expert can shake with laughter when he hears a piece which in good rhythm follows a sixteenth note with a punctuated eight, although this rhythm is more aggressive and in no way more provincial in character than the syncopated connection and renunciation of all counter-stress practised later. The regressive listeners are in fact destructive. The old-timer's insult has its ironic justification; ironic, because the destructive tendencies of the regressive listeners are in truth directed against the same thing that the old-fashioned hate, against disobedience as such, unless it comes under the tolerated spontaneity of collective excesses. The seeming opposition of the generations is nowhere more transparent than in rage. The bigots who complain to the radio stations in pathetic-sadistic letters of the jazzing up of holy things and the youth who delights in such exhibitions are of one mind. It requires only the proper situation to bring them together in a united front.

This furnishes a criticism of the 'new possibilities' in regressive listening. One might be tempted to rescue it if it were something in which the 'auratic' characteristics of the work of art, its illusory elements, gave way to the playful ones. However it may be with films, today's mass music shows little of such progress in disenchantment. Nothing survives in it more steadfastly than the illusion, nothing is more illusory than its reality. The infantile play has scarcely more than the name in common with the productivity of children. Otherwise, bourgeois sport would not want to differentiate itself so strictly from play. Its bestial seriousness consists in the fact that instead of remaining faithful to the dream of freedom by getting away from purposiveness, the treatment of play as a duty puts it among useful purposes and thereby wipes out the trace of freedom in it. This is particularly valid for contemporary mass music. It is only play as a repetition of prescribed models, and the playful release from responsibility which is thereby achieved does not reduce at all the time devoted to duty except by transferring the responsibility to the models, the following of which one makes into a duty for himself. In this lies the inherent pretence of the dominant music sport. It is illusory to promote the technical-rational moments of contemporary mass music – or the special capacities of the regressive listeners which may correspond to these moments – at the expense of a decayed magic, which nevertheless prescribes the rules for the bare functioning itself. It would also be illusory because the technical innovations of mass music really don't exist. This goes without saying for harmonic and melodic construction. The real colouristic accomplishment of modern dance music, the approach of the different colours to one another to the extent that one instrument replaces another without a break or one instrument can disguise itself as another, is as familiar to Wagnerian and post-Wagnerian orchestral technique as the mute effects of the brasses. Even in the techniques of syncopation, there is nothing that was not present in rudimentary form in Brahms and outdone by Schonberg and Stravinsky. The practice of contemporary popular music has not so much developed these techniques as conformistically dulled them. The listeners who expertly view these techniques with astonishment are in no way technically educated thereby, but react with resistance and rejection as soon as the techniques are introduced to them in those contexts in which they have their meaning. Whether a technique can be considered progressive and 'rational' depends on this meaning and on its place in the whole of society as well as in the organization of the particular work. Technical development as such can serve crude reaction as soon as it has established itself as a fetish and by its perfection represents the neglected social tasks as already accomplished. This is why all attempts to reform mass music and regressive listening on the basis of what exists are frustrated. Consumable art music must pay by the sacrifice of its consistency. Its faults are not 'artistic'; every incorrectly composed or outmoded chord bespeaks the backwardness of those to whose demand accommodation is made. But technically consistent, harmonious mass music purified of all the elements of bad pretence would turn into art music and at once lose its mass basis. All attempts at reconciliation, whether by market-oriented artists or collectively-oriented art educators, are fruitless. They have accomplished nothing more than handicrafts or the sort of products with which directions for use or a social text must be given, so that one may be properly informed about the deeper background.

The positive aspect for which the new mass music and regressive listening are praised – vitality and technical progress, collective breadth and relation to an undefined practice, into whose concepts there has entered the supplicant self-denunciation of the intellectuals, who can thereby finally end their social alienation from the masses in order to co-ordinate themselves politically with contemporary mass consciousness – this positive is a negative, the irruption into music of a catastrophic phase of society. The positive lies locked up solely in its negativity. Fetishized mass music threatens the fetishized cultural goods. The tension between the two spheres of music has so grown that it becomes difficult for the official sphere to hold its ground. However little it has to do with technical standards of mass music, if one compares the special knowledge of a jazz expert with that of a Toscanini worshipper the former is far ahead of the latter. But regressive listening represents a growing and merciless enemy not only to museum cultural goods but to the age-old sacral function of music as the locus for the taming of impulses. Not without penalty, and therefore not without restraint, are the debased products of musical culture surrendered to disrespectful play and sadistic humour.

In the face of regressive listening, music as a whole begins to take on a comic aspect. One need only listen to the uninhibited sonority of a choral rehearsal from outside. This experience was caught with great force in a film by the Marx brothers, who demolish an opera set as if to clothe in allegory the insight of the philosophy of history on the decay of the operatic form, or in a most estimable piece of refined entertainment, break up a grand piano in order to take possession of its strings in their frame as the true harp of the future, on which to play a prelude. Music has become comic in the present phase primarily because something so completely useless is carried on with all the visible signs of the strain of serious work. By being alien to solid people, music reveals their alienation from one another, and the consciousness of alienation vents itself in laughter. In music – or similarly in lyric poetry – the society which judged them comic becomes comic. But involved in this laughter is the decay of the sacral spirit of reconciliation. All music today can very easily sound as *Parsifal* did to Nietzsche's ear. It recalls incomprehensible rites and surviving masks from an earlier time, and is provocative nonsense.

The radio, which both wears out music and over-exposes it, makes a major contribution to this. Perhaps a better hour may at some time strike even for the clever fellows: one in which they may demand, instead of prepared material ready to be switched on, the improvisatory displacement of things, as the sort of radical beginning that can only thrive under the protection of the unshaken real world. Even discipline can take over the expression of free solidarity if freedom becomes its content. As little as regressive listening is a symptom of progress in consciousness of freedom, it could suddenly turn around if art, in unity with the society, should ever leave the road of the always-identical.

Not popular music but artistic music has furnished a model for this possibility. It is not for nothing that Mahler is the scandal of all bourgeois musical aesthetics. They call him uncreative because he suspends their concept of creation itself. Everything with which he occupies himself is already there. He accepts it in its vulgarized form; his themes are expropriated ones. Nevertheless, nothing sounds as it was wont to; all things are diverted as if by a magnet. What is worn out yields pliantly to the improvising hand; the used parts win a second life as variants. Just as the chauffeur's knowledge of his old second-hand car can enable him to drive it punctually and unrecognized to its intended destination, so can the expression of a beat-up melody, straining under the pressure of clarinets and oboes in the upper register, arrive at places which the approved musical language could never safely reach. Such music really crystallizes the whole, into which it has incorporated the vulgarized fragments, into something new, yet it takes its material from regressive listening. Indeed, one can almost think that in Mahler's music this experience was seismographically recorded forty years before it permeated society. But if Mahler stood athwart the concept of musical progress, neither can the new and radical music whose most advanced practitioners give allegiance to him in a seemingly paradoxical way any longer be subsumed exclusively under the concept of progress. It proposes to consciously resist the phenomenon of regressive listening. The terror which Schönberg and Webern spread, today as in the past, comes not from their incomprehensibility but from the fact that they are all too correctly understood. Their music gives form to that anxiety, that terror, that insight into the catastrophic situation which others merely evade by regressing. They are called individualists, and yet their work is nothing but a single dialogue with the powers which destroy individuality – powers whose 'formless shadows' fall gigantically on their music. In music, too, collective powers are liquidating an individuality past saving, but against them only individuals are capable of consciously representing the aims of collectivity.

Chapter two

The schema of mass culture

The commercial character of culture causes the difference between culture and practical life to disappear. Aesthetic semblance (Schein) turns into the sheen which commercial advertising lends to the commodities which absorb it in turn. But that moment of independence which philosophy specifically grasped under the idea of aesthetic semblance is lost in the process. On all sides the borderline between culture and empirical reality becomes more and more indistinct. Thorough efforts in this direction have long been underway. Since the beginning of the industrial era an art has been in vogue which is adept at promoting the right attitudes and which has entered into alliance with reification insofar as it proffers precisely for a disenchanted world, for the realm of the prosaic and even the banausic, a poetry of its own nourished upon the work ethic. Goebbels then prescribed it in the form of an iron romanticism for totalitarian purposes. It was not without good reason that writings like 'Hinter Pflug und Schraubstock' ('Behind Plough and Vice') and even 'Soll und Haben' ('Debit and Credit'), which were recommended to the young as particularly suitable fare, enjoyed such popularity in Germany. Such works are sited around the fundamental fracture within bourgeois education. Officially this education is oriented towards the realm of the ideal, towards 'alles Schöne und Gute' ('Everything that is beautiful and good'), it encourages admiration for the heroic individual and glorifies the values of candour, unselfishness and generosity. And yet from our earliest youth all of this is only admitted on the condition that it is not after all to be taken seriously. With every gesture the pupil is given to understand that what is most important is understanding the demands of 'real life' and fitting oneself properly for the competitive realm, and that the ideals themselves were either to be taken as a confirmation of this life or were to be immediately placed in its service. Enthusiasm for Schiller meant sowing one's wild oats in good time and an enthusiastic essay on *The Maid of*

Orleans was a sure promise of time-saving promotion into the higher class at Easter. Herein lies the tacit understanding between teacher and pupil which binds them so firmly together in spite of all other conflicts. The so-called teacher's witticisms and the fraternal gatherings of teachers and students at drinking parties and the like may deceptively conceal the misery of hierarchical subordination but they simultaneously reveal that identity on the basis of which the hierarchy is built. Nevertheless the very inexperience of the young, which is so tirelessly impressed upon us, can always mislead them into taking the ideals with which they have been pragmatically presented seriously: one can never be quite sure that the proper integration has been accomplished as early and as radically as it should have been. This is where the likes of Eyth and Freytag so promptly and helpfully step in. Beneath the mantle of adventure they smuggle in the contraband of utility and the reader is persuaded that he does not have to renounce any of his dreams if he eventually becomes an engineer or a shop assistant, those dreams which in a class society are already in thrall to the world of things and directed towards the imago of the train driver and the pastry cook even before the reliable 'children's literature' has been unleashed upon him. Perhaps the fantastical figure of Robinson Crusoe was already no different, who represented the very model of '*Homo oeconomicus*', being transported by a fortunate shipwreck out of the system of bourgeois society only to reproduce it again 'through his own effort', as the children's literature likes to put it.

Everything, including war, has its own poetry, if only Eyth's lyrics and the products of the 'worker poets'. Starting with 'Das Flaggenlied' ('The Banner Song') such poetry points the way, *mens sana in corpore sano*, towards colonial expansion and workers associations. Today total mass culture has replaced the 'Neue Universum' ('New World'). The most stylish photographs of aeroplanes soaring above the clouds, the brilliant play of light on moving machinery, the furrowed brows of well-chosen representatives of the 'common folk' emulate that perfidious innocence of 'The Golden Book of Technology' that lies resplendent among the Christmas gifts of the modern liberal child. In the cinema, this misalliance between photography and the novel, such pseudo-poetry becomes complete; it is now so present in every detail that it no longer even needs to express itself as such. It is solely the power which stands behind this everyday poetry today and impresses us with its colourfast and lavish presentation that can still deceive adult human beings about the extended childhood that is only prepared for them so that they might function in all the more 'adult' a fashion. A poetic tremor is expected of every example of emphatic objectivity. The 'Oh!' of astonishment which the objective close-up still stifled is blurted out by the lyrical musical accompaniment. The tremor lives off the excess power which technology as a whole, along with the capital that stands behind it, exercises over every individual thing. This is what transcendence is in mass culture. The poetic mystery of the product, in which it is more than itself, consists in the fact that it participates in the infinite nature of production and the reverential awe inspired by objectivity fits in smoothly with the schema of advertising. It is precisely this stress upon the mere fact of being which is supposed to be so great and strong that no subjective intention can alter it in any way – and this stress corresponds to the true impotence of art in relation to society today – that conceals the transfiguration against which all sober objectivity gestures. Reality becomes its own ideology through the spell cast by its faithful duplication. This is how the technological veil and the myth of the positive is woven. If the real becomes an image insofar as in its particularity it becomes as equivalent to the whole as one Ford car is to all the others of the same range, then the image on the other hand turns into immediate reality. We no longer even approach the much vaunted aesthetic image-consciousness. Any achievement of imagination, any expectation that imagination might of its own accord gather together the discrete elements of the real into its truth, is repudiated as an improper presumption. Imagination is replaced by a mechanically relentless control mechanism which determines whether the latest imago to be distributed really represents an exact, accurate and reliable reflection of the relevant item of reality. The only remnant of aesthetic semblance here is the empty abstract semblance of a difference between culture as such and practice as such, the division of labour as it were between different departments of production. The actual power of aesthetic image-consciousness with respect to the reception of works of art has always been highly questionable. It was bound up with educational privilege and conditions of leisure and in its pure form belonged more to the philosophical concept of art than it did to the social fate of works of art and the social conditions of their production. The prevalent concern with the material stratum of works of art, a persistent symptom of the failure of bourgeois civilisation, also betrays something of the untruth of aesthetic autonomy itself: its universality remains allied to ideology as long as real hunger is perpetuated in hunger for the material in the aesthetic domain. But if works of art have only intermittently been perceived as such, then mass art has taken that alienation of the masses from art, blindly sustained in life by society, up into the process of production as its presupposition, lives from it and deliberately reproduces it. The work of art becomes its own material and forms the technique of reproduction and presentation, actually a technique

[margin note: If something is generally accepted then it is true OR if one people then it is good?]

[margin note: essentially selling a lifestyle through idealistic imagery]

for the distribution of a real object. Radio broadcasts for children which intentionally play off image and reality against one another for the sake of advertising commodities and in the next moment have a Wild West hero proclaiming the virtues of some breakfast cereal, betraying the domination of image over the programme in the process, are as characteristic as the identification of film stars with their roles which is promoted by the advertising media, 'The lovers of "Burning Sarong" matched again' etc. The affair of Orson Welles' broadcast 'Invasion from Mars' was a test performed by the positivistic spirit to determine its own zone of influence and one which showed that the elimination of the distinction between image and reality has already advanced to the point of a collective sickness, that the reduction of the work of art to empirical reason is already capable of turning into overt lunacy at any moment, a lunacy which the fans who send trousers to the Lone Ranger and saddles to his horse already half affect. The successful fusion of waking life and dream life however can allow itself a certain tolerance with regard to ideals. They are accepted as an ahistorical given along with others and the honour which they owe to their opposition to life becomes a means of vindicating them as legitimate and successful elements of real life. A great poet is almost as good as a great inventor or talent scout, just as long as the standing of the work protects us from having to read any of it.

With the liquidation of its opposition to empirical reality art assumes a parasitic character. Inasmuch as it now appears itself as reality, which is supposed to stand in for the reality out there, it tends to relate back to culture as its own object. The monopolistic hold on culture, which forbids anything that cannot be grasped, necessarily refers us back to what has already been produced in the past and institutes self-reflection. This is the source of that glaring and yet ineliminable contradiction between the presentation, elegant technical finish and modish procedures on the one hand, and the old-fashioned traditionally individual and culturally derived decayed contents on the other, the contradiction that is revealed in the standardization of what is individual. The bourgeois works of art which mass culture withdraws from circulation on account of their defective fidelity to the real did not take pleasure in themselves precisely because of their strict formal immanence: Kant's doctrine of the sublime is the most striking expression of this. The mass culture which is so true to the facts absorbs the truth content and expends itself in the material but all it has left as material is itself. Hence all those musicals and biopics and all the biographies about artists etc. Self-reflection is provoked by the techniques of the sound film which can only introduce song into the action in a realistic manner by turning singers into the heroes who first lose and subsequently regain their voices. But the true source of self-reflection lies in the fact that decisive aspects of reality today elude representation through the aesthetic image. Monopoly scorns art. The sensuous individuation of the work, to which mass culture must continue to lay claim precisely if it is to be able to perform its complementary function profitably in a standardized society, contradicts the abstractness and self-sameness to which the world has shrunk. In so far as a film only recounts the fate of an individual, even if maintaining the most extreme critical awareness, it already succumbs to ideology. The case which is presented as one which is still worth recounting becomes for all its desperate nature an excuse for the world which has produced something so worthy of being related; while the real desperation expresses itself mutely in the fact there is nothing more to be recounted and that all we can do is recognize it for what it is. Perhaps the gesture of the narrator has always had something apologetic about it, but today it has become nothing but apology through and through. Even a radical film director who wished to portray crucially important social developments like the merger of two industrial concerns could only do so by showing us the dominant figures in the office, at the conference table or in their mansions. Even if they were thereby revealed as monstrous characters, their monstrousness would still be sanctioned as a quality of individual human beings in a way that would tend to obscure the monstrousness of the system whose servile functionaries they are. Yet if the director were to proceed in the most modern fashion and interrupt the life-story of the characters with montage technique in which the ominous balance sheets of the steel concern are intercut with images of the might and greatness of the plant itself, and both those intercut with images of the general director himself, this would not only be unintelligible and tedious for the audience but would also automatically transform itself into an artistic ornament on account of its arbitrary psychology. Finally, the magnate would come to acquire a negative symbolic function for those viewers with the least sociological awareness.

Anxious concern over the deplorable state of affairs agitates for reform and a society that is generous enough to anticipate its own critique: the ghost town of yesterday implies the full employment of tomorrow. No ideology even needs to be injected. Ever since the pressure from above has ceased to tolerate any longer the tension between the individual and the universal, then what is individual can no longer express the universal and art becomes a form of justification or at least a means of eliminating the period of fruitless expectation. This is not to say that art should seek its true vocation solely in the representation of the relations of production for precisely this is in all probability impossible for it.[1] But mass culture expressly claims to be close to reality only to betray this claim immediately by redirecting it to conflicts in the sphere of consumption where all psychology belongs today from the social point of view. The conflict which was once located in the realm of the superfluous now appears itself as a luxury: fashionable misfortune is its own consolation. In its mirror mass culture is always the fairest in all the land.

The self-reflection of culture brings a levelling down process in its wake. Inasmuch as any and every product refers back to what has already been preformed, the mechanism of adjustment towards which business interest drives it anyway is imposed upon it once again. Whatever is to pass muster must already have been handled, manipulated and approved by hundreds of thousands of people before anyone can enjoy it. Loudspeakers are installed in the smallest of night clubs to amplify the sound until it becomes literally unbearable: everything is to sound like radio, like the echo of mass culture in all its might. The saxophones stand in pre-established harmony with the sound of canned music in so far as the instruments themselves manage to combine individual expression and mechanical standardization, just as this is accomplished in principle throughout the process of mechanical reproduction. The 'digest' has become a particularly popular form of literary distribution and the average film now boasts of its similarity with the successful prototype rather than trying to conceal the fact. All mass culture is fundamentally adaptation. However, this adaptive character, the monopolistic filter which protects it from any external rays of influence which have not already been safely accommodated within its reified schema, represents an adjustment to the consumers as well. The pre-digested quality of the product prevails, justifies itself and establishes itself all the more firmly in so far as it constantly refers to those who cannot digest anything not already pre-digested. It is baby-food: permanent self-reflection based upon the infantile compulsion towards the repetition of needs which it creates in the first place. Traditional cultural goods are treated in just the same way. Nothing is left of them except the crudest materials of political and cultural history and the lustre of the great names handed down to us, those names to which all the 'top people' of today cling with unconditional solidarity. Through constant contact with the sold-off spirit 'amusement' in turn is elevated until it degenerates into dutiful exercises in the appreciation of cultural values. The difference between 'serious' and 'light' culture is either eroded or expressly organized and thus incorporated into the almighty totality. In the case of the socio-critical novels which are fed through the best-seller mechanism, we can no longer distinguish how far the horrors narrated in them serve the denunciation of society as opposed to the amusement of those who do not yet have the Roman circuses they are really waiting for. Schubert polished up to the highest finish now resembles Tchaikovsky or Rachmaninov. Gershwin's hits have derived their harmonic recipes from these sources and are accounted great art as a reward for having reconciled popular appeal with cultural distinction. There is no longer either kitsch or intransigent modernism in art. Advertising has absorbed surrealism and the champions of this movement have given their blessing to this commercialization of their own murderous attacks on culture in the name of hostility to the same. Kitsch fares no better as hatred towards it becomes its very element. Sentimentality is robbed of its implausible character, of that touching but impotent Utopian moment which for an instant might soften the hearts of those who have been hardened and take them beyond the reach of their even harder masters. The imported French director who cannot have too many bright ideas immediately takes back with glossy irony the tears almost as soon as they appear. To the jazzed-up classics there now belong the screen actresses of 'grande passion' who are undressed and depicted in compromising situations; no longer witnesses to passion, they are debased along with passion itself: the usual hazards of passion must play along with the universal 'fun'. It is true that such exhibitions do not alter the acceptability or respectability of what is made fun of. With the sense of order characteristic of a dominant housewife careful watch is kept lest the realistic harmony between image and object be disturbed, this flotsam and jetsam of the nineteenth century to which we remain truer the more we mock the beards and the fashions of the past. The tradition in question is that of the comfortable second-hand realism of the humanly accessible which was formerly administered by feature journalism and purveyed on a big scale by essayists from Sainte-Beuve right down to Herbert Eulenberg. Art which informs us about reality was always accompanied by 'instructions for use' which inform us about art and today both have been conflated. Empathy with the object not only reconciles us with it but with every object. No one should think themselves better than they are. The viewer is persuaded of the merit of his own averageness and he may one day receive the supreme prize as 'Mr Average Customer'. Not even the oldest are repelled by the modernism of mass culture and its presentation: they pour into the cinema as avidly as they read the novels of Werfel. What David Friedrich Strauss, who could write about Jesus as if he were Emil Ludwig even though he was wounded by Nietzsche's attacks, what he undertook on his own account today is performed irresistibly from above without any risk whatsoever. There is no longer a single idea which cannot be neutralized by recourse to the fate or psychology of its author so that the latest doctor can bask in the claim that his hysterical wife resembles Queen Elizabeth I of England and his jealous colleagues resemble those of Paul Ehrlich. Not enough that faded aristocratic values are fed to the fraternal millions, they are simultaneously translated into egalitarian terms and the jargon of unlimited communication. Spiritual nobility of soul and the sense of fraternity have melted together into slogans for the workforce.

But every individual product is levelled down in itself as well. There are no longer any real conflicts to be seen. They are replaced by the surrogate of shocks and sensations which seem to erupt from without and generally have no real consequences, smoothly insinuating themselves into the episodic action. The products are articulated in terms of episodes and adventures rather than in acts: the structure of the 'funnies' is overtly reproduced in the women serials and in more refined form in the class A picture. The defective power of recall on the part of the consumer furnishes the point of departure: no one is trusted to remember anything that has already happened or to concentrate upon anything other than what is presented to him in the given moment. The consumer is thus reduced to the abstract present. Yet the more narrowly the moment has to vouch for itself, all the more must it also avoid being burdened with calamity. The viewer is supposed to be as incapable of looking suffering in the eye as he is of exercising thought. However, even more essential than transparent affirmation is the predetermined resolution in the 'happy ending' of every tension whose purely apparent character is revealed by the ritual conclusion. Every specimen of mass culture in its very structure is as historical as the perfectly organized world of the future could wish it to be. It is the 'variety act', the techniques of which are clearly recalled by jazz and film as the two most characteristic forms of mass culture, that provides the model here. It was certainly no accident that the variety act was once so prized by those avant-garde writers who were so critical of the liberal bourgeois work of art, that is, the work determined by the idea of conflict. What really constitutes the variety act, the thing which strikes any child the first time he sees such a performance, is the fact that on each occasion something happens and nothing happens at the same time. Every variety act, especially that of the clown and the juggler, is really a kind of expectation. It subsequently transpires that waiting for the thing in question, which takes place as long as the juggler manages to keep the balls going, is precisely the thing itself. In variety the applause always comes a fraction too late, namely when the viewer perceives that what was initially imagined to be a preparation for something else was just the event of which he has been cheated as it were. The trick of the variety act consists in this betrayal of the temporal order, just as the event when it finally comes always displays a tendency to assume the character of a frozen pose or tableau, a symbolic suspension of the action to the accompaniment of the drum roll while all other music is stilled. Consequently the viewer who always comes too late can never be tardy after all: he jumps up as if to mount the merry-go-round, and in its first beginnings the cinema still resembled the fairground shooting-booth that you entered as you chanced upon it. The major film is too good for this, of course, but by technical necessity and especially in its more respectable examples it is constantly driven in the same direction. However, the trick is played upon time itself and not merely upon the viewer. Thus variety already represented the magical repetition of the industrial procedure in which the selfsame is reproduced through time – the very allegory of high capitalism which demonstrates its dominating character even as it appropriates its necessity as the freedom of play.

Variety celebrates the paradoxical fact that in our advanced industrial epoch there is still such a thing as history, while its archetypes, the first chimney and the first top-hat, already suggest the idea of technical control over time in which history comes to a standstill. Surrealism lives off the obsolescence of that which has no history and which presents itself as obsolescent, as if it had been destroyed by some catastrophe – this paradox is celebrated by the variety show. The act, the performance becomes the model of mechanical repetition and thus absolves itself of its nugatory historicality. Perhaps it was this disenchanting truth in 'variété' which outweighs any semblance of the historical, a semblance to which the bourgeois work of art still clung even in the advanced industrial age, which inspired Wedekind and Cocteau, Apollinaire and Kafka to praise the form so much. Impressionist music, a spurious synthesis of painting and music, imitated the procedure and it was not for nothing that Debussy chose the variety act as one of his musical subjects. With Debussy, who described his most mature piano pieces as 'Préludes' and 'Etudes', the inexperienced listener might well be tempted to take everything here as a prelude and wait for it all to begin, as with a firework display – which is what the last of the Préludes is actually called. As the form which subsumed the heritage of impressionist music for the purposes of mass culture, jazz was never so faithful to that style of music as in this: that as has been noticed before in a jazz piece, all the moments which succeed one another in time are more or less directly interchangeable with one another, that there is no real development, and that what comes later is not one whit richer in experience than what has preceded it. Both variété and impressionism objectively speaking represented an attempt to render the concept of industrial procedure serviceable for the autonomous work of art or to conceive of it, emancipated from every end, *in abstracto* as the pure domination of nature.

In so far as they made mechanization their privileged theme as it

61

were, they attempted like Chaplin to play a trick on it and transform the shock of the eversame into a Bergsonian laughter. But mass culture falls victim to its pre-ordained fate inasmuch as it adopts its law and simultaneously obscures it. Mass culture treats conflicts but in fact proceeds without conflict. The representation of living reality becomes a technique for suspending its development and thus comes to occupy that static realm which revealed the very essence of variété. This can be seen in those sectors in which dynamic bourgeois art is subjected to adaptation. Simply by virtue of what it does to the original the technique of mechanical reproduction as such already betrays the aspect of resistancelessness. Whatever problems of psychological fate the film may present, through parading the events past the viewer on the screen the power of the oppositions involved and the possibility of freedom within them is denied and reduced to the abstract temporal relationship of before and after. The eye of the camera which has perceived the conflict before the viewer and projected it upon the unresisting smoothly unfolding reel of film has already taken care that the conflicts are not conflicts at all. In so far as the individual images are played past in an uninterrupted photographic series on the screen they have already become mere objects in advance. Subsumed as they are, they pass us impotently by. Like the child who reads an adventure story in the first person and is relieved to know that nothing has happened to the hero since otherwise he would be unable to narrate his story in the first place, so it is to a certain extent with one who watches a filmed version of a novel as well. It is true that the hero may die but he cannot at least instigate anything and a filmed death is only half a death after all. It is similar with the biographies of great individuals: nothing can happen to them which didn't happen to them anyway and the finished story takes care of this. The historical accounts which so zealously exploit the fame of their heroic subjects decisively help to procure for them that Olympian existence which they had already begun to assume with their translation into the pantheon. Certainly every finished work of art is already predetermined in some way but art strives to overcome its own oppressive weight as an artefact through the force of its very construction. Mass culture on the other hand simply identifies with the curse of predetermination and joyfully fulfils it. Thus the technological changes which have been brought about with the advent of radio have inflicted a loss of history upon music.[2] Even the performance ideal of serious music in the sense of a perfect account of the work that takes no risks, as this has developed under monopoly conditions, has fallen under an iron grip of rigidity despite the ostentatious appearance of dynamism: the performance of a symphony in which nothing can go wrong is also one in which nothing happens any

more either.[3] The favoured compositions of mass culture are specifically selected in accordance with this trend. The best sellers here are
the late romantics like Tchaikovsky and Dvořák for whom the symphonic form is simply a face. They already weakened symphonic form
by turning it into a pot-pourri of melodies arbitrarily connected with
one another. The symphonic schema no longer performs any real
function here and all that is left of the dynamic form of the symphony,
antiphonic motivic elaboration and thematic development, are the
interludes of noisy excitement which unpleasantly interrupt the potpourri until it is resumed as if nothing had happened, as if everything
could begin all over again.

The lack of conflict which in mass culture stems from the all-
encompassing concerns of the monopoly can even be seen today in
great art within those very works which most resolutely resist the cultural monopoly. Schoenberg's dodecaphonic technique has put in
question the principle of development from which it first arose, and
Brecht's epic theatre, which has taken to constructing conflict specifically for the purpose of social critique and for the sake of a materialist
dialectic, has actually cancelled a dramatic dialectic: the idiosyncratic
sensitivity towards the concept of climax is the most obvious expression of this. The montage effects which Brecht introduced into drama
implies the almost complete interchangeability of time and the explicit captioning which refers to 'Life' and 'Rise', for example, in the
titles of his plays seems to deprive the dramatic characters of action
and transform them into experimental objects of a predetermined
thesis. Thus in spite of its discontinuous nature this procedure comes
to resemble the lack of resistance of cinematographic technique, just
as in fact all Brecht's innovations could be read as an attempt to salvage the theatre in an age of film after the disintegration of psychology. This approach presupposes in the viewer, envisaged as someone
smoking at ease who is not supposed to be 'centrally' moved, as a
political issue just that feebleness of thought and recall which mass
culture has produced: epic theatre is both a response to mass culture
and mass culture's own reversed consciousness of itself. This theatre
demonstrates how the relationship between the work of art and its
immanent temporality is changing. The overcoming of time represented the most crucial concern of drama and symphonic music, as is
revealed not only by the Aristotelian doctrine of the unity of time but
by the actual procedures employed in the great dynamic works of art
themselves. The empty passage of time, the meaningless transience
of life was to be seized upon through form and brought into participation with the 'idea' by virtue of the totality of this form. It was precisely this thematization of time which allowed its heteronomy to be
excluded from the aesthetic domain and which permitted the artist to

inject into the work of art at least the appearance of a timelessness. This appearance transformed the work into the essence and pure reflection of mere existence and thus served to express transcendence. Conflict was the means by which time was overcome through sustaining intra-temporal tension within the work. Conflict concentrates past and future in the present. Ibsen's dramaturgy expressed this with the formula: the measure of conflict is the power of the past in the present as the threat of the future. In the very idea of drama the interconnection of intra-temporal moments becomes so condensed and the relationships between them so comprehensively articulated that the mere passage of time takes on form and shape as a powerful configuration of meaningful relationships on the level of conflict before ultimately finding resolution. The temporality of absolute drama would be the instant which reveals itself in a flash from the crystallization of all the temporal relationships within the action. It is no different in the case of the symphony which by means of its universal motivic elaboration, the musical equivalent for the dramatic dynamics of conflict, not merely fulfils its own time but actively imposes meaning upon it and causes it to disappear: Beethoven's Seventh Symphony provides an exemplary case of the dialectical arrest of time. Yet this intention has only ever represented one side of bourgeois art: the truth concerning the existence of pre-history, a truth which is constituted in reflection upon the timelessly governing unity of time, as timeless truth becomes a lie, as governing truth always becomes an injustice and the dams it has erected are constantly and repeatedly broken by the time it has tried to exorcise. By virtue of its overcoming of time art remains impotent really to accomplish the transcendence of existence in the mere commemoration of it. Consequently the demand to transcend existence through the integration of time has always been accompanied by the other demand to renounce all pre-ordained meaning and through an unfettered, as it were passive, 'empiricist' abandonment to the temporal element which we have given up trying to master and thus to allow this absence of meaning to emerge and reveal it precisely in its very negativity: 'the rest is silence'. From Shakespeare's chronicle dramas through the struggles of Lessing and the Swiss school against classicist poetics right up to the psychological novel this tendency, under the massive shadow of bourgeois culture, has become more and more powerful. Today it has sprung over into the two poles of the avant-garde on the one hand and mass culture on the other. The last great novels, namely those of Proust and Joyce, surrender themselves so unreservedly to time that time itself, the meaningless passing of which still constitutes the real content of the novel in Flaubert's work according to Lukács, now becomes as dissociated as the individuals who live through it. The renunciatory surrender to the purely temporal explodes the temporal continuum. The temporal moments into which the narrative has disintegrated now even begin to escape from the relationship of temporal succession and through the power of memory draw all temporal events back into themselves like a whirlpool. Finally, Brecht's dramatic procedure already presupposes the collapse of time as well as that of the individual. The epic element is supposed to cut through the intensive unity of the dramatic action and reveal its illusory and ideological character, but it is certainly not intended to replace the unity of action with that of the temporal continuum. The Brechtian drama is governed by a kind of time-space, an experimental time which more closely resembles that of the repeatable 'laboratory experiment' than it does the time of history. It is true that this experimental time is no more protected from the irruption of empirical time than is its counterpart of dramatically contained time. For empirical time, which is the most profound expression of the relations of domination within the field of consciousness, persists as long as domination lasts and lies embedded in art itself because art is constituted in the protest against the time of fate. While such time is excluded by the relationship of spatial simultaneity created by the 'mounted' scenes, it creeps into the conflictless succession of events. As long as drama in general remains bound to the principle of succession it becomes all the more subject to abstract time the more resolutely it refuses to wrap up time by means of the dramatic action. Mass culture which tolerates neither conflict nor any obvious form of montage must pay tribute to time in every one of its products. This is the paradox of mass culture. The more ahistorical and pre-ordained its procedures are, the less temporal relationships become a problem for it and the less it succeeds in transposing these relationships into a dialectical unity of temporal moments, the more craftily it employs static tricks to deceive us into seeing new temporal content in what it does, then the less it has left to oppose to the time beyond itself and all the more fatally does it fall victim to that time. Its ahistoricality is the tedium which it affects to relieve. It evokes the question whether or not the one-dimensional time which is characteristic of the blind course of history is even identical with the timelessness of the ever-same, identical with fate.[4]

Yet the liquidation of conflict in mass culture is not merely an arbitrary matter of manipulation. Conflict, intrigue and development, the crucial elements of autonomous literature and music, are unconditionally bourgeois as well. It is no accident that ever since the time of Attic comedy drama has looked for its intriguers among the bourgeois. As an attempt on the part of the powerless to acquire power through their own intelligence, intrigue is the aesthetic cipher for the bourgeois triumph over the feudal order, the triumph of calculation and money over the static wealth of land and the immediate repression through armed force. The business and bustle of the intriguer, as this could still be perceived in the early period of great symphonic music in Haydn, in genially confident affirmative form before, with a critical turn, it came to constitute the essence of Beethovinian humour, originally derives from the unlimited effort demanded by competition, that zealous and conscientious industriousness which unintentionally put the noose around the neck of anyone who couldn't keep up. The intriguer is the negative image of the bourgeois individual and embodies the inevitable contradiction with solidarity that such an individual implies, just as the hero and his spirit of freedom and sacrifice is supposed to represent the very same individual. They both belong to one another like two fragments of a broken world which have been welded together, one might almost say welded together like the bourgeois world and art itself. Today the life of both is at stake as they draw ever closer together. The hero no longer makes any sacrifices but now enjoys success. He does not come of age and assume freedom through his deeds for his career is simply the revelation of his conformity. Thus he is the intriguer who has 'arrived', whose confiscated appearance reveals itself with all its irresistability in the form of Clark Gable. Monopoly establishes the successful competitor in just the same way. Thus the petty intriguer disappears along with the small competitor: his conspiracy would only be a bankruptcy. His success is sanctioned as a fate which renders all action illusory and pre-ordained. The last intriguers were the triumphant ones who helped bring the Fascists to the reins of power and establish them firmly in the Kaiserhof through the secret dealings of the banker Shroder, who advanced on Rome by sleeping-car, and who took part in the murder of the old guard [in the Night of the Long Knives].

Nobody is deceived by intrigue any more now that its law has established itself directly in all its omnipotence. Mass art registers this fact inasmuch as it repudiates conflict as outmoded or if it borrows it from the store of traditional culture removes it from the realm of genuine spontaneity by predetermining its character. The bourgeois types generally associated with intrigue and conflict seem to appear in the prison clothing which they are supposed to have acquired in the liberal past. The word 'banker' has become a term of abuse even in the United States, like 'lawyer' and 'professional politician', and the dissatisfied ambitious woman fares no better when she is depicted as a vamp. Reporters and impresarios are still tolerated as comic relics. History is extruded from tales which have become cultural commodities, even and especially there where historical themes are exploited. History as such becomes a costume identified with the individual concealing the frozen modernity of monopoly and state capitalism. Hence the emergence of that false reconciliation, the absorption of every negative counter-instance by an omnipotent reality, the elimination of dissonance in the bad totality. Lack of conflict within the work of art ensures that it can no longer endure any conflict with the life outside itself because life banishes all conflicts into the deepest hidden places of suffering and keeps them out of sight with pitiless force. Aesthetic truth was bound to the expression of the untruth of bourgeois society. Art really only exists as long as it is impossible by virtue of the order which it transcends. That is why the existence of all the great forms of art is paradoxical, and more than all the others that of the novel, the bourgeois art form *par excellence* which the film has now appropriated for itself. Today with the most extreme increase of real tension the possibility of the work of art itself has become utterly questionable. Monopoly is the executor: eliminating tension, it abolishes art along with conflict. Only in this consummated conflictlessness does art wholly become one moment of material production and thus turn completely into the lie to which it has always contributed its part in the past. Yet at the same time it here approaches more closely to the truth than those remnants of traditional art that still continue to flourish, to the extent that all preservation of individual conflict in the work of art, and generally even the introduction of social conflict as well, only serves as a romantic deception. It transfigures the world into one in which conflict is still possible rather than revealing it as one in which the omnipotent power of production is beginning ever more obviously to repress such a possibility. It is a delicate question whether the liquidation of aesthetic intrication and development represents the liquidation of every last trace of resistance or rather the medium of its secret omnipresence.

'One doesn't do that sort of thing', says the smart court official Brack when Hedda Gabler shoots herself. The monopoly now assumes his position. It disenchants conflict and the individual by means of its plain objectivity (*Sachlichkeit*). The omnipresence of technology imprints itself upon objects and everything historical, the race of past suffering in men and things it taboos as kitsch. Prototypical here is the actress who manages to appear fresh and painstakingly made up with her hair perfectly arranged even in the midst of the most appalling dangers, in a tropical typhoon or in the clutches of white slave traders. She is so closely, so precisely and so pitilessly photographed that the magic which her make-up is intended to exert is heightened by the lack of illusion with which it is thrust before the viewer as literally true and unexaggerated. Mass culture is unadorned make-up. It assimilates itself to the realm of ends more than to anything else with a sober look that knows no nonsense. The new objectivity which it apes was developed in architecture. In this purposive domain it defended the aesthetic rights of purposiveness against the barbarism which the semblance of purposivelessness brings with it in that context. It has made standardization and mass production into a matter of art, where its opposite scorns every law of form that is derived from without. The practical is all the more beautiful, the more it repudiates the semblance of beauty. But as soon as objectivity is wrenched free of ends, it degenerates into precisely that kind of ornamentation which it had originally denounced as a crime. Wherever film and radio abandon themselves to technocratic visions and Utopian techniques, they resemble that advanced architecture before it made its peace with the world, when it still dishonestly struggled against it with all its might. If we wish to compare the mass-produced music 'Tin Pan Alley' with architecture, we should not think of those plain new rows of dwellings but rather of the detached family houses which fill such a large part of Old and New England: standardized mass products which even standardize the claim of each one to be irreplaceably unique, to be a villa of its own. It is not the standardization as such which makes these houses from the nineteenth century look so uncanny today as much as the relentless repetition of the unrepeatable, all those pillars and bay windows, little stairs and turrets. We can perceive this atmosphere of 'presentation' in all its first bloom in every product of mass culture and the process of consumption under monopolistic direction only reveals it all the more clearly year by year. Mass culture is incompatible with its own objectivity. It constantly refers back to materials whose essence resists such an objective presentation. At the same time it demonstrates its connection with the prevailing practice from the first by borrowing industrial methods through which it produces objectivity as style. The relationship between objectivity and the object itself is not an objective one: it is determined and disrupted by calculation. The perfection of the technical 'how', of trick and presentation, combined with the indispensable fatuity of the 'what', is the ultimate expression of this. The virtuosity of the jazz band which abandons itself to the eight-bar rhythms of the hit composer like a wild animal in a cage, the clever camera shots which can create to order the sensitive cloud effects of the nineteenth-century novel, the frequency modulation which allows us to hear Gounod's 'Ave Maria' with such astonishing clarity, all of this represents more than a mere disparity between moments that find themselves at different stages of development. The time lag itself arises out of the compulsive quid pro quo of dream and purposiveness in mass culture, just as old-world German national costume and folk-dancing were instigated not in spite of the reality of the tank but because of it. In a highly industrialized society, so it is argued by the new realists in the name of mass culture, the intellectual and cultural needs of the consumer adapt themselves to material needs. They are subject to exactly the same standardization and it would surely be retrogressive to try and avoid this process which is the technical presupposition of the realistic attitude. The Ford model and the model hit song are all of a piece. But the very thought of such adaptation already implies the acceptance of the manipulation of needs by the might of production. Yet the spirit which is supposed to adapt itself in this way has the tendency and not merely the opportunity to resist such manipulation. The difference between practice and culture, upon which the monopoly lays such value by turning it into the administrative problem of co-ordinating the appropriate departments, consists precisely in the denial of co-ordination and the supremacy of those purposes dictated by the relations of production. Since in order to assert itself in its departmental character this co-ordinated culture must take account of this fact, it gets caught up in an irresolvable contradiction which it must constantly admit despite itself in every attempted evasion. Even the current hits, the most contemptible of standard products have something immaterial as their subject. They all obey the absurd slogan which one of them once advertised as a title: 'Especially for You'. In view of such close interconnection it is not enough merely to point out this ineliminable opposition between art and the real purposes from which such objective art adopts its standards. For mass art lives precisely from the fact that it maintains the opposition between practice and culture in a world where that opposition has become an ideology. Mass art falls victim to the realm of practice through its insistence over against material life upon the thing-like and fetishized character of the cultural goods which it has packed up and dispatched for use.

Permanent self-reflection is good for it in this respect. On the other hand that art which is seriously concerned with the critique of bourgeois purposiveness focuses upon a world which has been wholly claimed by purposiveness. It must measure itself against that world not only materially but in accordance with its own formal constitution. If objective art finds itself in danger of degrading its purposive forms into a false façade for the sake of its own purposivelessness, then non-objective art which avoids the transposition of purposive forms betrays a tendency towards the apologetic. Its poetry confidingly complements the jauntiness of its opposite and thus both antagonistic schools get along amicably with one another. The Wiener Werkstätte and suchlike right up to Rilke and T.S. Eliot with their attempts at the preservation of the soul are actually no further from monopoly capital than the streamlined products which nestle up to the soul all the more obligingly as its ornament to the extent they imitate monopoly more literally. Every yellow-bound Ullstein novel, every film produces the required synthesis. The cracked surface of the commodities betrays the fracture of all art today. Responsible art sees itself confronted with a paradoxical choice: either it develops purposive forms so unrelentingly in their purposiveness that they come into open conflict with all external purposes when pursued to the bitter end, or it abandons itself so unreservedly to describing the existent without paying the slightest attention to special aesthetic considerations that its very refusal to intervene in the aesthetic formation of the object actually reveals itself as a purer law of form free of any decorative ingredients. Mass culture is not to be reproached for contradiction, any more than for its objective or non-objective character, but rather on account of the reconciliation which bars it from unfolding the contradiction into its truth. Its objectivity is not that which belongs to the immanent necessity of all the moments in a work but is merely the reflection of an objective style of life and perception. Its non-objective character on the other hand does not declare war upon the world of business but merely exploits its worn out expressive schemata – the myth of personification and platitudes about 'humanity' as a crude material resource. The objective practices are designed from the first to serve the promptness and precision of the information which is conveyed to the captive consumer. Reduced as it is to the pursuit of cultural goods, the spirit demands that these goods themselves are not genuinely experienced. The consumer must only know how to deal with them in order to justify his claim to be a cultivated person. Even the solemn transmission of Beethoven's Ninth Symphony, much publicized and impressively mounted as it is and never missing an opportunity to present itself as a truly historic event, is more concerned with instructing the listener about the event he is about to witness and the powers that have staged it than about encouraging him to participate in the work itself.

The current practice of musical commentators who prefer talking about the history of the work's conception to telling us about the specific nature of its construction is tailored in advance to this tendency. What we are actually informed about is mass culture itself. All genuine experience of art is devalued into a matter of evaluation. The consumer is encouraged to recognize what is offered to him: the cultural object in question is represented as the finished product it has become which now asks to be identified. This universal informational character sets the seal upon the radical alienation between the consumer and the inescapable proximity of the product. He finds himself dependent upon information when his own experience proves inadequate and the apparatus trains him to appear well-informed on pain of losing prestige among other people and to renounce the more arduous process of real experience. If mass culture has already become one great exhibition, then everyone who stumbles into it feels as lonely as a stranger on an exhibition site. This is where information leaps in: the endless exhibition is also the endless bureau of information which forces itself upon the hapless visitor and regales him with leaflets, guides and radio recommendations, sparing each individual from the disgrace of appearing as stupid as everyone else. Mass culture is a system of signals that signals itself. The millions who belong to the underclasses formerly excluded from the enjoyment of cultural goods but now ensnared provide a welcome pretext for this new orientation towards information. But this grandiose system of elucidation, transmission and rapid familiarization in the sudden shock of imposition destroys everything that the ideology of cultural products claims to promote so widely. The jokes which were made in the symptomatic programme called 'Information Please' not only express the truth about the system of information but also the truth about what the information is about. Information emphatically promotes the decay of the aesthetic image. Even the entertainment film becomes a newsreel and an extension of its own publicity: we learn what Lana Turner looks like in a sweater, how the latest cinematographic techniques of Orson Welles actually work, whether FM transmission is really so different from the old radio sound. The type of concert-goer who only notices whether the piano is slightly out of tune or not, as a direct or indirect consumer of the latest innovations dispensed by the monopoly, has been turned into the ideal object for those cultural commodities which he has come to resemble so closely. The products are all the more respectable the more they recommend themselves to the world of information: they become unbearable on the other hand when they attempt to restore information as what is obscured by its over-illumination, through aesthetic form-giving in the work.

Information counts upon curiosity as the attitude with which the viewer approaches the product. The indiscretion formerly the prerogative of the most wretched of journalists has become part of the very essence of official culture. The information communicated by mass culture constantly winks at us.

In an edition of millions the popular magazine disseminates its 'inside stories' with an air of self-importance and the camera concentrates upon every physical detail just as the old opera-glasses used to do. With an illusionless mien and a bad conscience both wish to encourage the subject in the illusion that here too he is in on the act, that he is excluded nowhere. Heidegger accorded a place of honour to curiosity as an invariant feature in the 'fallenness' of human existence, as a fundamental existential-ontological 'constitution' within the 'ontological tendency of everydayness'.[5] Although he clearly saw the function of curiosity as the cement of mass activity, probably expressing a diluted form of collective mimesis of the desire to equal everyone else by knowing everything about them, he nevertheless committed an injustice upon mankind by ascribing curiosity to man as such and virtually making the victim responsible rather than the jail-keeper. Whatever Aristotle knew about the intrinsic desire to see, today visibility is thrust upon everything that can possibly be seen. This is the anthropological sediment of that monopolistic compulsion to handle, to manipulate, to absorb everything, the inability to leave anything beyond itself untouched. The less the system tolerates anything new, the more those who have been forsaken must be acquainted with all the latest novelties if they are to continue living in society rather than feeling themselves excluded from it. Mass culture allows precisely this reserve army of outsiders to participate: mass culture is an organized mania for connecting everything with everything else, a totality of public secrets. Everyone who is informed has his share in the secret, just as under National Socialism the privilege of esoteric blood-brotherhood was actually offered to everyone. But the tendency towards extortion in which both curiosity and indiscretion find their fulfilment is a part of that violence which the fascist is always ready to employ against the underprivileged. The satisfaction of curiosity by no means serves only the psychological economy of the subject, but directly serves material interests as well. Those who have been thoroughly informed lend themselves to thorough utilization. The German hit song from the era of incipient fascism 'Kannst du tanzen, Johanna? Gewiss kann ich das' ('Can you dance, Joanna? I certainly can'), in which the erotic accomplishments of the object of desire appear as qualities in a saturated labour-market, has preserved this historical aspect of curiosity in a particularly drastic form. Such curiosity belongs to those deformations of human behaviour produced by the market economy which have become independent since the demise of the latter and attained a diseased pitch of irrationality. In the epoch of total anti-semitism, everyone has chosen little Moritz as an idol: this has become an institution among the quiz kids and their ilk. This curiosity is perfectly attuned to the information which in turn socializes curiosity. It refers constantly to what has been preformed, to what others already know. To be informed about something implies an enforced solidarity with what has already been judged. We agree with the majority about it, yet simultaneously we wish to deprive them of it and take possession of it ourselves. With the gesture for which one is always prepared and which exercises a dictatorial power from the joke to the social research project, namely that of 'But we know that already', one doesn't merely ingratiate oneself with the system personally, one also simultaneously disparages anyone who tries to persuade us of inconvenient facts which are devalued instantly since we know them ourselves already. Curiosity is the enemy of the new which is not permitted to exist anyway. It lives off the claim that there cannot be anything new and that what presents itself as new is already predisposed to subsumption on the part of the well-informed. The passionate intensity with which curiosity comes on the scene squanders in the process of reproduction and appropriation the very power which might have contributed to the experience or the creation of something really new. The blindness of this passion renders the data towards which it is directed indifferent and irrelevant. However useful it might be from a practical point of view to have as much information as possible at one's disposal, there still prevails the iron law that the information in question shall never touch the essential, shall never degenerate into thought. This is ensured by the restriction of information to what the monopoly has supplied, to commodities, or to those people whose function in the business world has turned them into commodities. But as if this were not enough, there is a taboo against inaccurate information, a charge that can be invoked against any thought. The curiosity for information cannot be separated from the opinionated mentality of those who know it all. Today the curious individual becomes a nihilist. Anything that cannot be recognized, subsumed and verified he rejects as idiocy or ideology, as subjective in the derogatory sense. But what he already knows and can identify becomes valueless in the process, mere repetition, so much wasted time and money. This aporia of mass culture and the science affiliated to it reduces its victims to its own kind of praxis, namely a blunted perseverance. But this hopeless figure of curiosity is wholly determined by the monopoly. The attitude of the well-informed derives from that of the buyer who knows his way about the market. To this extent it is directly related to the advertising business.

Advertising becomes information when there is no longer anything to choose from, when the recognition of brand names has taken the place of choice, when at the same time the totality forces everyone who wishes to survive into consciously going along with the process. This is what happens under monopolistic mass culture. We can distinguish three stages in the developing domination of needs: advertising, information and command. As a form of omnipresent familiarization mass culture dissolves these stages into one another. The curiosity which it kindles brutally reproduces that of the child

73

which already derives from compulsion, deception and renunciation. The child becomes curious when its parents refuse to provide it with genuine information. It is not that original desire to look with which ontologies ancient and modern have obscurely connected it, but a gaze narcissistically turned upon itself. The curiosity which transforms the world into objects is not objective: it is not concerned with what is known but with the fact of knowing it, with having, with knowledge as a possession. This is precisely how the objects of information are organized today. Their indifferent character predestines their being and they are incapable of transcending the abstract fact of possession through any immanent quality of their own. As facts they are arranged in such a way that they can be grasped as quickly and easily as possible. Wrenched from all context, detached from thought, they are made instantly accessible to an infantile grasp. They may never be broadened out in any way but like favourite dishes they must obey the rule of identity if they are not to be rejected as false or alien. They must always be accurate but never true. Thus they tend towards deceit and the journalist's canard and the feeble invented anecdotes of the radio reporter are merely an explosion of the untruth which already lies within the blindness of the facts themselves. The curious individual who falls victim here, the raving autograph-chaser at the film studio, the child under fascism who suffers under the new-fangled disease of compulsive reading, is simply the citizen who has come to consciousness of himself, the person who has learnt how to come to terms with reality and whose apparent insanity merely confirms the objective insanity which men have finally succeeded in catching up with.

The more participation in mass culture exhausts itself in the informed access to cultural facts, the more the culture business comes to resemble contests, those aptitude tests which check suitability and performance, and finally sport. While the consumers are tirelessly encouraged to compete, whether by virtue of the way in which goods are offered to them or through the techniques of advertising, the products themselves right down to the details of technical procedure begin to exhibit sport-like characteristics. They require extreme accomplishments that can be exactly measured. The task of the screen actor breaks down into a set of precisely defined obligatory exercises each of which is compared with the corresponding one in the work of all the other competitors in the same group. And then in the end we have the final spurt, the ultimate exertion which has been kept in reserve all along, the culmination without antecedent intensification isolated from the previous action, the opposite of the dramatic climax. The film is articulated into so many sequences but its total duration, like that of the hit song, is regulated as if by stopwatch. In a space of one and a half hours the film should have knocked out its audience as planned. The detective story actually organises a match not merely between criminal and detective but between author and reader as well. The paradigm of this cultural sport is the competition, that ancient challenging of feudal style and bourgeois spirit. Here the integrity of memory, the substance of individuality, is fragmented and torn from the protective cover of oblivion, caught up in the dynamics of exchange value and free competition and finally disposed of as supposed knowledge. The wretched fate here is like that which be-falls the joke specially committed to paper so that we can remember it. The bourgeois citizen comes to terms with spirit by inscribing it among the world of facts. It all comes down to making himself suffi-ciently like that world on the one hand while, as a small property owner, making a sufficient bed to lie on out of it on the other: 'He knows such a lot' as they say. This knowledge is then tried and tested in competitions. Mass culture has finally rewritten the whole of Hegel's *Phenomenology of Spirit* in accordance with the principle of the competition. The sensuous moment of art transforms itself under the eyes of mass culture into the measurement, comparison and as-sessment of physical phenomena. This is most clearly to be seen in the case of jazz which is directly indebted to the sport of competitive dancing although it has gone its own independent way by pursuing this debt far beyond the real possibilities of the dance. If we may seek the enjoyment of the dancer at a jazz event in the obsession with syn-copation as the very formula of his own crippling which he does not allow to confuse him about his collective function, then the enjoy-ment of the jazz player should be compared with that of the sports-man who also labours under testing self-imposed conditions. All bourgeois art has preserved this moment in the phenomenon of the virtuoso performer. 'The bourgeois class demands something astonishing, something mechanical which I cannot offer them. The refined and much travelled world is arrogant but also cultivated and discriminating when it is prepared to consider something more close-ly. But it is so occupied with a thousand other things, so imprisoned in its conventional tedium, that it is a matter of complete indifference to it whether the music which it insists on hearing from morning till night is good or bad.'[6] So wrote Chopin in 1848. In the last hundred years since then the bourgeois class has quite lost the privilege of not having to listen to music all the time although it has not relinquished the need for mechanical and astonishing display. It is simply the case that this need has become so universally widespread that the mech-anical moment has utterly consumed the element of the astonishing. The romantic dissolution of the preconceived unity into its details, something which once pressed the right of the individual against the inflexibility of the totality, nevertheless harboured its opposite, the process of mechanization, in its very principle: the emancipated detail first becomes an effect and finally a trick. Under the sign of such details the work of art has fallen into the hands of competing specialists, a victim of that division of labour whose hegemony it tries to challenge. The original, authentically bourgeois reduction of truth to what we have the power to do, as Bacon formulated the idea,[7] affects the content of the work of art. This content is sought in the fabrication of the work itself, social production as such is glorified and the untruth of this form of production, the cult of labour conspicuously embodied in consumer goods, conceals the appropriation of its own surplus value in the products.[8] When mass culture exhibits itself it also loves to show how its products are made and how everything in it functions. For the citizen the free capacity to produce replaces the idea of a life free from domination and he seeks in the world of achievement the human significance that this realm specifically denies him. Virtuosity, which can yet never be detached wholly from art to the extent that a moment of nature-domination inheres in all art, has always pointed towards accomplishment and achievement. In mass culture such virtuosity is all that remains. In this respect, of course, it differs fundamentally from the virtuosity which was characteristic of an earlier liberal century. Ultimate achievement now consists not in triumphing over difficulty but in a process of subordination. It produces an aesthetic attitude which cannot be disturbed by external contingency or any other obtrusive factors. Whenever possible the disturbing factors are expressly produced without even allowing any longer the image of an autonomy which might master the alien elements as something not already preformed and thus establish its rule from out of freedom itself. If the piano virtuoso still recalled the acrobat or the juggler, who would only appear for money after the most arduous preparation, the jazz musician without entirely relinquishing these models comes more and more to resemble the goalkeeper. The virtues required of him are undistractability, attention, preparedness and concentration. He becomes an improviser in a compulsory situation. The illusionlessness of his performance is turned into that sporting facility which consists in being unsettled by nothing. Nothing is more frowned upon than rubato. Under monopoly conditions the heir to the virtuoso is he who accommodates himself most efficiently to the team. In so far as he does stand out personally in any way, this is regulated by the function which he performs in the team, in the ideal case by effacing himself, leaping to save a goal and thus serving the collective. The jazz musician and everyone in front of the microphone or the camera are forced to inflict violence upon themselves. Indeed the most rewarded are those who do not even require this violence to be exercised upon them in the first place, those who are so utterly compliant with the expected behaviour that they can even simulate the signs of resistance spontaneously precisely because they no longer feel such resistance in themselves.

The sporting events from which the schema of mass culture borrows so many of its features and which represent one of its favourite themes have divested themselves of all meaning. They are nothing but what they are. So it is that 'sportification' has played its part in the dissolution of aesthetic semblance. Sport is the imageless counterpart to practical life. And aesthetic images increasingly participate in this imagelessness the more they turn into a form of sport themselves. Indeed one might perceive in this an anticipation of a kind of play which in a classless society might do away with semblance along with the principle of utility whose complement it is. But if in fact the principles of the classless society do mature under the conditions of monopoly capitalism, they certainly do not do so in such a way that they only need liberating from the fetters of domination before being realized. Monopoly does not merely abuse these principles but actually inhabits them. They contain future possibilities mediated by the unbearable opposition which is still burned into the traces of freedom. Sport itself is not play but ritual in which the subjected celebrate their subjection. They parody freedom in their readiness for service, a service which the individual forcibly exacts from his own body for a second time. In the freedom which he exercises over his body the individual confirms what he is by inflicting upon this slave the same injustice he has already endured at the violent hands of society. The passion for sport, in which the masters of mass culture sense the real mass basis of their dictatorial power, is grounded in this fact. One can play the master by inflicting the original pain upon oneself and others again symbolically through a kind of compulsive repetition. While the act of repetition schools obedience, it absorbs the fateful damage in the perpetual potential for anxiety, and so it continues. At the same time the border line between acting and suffering, between internal and external force, is eliminated in the symbolic performance. This is the school for that integration which finally succeeded politically in transforming the powerless into a band of applauding hooligans. One is allowed to inflict pain according to the rules, one is maltreated according to the rules and the rule checks strength in order to vindicate weakness as strength: the screen heroes enjoy being tortured on film. The rules of the game resemble those of the market, equal chances and fair play for all, but only as the struggle of all against all. Thus it is that sport permits competition, now reduced to a form of brutality, to survive in a world in which competition has actually been eliminated. While sport does indeed express competition as a form of immediate activity, it also expressly thematizes a historical tendency which has done away with competition proper. From being a kind of deception or trick practised upon others it has become a coup. But the record achievements in which sport culminates already proclaim the undisguised law of the strongest which arises so naturally from the competitive domain precisely because it has always dominated that domain so relentlessly. In the triumph of this practical spirit, far as it is from the acquisitive pursuit of the necessities of life, sport becomes a pseudo-praxis in which those who are practically active are no longer capable of helping themselves but now turn themselves once again into the objects they have already become. In its naked literalness, in the brutish seriousness which hardens every gesture of play into an automatic reflex, sport becomes the colourless reflection of a hardened callous life. Sport only preserves the joy of movement, the thought of bodily liberation, the suspension of practical ends in a completely external distorted form. Yet perhaps because the violence which sport inflicts upon people might help them towards understanding how they could one day finally put an end to violence itself, mass culture takes sport into custody. Even if the sportsman might possibly be able to develop certain virtues like solidarity, readiness to help others or even enthusiasm which could prove valuable in critical political moments, nothing of this kind is to be found in the spectator. Here a crude contemplative curiosity replaces the last traces of spontaneity. But mass culture is not interested in turning its consumers into sportsmen as such but only into howling devotees of the stadium. In so far as mass culture reflects the totality of life as a complete system of open or covert sportive competitive struggles, it enthrones sport as life itself and even eliminates the tension between sport on the Sunday day off and the wretchedness of the working week, a tension in which the better part of sport used to consist. This is what it achieves with the final liquidation of aesthetic semblance. Mass culture even neutralizes this pseudo-praxis into the image-quality which is simultaneously renounced in the sportification of the product.

Under monopoly conditions the more life forces anyone who wishes to survive into deceit, trickery and insinuation and the less the individual can depend any longer upon a stable profession for his living, upon the continuity of labour, then all the greater becomes the might of sport in mass culture and the outside world in general. Mass culture is a kind of training for life when things have gone wrong.

The schema of mass culture now prevails as a canon of synthetically produced modes of behaviour. The following which mass culture can still count on even there where tedium and deception seem almost calculated to provoke the consumers is held together by the hope that the voice of the monopoly will tell them as they wait in line precisely what is expected of them if they want to be clothed and fed. The first commandment of course is that one should already be properly dressed and tolerably well fed. The good manners which the system teaches them presupposes all this. Anyone who fails openly to parade their freedom, their courtesy, their sense of security, who fails to observe and propagate the established guidelines, is forced to remain outside the pale. It is not so much that misery is concealed in the medium of film for example, indeed it is often enough depicted with some relish, but that the viewer is taught to behave everywhere as if there really were no such thing. In spite of all sententious humanitarianism the obedient adept becomes ever colder, harder and more pitiless. The more industry exhausts what has already been perverted into commodities in the very name of culture, the more the omnipresence of culture proclaims itself. The shots of leading figures in economic life and other prominent people in their straw hats and padded suits can only be distinguished from those of gangsters by the fact that they take their hats off when they enter the room while they exploit the robust speech of the gangster for the sake of popularity. Thus they prepare the *fata Morgana* of a fine society which once again reinforces in the medium of the image the actual destruction of society proper and the transformation of its members into the mannequins of the society page even as it denies them. Mass culture only recognizes refined people. Even the slang of the street kids that can never be reproduced too realistically merely serves to ensure that the laughing viewer is never tempted to use such language himself. The totality of mass culture culminates in the demand that no one can be any different from itself. The scientific tests upon which employment depends simply follow its example in this. The monopoly shuts its doors on anyone who fails to learn from the cinema how to move and speak according to the schema which it has fabricated: because of their position in the productive process women are particularly susceptible in this respect and this may partially explain why they are so dependent upon the dismal pleasures of screen entertainment. The old slogan of bourgeois entertainment, 'But you must have seen this', which just represented a swindle in the market place becomes a matter of deadly seriousness with the elimination of amusements and the market alike. Formerly the supposed penalty merely lay in not being able to participate in what everyone else was talking about. Today anyone who is incapable of talking in the prescribed fashion, that is of effortlessly reproducing the formulas, conventions and judgements of mass culture as if they were his own, is threatened in his very existence, suspected of being an idiot or an intellectual. Looking good, make-up, the desperately strained smile of eternal youth which only cracks momentarily in the angry twitching of the wrinkles of the brow, all this bounty is dispensed by the personnel manager under threat of the stick. People give their approval to mass culture because they know or suspect that this is where they are taught the mores they will surely need as their passport in a monopolized life. This passport is only valid if paid for in blood, with the surrender of life as a whole and the impassioned obedience to a hated compulsion. This is why mass culture proves so irresistible and not because of the supposed 'stultification' of the masses which is promoted by their enemies and lamented by their philanthropic friends. The psychological mechanisms involved are secondary. Today the rationality of adjustment has already reached such a point that the slightest jolt would be sufficient to reveal its irrationality. The renunciation of resistance is ratified by regression. The masses draw the correct conclusion from their complete social powerlessness over against the monopoly which represents their misery today. Through this adjustment to the technical forces of production, an adjustment which the system imposes upon them in the name of progress, men become objects that can be manipulated without further objection and thus fall far behind the potential which lies in the technical forces of production. But since as subjects men themselves still represent the ultimate limit of reification, mass culture must try and take hold of them again and again: the bad infinity involved in this hopeless effort of repetition is the only trace of hope that this repetition might be in vain, that men cannot wholly be grasped after all.

As a focus of regression mass culture assiduously concerns itself with the production of those archetypes in whose survival fascistic psychology perceives the most reliable means of perpetuating the modern conditions of domination. Primeval symbols are constructed on the production line. The dream industry does not so much fabricate the dreams of the customers as introduce the dreams of the suppliers among the people. This is the thousand-year empire of an industrial caste system governed by a stream of never ending dynasties.[9] In the dreams of those in charge of mummifying the world mass culture represents a priestly hieroglyphic script which addresses its images to those who have been subjugated not in order that they might be enjoyed but only that they be read. The authentic images of the film screen as well as the inauthentic ones encountered in hit melodies and the well-worn written phrase appear so rigidly and so frequently that they are no longer perceived in their own right but only as repetitions whose perpetual sameness always expresses an identical meaning. The looser the connection in the sequence of events or the development of the action, the more the shattered image becomes an allegorical seal. Even from the visual point of view the sudden evanescent images of the cinema come to resemble a sort of script. The images are seized but not contemplated. The film reel draws the eye along just like a line of writing and it turns the page with the gentle jolt of every scene change. On occasion aesthetically crafted films like Guitry's *Perles de la Couronne* have emphasized this book-like character of the film as an explicit framework. Thus the technology of the mass work of art accomplishes that transition from image to writing in which the absorption of art by monopolistic practice culminates.[10] But the secret doctrine which is communicated here is the message of capital. It must be secret because total domination likes to keep itself invisible: 'No shepherd and a herd'. Nonetheless it is directed at everyone. Its meaning has little to do with the ephemeral character of the cultural product and the very frailty of this product calls out to be deciphered. When a film presents us with a strikingly beautiful young woman it may officially approve or disapprove of her, she may be glorified as a successful heroine or punished as a vamp. Yet as a written character she announces something quite different from the psychological banners draped around her grinning mouth, namely the injunction to be like her. The new context into which these pre-prepared images enter as so many letters is always that of the command. The viewer is required constantly to translate the images back into writing. The exercise of obedience inheres in the fact of translation itself as soon as it takes place automatically. The more the film-goer, the hit song enthusiast, the reader of detective and magazine stories anticipates the outcome, the solution, the structure and so on, the more his attention is displaced towards the question of *how* the nugatory result is achieved, to the rebus-like details involved, and in this searching process of displacement the hieroglyphic meaning suddenly reveals itself. It articulates every phenomenon right down to the subtlest nuance according to a simplistic two-term logic of 'dos' and 'don'ts', and by virtue of this reduction of everything alien and unintelligible it overtakes the consumers. The emergence of this tendency towards the hieroglyphic represents a decisive stage in the previous history of mass culture for it marks the transition from the silent film to the sound film. In the older type of film images and written signs still alternated with one another and the antithesis of the two lent emphasis to the image-character of the images. But this dialectic like every other was unbearable to mass culture. It has expelled writing from the film as an alien presence but only to transform the images themselves completely into the writing which they have then absorbed in turn. Chaplin's patient sabotage of sound film, especially the forlorn neon light advertisement with which he prefaced *Modern Times*, proved itself as a conscious expression of this process in the medium itself. But the speaking images are only masks. The 'Ur-phenomenon' of this latest pictorial script is the same as the oldest of all. Through fixation the mask transforms what is utterly un-thinglike, expression itself, into horror over the fact that a human face can be so arrested, and then transforms the horror into obedience before the mortified face. That is the secret of the 'keep smiling' attitude. The face becomes a dead letter by freezing the most living thing about it, namely its laughter. The film fulfils the old children's threat of the ugly grimace which freezes when the wind changes or the clock strikes. And here it strikes the hour of total domination. The masks of the film are so many emblems of authority. Their horror grows to the extent that these masks are able to move and speak, although this does nothing to alter their inexorability: everything that lives is captured in such masks.[11] As far as mass culture is concerned reification is no metaphor: it makes the human beings that it reproduces resemble things even where their teeth do not represent toothpaste and their care-worn wrinkles do not evoke cosmetics. Whoever goes to a film is only waiting for the day when this spell will be broken, and perhaps ultimately it is only this well concealed hope which draws people to the cinema. But once there they obey. They assimilate themselves to what is dead. And that is how they become disposable. Mimesis explains the enigmatically empty ecstasy of the fans in mass culture. Ecstasy is the motor of imitation. It is this rather than self-expression and individuality which forcibly produces the behaviour of the victims which recalls St Vitus's dance or the motor reflex spasms of the maimed animal. The gestures are not identical with those in transports of ecstasy and yet they are the most impassioned expression of these same human beings: under the force of immense pressure the identity of the personality gives way, and since this identity itself already originates in pressure, this is felt as a liberation. When people dance to jazz for example, they do not dance for sensuous pleasure or in order to obtain release. Rather they merely depict the gestures of sensuous human beings, just as in a film individual allegorical gestures on their own represent modes of behaviour in general, and that is precisely the release. They fasten on the culture-masks proffered to them and practise themselves the magic which is already worked upon them. They become a collective through the adaptation to an over-mastering arbitrary power. The terror for which the people of every land are being prepared glares ever more threateningly from the rigid features of these culture-masks: in every peal of laughter we hear the menacing voice of extortion and the comic types are legible signs which represent the contorted bodies of revolutionaries. Participation in mass culture itself stands under the sign of terror. Enthusiasm not merely betrays an unconscious eagerness to read the commands from above but already reveals the fear of disobedience, of those unconventional desires from the suspicion of which the sex murderer who kills his own beloved passionately strives to cleanse himself. This anxiety, the ultimate lesson of the fascist era, is already harboured within the very medium of technological communication. Anyone who has not yet been wholly inured by the oppressive self-importance of big business is unnerved to receive a telegram. The mutilated language condensed to carry the maximum information combined with the urgency of delivery imparts the shock of immediate domination in the form of immediate horror. The fear of the disaster which the telegram might announce is only a mantle for the fear of the omnipresent disasters that can overtake us at any time. Above all on the radio the authority of society standing behind every speaker immediately addresses its listeners unchallenged. If indeed the advances of technology largely determine the fate of society, then the technicized forms of modern consciousness are also heralds of that fate. They transform culture into a total lie, but this untruth confesses the truth about the socio-economic base with which it has now become identical. The neon signs which hang over our cities and outshine the natural light of the night with their own are comets presaging the natural disaster of society, its frozen death. Yet they do not come from the sky. They are controlled from earth. It depends upon human beings themselves whether they will extinguish these lights and awake from a nightmare which only threatens to become actual as long as men believe in it.

and of chpt 04 / conclusion

Notes

1 In the attempt to denounce class society in a non-psychological manner, the best Russian films, above all *Battleship Potemkin*, have not actually depicted the process of material production at all but the realities of war and of political-military oppression. They maintain aesthetic concreteness by showing what is immediately inflicted upon human beings rather than by depicting what takes place in the abstract order of property relations. But in so far as these films present men as objects of domination who become subjects in the struggle against such domination, they penetrate to what is essential. The success of such films is of a highly paradoxical and precarious kind when we consider how in the subsequent Russian cinematographic tradition it was the war subjects which proved most susceptible to being transformed into patriotic propaganda.

2 Cf. T.W. Adorno (1941) 'The Radio Symphony. An Experiment in Theory', in P.F. Lazarsfeld and F.F. Stanton (eds) *Radio Research* , New York, pp. 110ff.

3 Cf. T.W. Adorno, 'On the Fetish Character of Music and the Regression of Listening', Chapter 1 of this book.
4 Cf. 'Odysseus or Myth and Enlightenment' in M. Horkheimer and T.W. Adorno (1972) *Dialectic of Enlightenment*, New York: Herder & Herder, pp. 43ff.
5 Martin Heidegger (1927) *Sein und Zeit*, Halle, p. 170, English Translation, pp. 214ff.
6 Frédéric Chopin (1928) *Gesammelte Briefe*, edited by Alexander Guttry, Munich, pp. 382ff.
7 See 'The Concept of Enlightenment' in *Dialectic of Enlightenment*, op. cit., pp. 4–5.
8 The fact that as far as the mature bourgeois work of art is concerned the way in which it is produced must be completely obscured, that it must appear as a 'second nature', merely expresses the deification of the process of fabrication itself. The opacity of labour belongs to its sanctification: if the semblance of sacredness were to dissolve, then labour itself would reveal itself as the labour of others. See T.W. Adorno (1981) *In Search of Wagner*, translated by R. Livingstone, London: New Left Books.
9 In this connection Huxley coined the motto of 'Identity, Community, Stability' which certainly captures the innermost tendency of emergent state capitalism, even if it was chosen with the apologetic intention of defending the individual in such a way that it works to the advantage of the monopoly itself.
10 See *Dialectic of Enlightenment*, op. cit., pp. 17ff.
11 In the account of dreams in his *Tage und Taten*, the only work in which he describes his most profound experience of it, Stefan George singled out the image of the speaking mask as one of the utmost horror: 'I had been given a clay mask which was now mounted on the wall of my room. I invited my friends to come and see how I incited the head to speak. I requested aloud that the head tell me the name of the one to whom I was pointing. When it refused to speak I attempted to force open its lips with my finger. Suddenly it distorted its features and bit my finger. In a state of extreme agitation I now repeated aloud my original demand and pointed at someone else. Thereupon the head named the name. Horrified we all left the room and I knew that I would never again set foot inside it.' – Stefan George (1933) *Tage und Taten. Aufzeichnungen und Skizzen*, Gesamt-Ausgabe, vol. 17, Berlin, p. 32. This is a prophecy of sound film.

Chapter three

Culture industry reconsidered

The term culture industry was perhaps used for the first time in the book *Dialectic of Enlightenment*, which Horkheimer and I published in Amsterdam in 1947. In our drafts we spoke of 'mass culture'. We replaced that expression with 'culture industry' in order to exclude from the outset the interpretation agreeable to its advocates: that it is a matter of something like a culture that arises spontaneously from the masses themselves, the contemporary form of popular art. From the latter the culture industry must be distinguished in the extreme. The culture industry fuses the old and familiar into a new quality. In all its branches, products which are tailored for consumption by masses, and which to a great extent determine the nature of that consumption, are manufactured more or less according to plan. The individual branches are similar in structure or at least fit into each other, ordering themselves into a system almost without a gap. This is made possible by contemporary technical capabilities as well as by economic and administrative concentration. The culture industry intentionally integrates its consumers from above. To the detriment of both it forces together the spheres of high and low art, separated for thousands of years. The seriousness of high art is destroyed in speculation about its efficacy; the seriousness of the lower perishes with the civilizational constraints imposed on the rebellious resistance inherent within it as long as social control was not yet total. Thus, although the culture industry undeniably speculates on the conscious and unconscious state of the millions towards which it is directed, the masses are not primary, but secondary, they are an object of calculation; an appendage of the machinery. The customer is not king, as the culture industry would have us believe, not its subject but its object. The very word mass-media, specially honed for the culture industry, already shifts the accent onto harmless terrain. Neither is it a question of primary concern for the masses, nor of the techniques of communication as such, but of the spirit which sufflates them, their

master's voice. The culture industry misuses its concern for the masses
in order to duplicate, reinforce and strengthen their mentality, which
it presumes is given and unchangeable. How this mentality might be
changed is excluded throughout. The masses are not the measure but
the ideology of the culture industry, even though the culture industry
itself could scarcely exist without adapting to the masses.

Making
profit

The cultural commodities of the industry are governed, as Brecht
and Suhrkamp expressed it thirty years ago, by the principle of their
realization as value, and not by their own specific content and harmonious formation. The entire practice of the culture industry trans-
fers the profit motive naked onto cultural forms. Ever since these
cultural forms first began to earn a living for their creators as commodities in the market-place they had already possessed something
of this quality. But then they sought after profit only indirectly, over
and above their autonomous essence. New on the part of the culture
industry is the direct and undisguised primacy of a precisely and thoroughly calculated efficacy in its most typical products. The autonomy
of works of art, which of course rarely ever predominated in an entirely
pure form, and was always permeated by a constellation of effects, is
tendentially eliminated by the culture industry, with or without the conscious will of those in control. The latter include both those who
carry out directives as well as those who hold the power. In economic
terms they are or were in search of new opportunities for the realization of capital in the most economically developed countries. The
old opportunities became increasingly more precarious as a result of
the same concentration process which alone makes the culture industry possible as an omnipresent phenomenon. Culture, in the true
sense, did not simply accommodate itself to human beings; but it always simultaneously raised a protest against the petrified relations
under which they lived, thereby honouring them. In so far as culture
becomes wholly assimilated to and integrated in those petrified relations, human beings are once more debased. Cultural entities typical
of the culture industry are no longer *also* commodities, they are commodities through and through. This quantitative shift is so great that
it calls forth entirely new phenomena. Ultimately, the culture industry no longer even needs to directly pursue everywhere the profit interests from which it originated. These interests have become
objectified in its ideology and have even made themselves independent of the compulsion to sell the cultural commodities which
must be swallowed anyway. The culture industry turns into public relations, the manufacturing of 'goodwill' per se, without regard for
particular firms or saleable objects. Brought to bear is a general un-
critical consensus, advertisements produced for the world, so that
each product of the culture industry becomes its own advertisement.

Nevertheless, those characteristics which originally stamped the transformation of literature into a commodity are maintained in this process. More than anything in the world, the culture industry has its ontology, a scaffolding of rigidly conservative basic categories which can be gleaned, for example, from the commercial English novels of the late seventeenth and early eighteenthth centuries. What parades as progress in the culture industry, as the incessantly new which it offers up, remains the disguise for an eternal sameness; everywhere the changes mask a skeleton which has changed just as little as the profit motive itself since the time it first gained its predominance over culture.

Thus, the expression 'industry' is not to be taken too literally. It refers to the standardization of the thing itself – such as that of the Western, familiar to every movie-goer – and to the rationalization of distribution techniques, but not strictly to the production process. Although in film, the central sector of the culture industry, the production process resembles technical modes of operation in the extensive division of labour, the employment of machines and the separation of the labourers from the means of production – expressed in the perennial conflict between artists active in the culture industry and those who control it – individual forms of production are nevertheless maintained. Each product affects an individual air; individuality itself serves to reinforce ideology, in so far as the illusion is conjured up that the completely reified and mediated is a sanctuary from immediacy and life. Now, as ever, the culture industry exists in the 'service' of third persons, maintaining its affinity to the declining circulation process of capital, to the commerce from which it came into being. Its ideology above all makes use of the star system, borrowed from individualistic art and its commercial exploitation. The more dehumanized its methods of operation and content, the more diligently and successfully the culture industry propagates supposedly great personalities and operates with heart-throbs. It is industrial more in a sociological sense, in the incorporation of industrial forms of organization even when nothing is manufactured – as in the rationalization of office work – rather than in the sense of anything really and actually produced by technological rationality. Accordingly, the misinvestments of the culture industry are considerable, throwing those branches rendered obsolete by new techniques into crises, which seldom lead to changes for the better.

The concept of technique in the culture industry is only in name identical with technique in works of art. In the latter, technique is concerned with the internal organization of the object itself, with its inner logic. In contrast, the technique of the culture industry is, from the beginning, one of distribution and mechanical reproduction, and

87

therefore always remains external to its object. The culture industry finds ideological support precisely in so far as it carefully shields itself from the full potential of the techniques contained in its products. It lives parasitically from the extra-artistic technique of the material production of goods, without regard for the obligation to the internal artistic whole implied by its functionality (*Sachlichkeit*), but also without concern for the laws of form demanded by aesthetic autonomy. The result for the physiognomy of the culture industry is essentially a mixture of streamlining, photographic hardness and precision on the one hand, and individualistic residues, sentimentality and an already rationally disposed and adapted romanticism on the other. Adopting Benjamin's designation of the traditional work of art by the concept of aura, the presence of that which is not present, the culture industry is defined by the fact that it does not strictly counterpose another principle to that of aura, but rather by the fact that it conserves the decaying aura as a foggy mist. By this means the culture industry betrays its own ideological abuses.

It has recently become customary among cultural officials as well as sociologists to warn against underestimating the culture industry while pointing to its great importance for the development of the consciousness of its consumers. It is to be taken seriously, without cultured snobbism. In actuality the culture industry is important as a moment of the spirit which dominates today. Whoever ignores its influence out of scepticism for what it stuffs into people would be naive. Yet there is a deceptive glitter about the admonition to take it seriously. Because of its social role, disturbing questions about its quality, about truth or untruth, and about the aesthetic niveau of the culture industry's emissions are repressed, or at least excluded from the so-called sociology of communications. The critic is accused of taking refuge in arrogant esoterica. It would be advisable first to indicate the double meaning of importance that slowly worms its way in unnoticed. Even if it touches the lives of innumerable people, the function of something is no guarantee of its particular quality. The blending of aesthetics with its residual communicative aspects leads art, as a social phenomenon, not to its rightful position in opposition to alleged artistic snobbism, but rather in a variety of ways to the defence of its baneful social consequences. The importance of the culture industry in the spiritual constitution of the masses is no dispensation for reflection on its objective legitimation, its essential being, least of all by a science which thinks itself pragmatic. On the contrary: such reflection becomes necessary precisely for this reason. To take the culture industry as seriously as its unquestioned role demands, means to take it seriously critically, and not to cower in the face of its monopolistic character.

Among those intellectuals anxious to reconcile themselves with the phenomenon and eager to find a common formula to express both their reservations against it and their respect for its power, a tone of ironic toleration prevails unless they have already created a new mythos of the twentieth century from the imposed regression. After all, those intellectuals maintain, everyone knows what pocket novels, films off the rack, family television shows rolled out into serials and hit parades, advice to the lovelorn and horoscope columns are all about. All of this, however, is harmless and, according to them, even democratic since it responds to a demand, albeit a stimulated one. It also bestows all kinds of blessings, they point out, for example, through the dissemination of information, advice and stress reducing patterns of behaviour. Of course, as every sociological study measuring something as elementary as how politically informed the public is has proven, the information is meagre or indifferent. Moreover, the advice to be gained from manifestations of the culture industry is vacuous, banal or worse, and the behaviour patterns are shamelessly conformist.

The two-faced irony in the relationship of servile intellectuals to the culture industry is not restricted to them alone. It may also be supposed that the consciousness of the consumers themselves is split between the prescribed fun which is supplied to them by the culture industry and a not particularly well-hidden doubt about its blessings. The phrase, the world wants to be deceived, has become truer than had ever been intended. People are not only, as the saying goes, falling for the swindle; if it guarantees them even the most fleeting gratification they desire a deception which is nonetheless transparent to them. They force their eyes shut and voice approval, in a kind of self-loathing, for what is meted out to them, knowing fully the purpose for which it is manufactured. Without admitting it they sense that their lives would be completely intolerable as soon as they no longer clung to satisfactions which are none at all.

The most ambitious defence of the culture industry today celebrates its spirit, which might be safely called ideology, as an ordering factor. In a supposedly chaotic world it provides human beings with something like standards for orientation, and that alone seems worthy of approval. However, what its defenders imagine is preserved by the culture industry is in fact all the more thoroughly destroyed by it. The colour film demolishes the genial old tavern to a greater extent than bombs ever could: the film exterminates its imago. No homeland can survive being processed by the films which celebrate it, and which thereby turn the unique character on which it thrives into an interchangeable sameness.

That which legitimately could be called culture attempted, as an expression of suffering and contradiction, to maintain a grasp on the idea of the good life. Culture cannot represent either that which merely exists or the conventional and no longer binding categories of order which the culture industry drapes over the idea of the good life as if existing reality were the good life, and as if those categories were its true measure. If the response of the culture industry's representatives is that it does not deliver art at all, this is itself the ideology with which they evade responsibility for that from which the business lives. No misdeed is ever righted by explaining it as such.

The appeal to order alone, without concrete specificity, is futile; the appeal to the dissemination of norms, without these ever proving themselves in reality or before consciousness, is equally futile. The idea of an objectively binding order, huckstered to people because it is so lacking for them, has no claims if it does not prove itself internally and in confrontation with human beings. But this is precisely what no product of the culture industry would engage in. The concepts of order which it hammers into human beings are always those of the status quo. They remain unquestioned, unanalysed and undialectically presupposed, even if they no longer have any substance for those who accept them. In contrast to the Kantian, the categorical imperative of the culture industry no longer has anything in common with freedom. It proclaims: you shall conform, without instruction as to what; conform to that which exists anyway, and to that which everyone thinks anyway as a reflex of its power and omnipresence. The power of the culture industry's ideology is such that conformity has replaced consciousness. The order that springs from it is never confronted with what it claims to be or with the real interests of human beings. Order, however, is not good in itself. It would be so only as a good order. The fact that the culture industry is oblivious to this and extols order *in abstracto*, bears witness to the impotence and untruth of the messages it conveys. While it claims to lead the perplexed, it deludes them with false conflicts which they are to exchange for their own. It solves conflicts for them only in appearance, in a way that they can hardly be solved in their real lives. In the products of the culture industry human beings get into trouble only so that they can be rescued unharmed, usually by representatives of a benevolent collective; and then in empty harmony, they are reconciled with the general, whose demands they had experienced at the outset as irreconcileable with their interests. For this purpose the culture industry has developed formulas which even reach into such non-conceptual areas as light musical entertainment. Here too one gets into a 'jam', into rhythmic problems, which can be instantly disentangled by the triumph of the basic beat.

Even its defenders, however, would hardly contradict Plato openly who maintained that what is objectively and intrinsically untrue cannot also be subjectively good and true for human beings. The concoctions of the culture industry are neither guides for a blissful life, nor a new art of moral responsibility, but rather exhortations to toe the line, behind which stand the most powerful interests. The consensus which it propagates strengthens blind, opaque authority. If the culture industry is measured not by its own substance and logic, but by its efficacy, by its position in reality and its explicit pretensions; if the focus of serious concern is with the efficacy to which it always appeals, the potential of its effect becomes twice as weighty. This potential, however, lies in the promotion and exploitation of the ego-weakness to which the powerless members of contemporary society, with its concentration of power, are condemned. Their consciousness is further developed retrogressively. It is no coincidence that cynical American film producers are heard to say that their pictures must take into consideration the level of eleven-year-olds. In doing so they would very much like to make adults into eleven-year-olds.

It is true that thorough research has not, for the time being, produced an airtight case proving the regressive effects of particular products of the culture industry. No doubt an imaginatively designed experiment could achieve this more successfully than the powerful financial interests concerned would find comfortable. In any case, it can be assumed without hesitation that steady drops hollow the stone, especially since the system of the culture industry that surrounds the masses tolerates hardly any deviation and incessantly drills the same formulas on behaviour. Only their deep unconscious mistrust, the last residue of the difference between art and empirical reality in the spiritual make-up of the masses explains why they have not, to a person, long since perceived and accepted the world as it is constructed for them by the culture industry. Even if its messages were as harmless as they are made out to be – on countless occasions they are obviously not harmless, like the movies which chime in with currently popular hate campaigns against intellectuals by portraying them with the usual stereotypes – the attitudes which the culture industry calls forth are anything but harmless. If an astrologer urges his readers to drive carefully on a particular day, that certainly hurts no one; they will, however, be harmed indeed by the stupefication which lies in the claim that advice which is valid every day and which is therefore idiotic, needs the approval of the stars.

Human dependence and servitude, the vanishing point of the culture industry, could scarcely be more faithfully described than by the American interviewee who was of the opinion that the dilemmas of the contemporary epoch would end if people would simply follow the lead of prominent personalities. In so far as the culture industry arouses a feeling of well-being that the world is precisely in that order suggested by the culture industry, the substitute gratification which it prepares for human beings cheats them out of the same happiness which it deceitfully projects. The total effect of the culture industry is one of anti-enlightenment, in which, as Horkheimer and I have noted, enlightenment, that is the progressive technical domination of nature, becomes mass deception and is turned into a means for fettering consciousness. It impedes the development of autonomous, independent individuals who judge and decide consciously for themselves. These, however, would be the precondition for a democratic society which needs adults who have come of age in order to sustain itself and develop. If the masses have been unjustly reviled from above as masses, the culture industry is not among the least responsible for making them into masses and then despising them, while obstructing the emancipation for which human beings are as ripe as the productive forces of the epoch permit.

Chapter four

Culture and administration

Whoever speaks of culture speaks of administration as well, whether this is his intention or not. The combination of so many things lacking a common denominator – such as philosophy and religion, science and art, forms of conduct and mores – and finally the inclusion of the objective spirit of an age in the single word 'culture' betrays from the outset the administrative view, the task of which, looking down from on high, is to assemble, distribute, evaluate and organize. The word culture itself, in its specific use, is scarcely older than Kant, and its beloved adversary, civilization, did not establish itself – at least in Germany – until the nineteenth century; it was then elevated to the level of a slogan by Spengler. In any case, the present-day proximity of the concepts 'culture' and 'administration' is easily detected within the practices of language, which in radio broadcasting attach the title 'The Cultural World' to a province where everything possible is encountered, in so far as it corresponds to a more or less precise idea of niveau and cultivation – in contrast to the sphere of entertainment – that province of administration, in other words, which is reserved for a spirit which is not spirit at all, but rather a service to listeners, devoted to light music along with its literary and dramatic pendants.

At the same time, however – according to German concepts – culture is opposed to administration. Culture would like to be higher and more pure, something untouchable which cannot be tailored according to any tactical or technical considerations. In educated language, this line of thought makes reference to the autonomy of culture. Popular opinion even takes pleasure in associating the concept of personality with it. Culture is viewed as the manifestation of pure humanity without regard for its functional relationships within society. In spite of its self-righteous assonance, the word culture cannot be avoided; this proves to what a degree the category, correctly criticized hundreds of times, is both fitting for and dedicated to the world as it is – namely to the administrated world. Nonetheless, no half-way sensitive person can overcome the discomfort conditioned by his consciousness of a culture which is indeed administrated. As Eduard Steuermann once formulated it, the more that is done for culture, the worse it fares. This paradox could be developed as follows: culture suffers damage when it is planned and administrated; when it is left to itself, however, everything cultural threatens not only to lose its possibility of effect, but its very existence as well. It is neither possible to accept uncritically the concept of culture, long permeated by ideas of departmentalization, nor to continue to shake one's head conservatively about what is being done to culture in the age of integral organization.

The aversion towards the words culture and administration – an aversion by no means free of barbarism and overshadowed by the urge to release the safety catch on a revolver – must not conceal that a certain truth is involved in it. This makes possible the treatment of culture as something of a unity, as for example the heads of cultural departments of cities are wont to do when they unite in the hands of an expert a series of objects which for the moment actually do have something in common. This common factor stands in contrast to everything which serves the reproduction of material life, the literal self-preservation of the human being in general, and the needs of his mere existence. Everyone knows that these boundaries cannot be clearly fixed. From the beginning it has been argued whether the spheres of justice and politics are to be included in culture; they are, at any rate, not to be found in the cultural departments organized by administration. It is further difficult to deny that due to the total tendencies at work in the present, many facets traditionally allotted to culture come to resemble material production more and more: the natural sciences far into the highest reaches of theoretical discipline – 'philosophic' according to older ways of thinking, in a manner hardly expected from the traditional perspective of culture – determine to an ever greater degree the down-to-earth fate of man. The progress of these sciences is, in turn, directly dependent upon the forces of material life, that is, of economics. This is the situation before which man stands today and which is so discomforting to him. The point is missed, however, if this situation is merely discussed to death by concentrating upon supposedly transitional phenomena. The current inclination to deny embarrassing contradictions in this matter by means of conceptual distinctions and manipulations – a type of vulgarized epistemology – must be resisted. For the moment the simple fact must be recognized that that which is specifically cultural is that which is removed from the naked necessity of life.

This, however, does not offer dispensation from the consideration of the meaning of administration, for this is no longer merely a national or communal institution existing in clear separation from the free play of social forces. The tendency of every institution towards expansion – both quantitatively and qualitatively – was designated as immanent by Max Weber in *The Theory of Social and Economic Organization* (Part III, Chapter VI).[1] Weber did this in keeping with the formally definitional method of his late work. In Weber's view, bureaucracies, following their own law, are destined to expand. In the recent past the Nazi SS offers the most horrid example of this thesis. Weber finds the foundation for his thesis in the technical superiority of the organizational type of administration in contrast to traditionalist organization: 'The decisive reason for the advance of bureaucratic organization has always been its purely technical superiority over every other form of organization. A fully-developed bureaucratic mechanism stands in the same relationship to other forms as does the machine to the non-mechanical production of goods. Precision, speed, clarity, documentary ability, continuity, discretion, unity, rigid subordination, reduction of friction and of material and personal expenses are unique to bureaucratic organization. In the case of monocratic administration, these factors are intensified to the optimum through schooled individual officials in contrast to colleague-like older forms which are either honorary or extra-official' (p. 600f). It is precisely the example of the SS, however, which shows to what degree the formal concept of rationality, imputed by Weber and restricted to an ends-means relationship, impedes judgement on the rationality of means. In Weber's own theory of rationality, there is a suspicion of the imprint of administrated thought. The mechanism through which independence is established by organizations would have to be defined more specifically than was done by Weber or even in the formal sociology of Simmel, who simply contrasted phenomena of social ossification with life as a metaphysical actuality. Organizations of convenience in an antagonistic society must necessarily pursue particular ends; they do this at the expense of the interests of other groups. Therefore, obduracy and reification necessarily result. If such organizations continued to occupy a subordinate position within which they were totally open and honest towards their membership and its direct desires, they would be incapable of any action. The more firmly integrated they are, the greater is their prospect for asserting themselves in relation to others. The advantage of totalitarian 'monolithic' nations over liberalist nations in power politics which can be internationally observed today is also applicable to the structure of organizations of small format. Their external effectivity is a function of their inner homogeneity, which in turn is dependent upon the so-called totality gaining primacy over individual interests, so that the organization *qua* organization takes the place of such interests. An organization is forced into independence by self-preservation; at the same time this establishment of independence leads to alienation from its purposes and from the people of whom it is composed. Finally – in order to be able to pursue its goals appropriately – it enters into a contradiction with them.

It is difficult to accept the immanent tendency of administration towards expansion and the establishment of independence as a simple form of control as the explanation for the transition from administrative apparatuses in the older sense of the word into those of the administrated world, along with their entry into regions not previously subject to administration. Responsibility for this might lie in the extension of conditions of exchange throughout the entirety of life in the face of increasing monopolization. Thinking in equivalents is in itself a form of production in so far as it produces the commensurability of all objects along with their subsumability under abstract rules. Qualitative differences between spheres as well as those within each individual sphere are reduced and therewith the resistance against administration is lessened. At the same time, growing concentration brings about units of such scope that traditionalist – in any way 'irrational' methods – are no longer of any help. Economically, risk increases along with the size of the unit and this calls for planning – at least planning of the type demanded up to now by the type in control, defined by Max Weber as the 'monocratic' type. However, the immoderate size even of those institutions not concerned about profit – such as education and radio – furthers the practices of administration through the demand for organizational gradation. These practices are strengthened by technological development; in the case of radio, for example, that which is to be communicated is concentrated to the extreme and disseminated as far as possible. Max Weber was still in a position to restrict his thought essentially to administration in the narrow sense, that is, to bureaucratic hierarchies. He made note – in agreement with Robert Michels – of analogous tendencies only in political parties and, of course, in the sector of education and instruction as well. Meanwhile, this tendency has left all this far behind and achieved total development; this it has done by no means only in economic monopolies. The increase in the quantity of administrative apparatus has brought about a new quality. Mechanisms conceived according to a liberalistic model are no longer roofed over or interpenetrated by administration; they have rather assumed the upper hand towards spheres of freedom to such a degree that the latter appear only to be tolerated. Precisely this was anticipated in the era of pre-fascism by Karl Mannheim.

Even culture is not taboo to this tendency. Within the economic sector, Weber asks whether the understanding of the administrators for the objective problems which they have to solve is equal to the powers which they wield. This is so because precise factual knowledge in their field is a matter of immediate economic existence: 'errors in official statistics bring no direct consequences for the guilty official; errors in the calculation of a capitalistic concern result in losses to the firm, indeed, perhaps even in the loss of its existence' (p. 673). However, the question regarding the competence of bureaucracies, formulated by Weber in regard to economics, has in the meantime magnified in scope to the same degree as has administration itself within society. This question becomes critical in the cultural sphere. Weber touches upon what is coming in a parenthetical remark without realizing the significance of his observation, made over forty years ago during the conception of his great work. Within the highly-specialized context of the educational-sociological annotation to this chapter on bureaucracy he mentions that the possession of educational patents increasingly represses talent – or 'charisma', for the spiritual cost of educational patents is always slight and does not particularly decrease with mass production (p. 676). According to this thought, that irrational mission which is not to be planned progressively withdraws from the spirit itself, while this remains a mission for which the spirit is uniquely suited according to traditional views. In an excourse, Weber underscores this view: 'Behind all pronouncements of the present day on the bases of education is to be found at some decisive point that struggle of the "specialist" type against "old cultured humanity", a struggle which penetrated into all the most intimate questions of culture and which is conditioned by the irrevocable expansion of the control of all public and private relations through bureaucraticization and the steadily-increasing significance of specialized knowledge' (p. 677). Weber's opposition to 'specialized humanity' expressed here is of the type common in late-liberal society since Ibsen's *Hedda Gabler*. Inseparable from this, however, is the obligatory increase of administrative control in regions in which administration is without objective competence. Specialists must exercise authority in fields in which they cannot be professionally qualified, while their particular aptitude in abstractly technical matters of administration is needed in order that the organization continues to function.

The dialectic of culture and administration nowhere expresses the sacrosanct irrationality of culture so clearly as in the continually growing alienation of administration from culture – both in terms of its objective categories and its personal composition. (And culture, of course, seems most thoroughly irrational to those who have had the smallest experience of it.) For that which is administrated, administration is an external affair by which it is subsumed rather than comprehended. This is precisely the essence of administrated rationality itself, which does nothing but order and cover over. In the chapter on amphiboly in the *Critique of Pure Reason*, Kant – in opposition to Leibniz – denied rationality the ability of cognition of 'the interior of things'. Aporia prevails between the absolute purpose of the cultural and the absolute rationality of administration, which is nothing but the rationality of scientific ratio. What is called cultural with good reason must recollectively assimilate whatever has been left along the way in the process of the progressive control of nature, reflected in increasing rationality and ever more rational forms of control. Culture is the perennial claim of the particular over the general, as long as the latter remains unreconciled to the former. At least, this was envisioned in the distinction between the nomothetic and the idiographic – problematic as this distinction might be – made in the Southwest German School towards which Max Weber was philosophically inclined. However, administration necessarily represents – without subjective guilt and without individual will – the general against this particular. The twisted feeling of irreconcilability in the relation of culture and administration is characteristic of this situation. It bears witness to the continuing antagonistic character of a world which is growing ever more unified. The demand made by administration upon culture is essentially heteronomous: culture – no matter what form it takes – is to be measured by norms not inherent to it and which have nothing to do with the quality of the object, but rather with some type of abstract standards imposed from without, while at the same time the administrative instance – according to its own prescriptions and nature – must for the most part refuse to become involved in questions of immanent quality which regard the truth of the thing itself or its objective bases in general. Such expansion of administrative competence into a region, the idea of which contradicts every kind of average generality inherent to the concept of administrative norms, is itself irrational, alien to the immanent ratio of the object – for example, to the quality of a work of art – and a matter of coincidence as far as culture is concerned. The self-consciousness of this antinomy and the consequences thereof are the first demands which would have to be made upon an administrative praxis which is mature and enlightened in the Kantian sense.

At an early point – beginning around the middle of the nineteenth century – culture began to resist this rationality of purpose. During the age of symbolism and art nouveau, artists such as Oscar Wilde provocatively called culture useless. In bourgeois society, however, a terribly complex relation prevails between the useful and the useless, a situation which is by no means new today. The usefulness of the useful is itself by no means beyond doubt and the useless occupies the place of that which can no longer be distorted by profit. Much which is classified as useful goods goes beyond the directly biological reproduction of life. This reproduction itself is in no sense a great beyond of history, but rather is dependent upon that which is looked upon as culture. If human beings of the industrial era were to spend the days of their existence under those conditions which characterized the vegetative life of the Stone Age, they would no doubt perish. Critical theory, in its view of society, has expressed this in the hypothesis that reproduction of the labour force corresponds to the cultural state historically achieved by any given age; this is not necessarily a static natural category. It is not necessary to be a follower of the American economist Veblen, back to whom technocracy dates and who tendentiously viewed all goods not drastically necessary as the expression of control, status and ostentation; he further designated all of culture as that looked upon in the slovenly jargon of the administrated world as 'show'. It is not possible, however, to be blind to the fact that the useful – that which is of advantage to man in all previous history – is nothing immediate, existing for its own sake, but rather that within the total system which has its eye directed towards profit. The useful per se has been relegated to a secondary position, where it is produced by the machinery of the system as well. There is hardly another point to which the consciousness of society is so allergic as it is to this one. Precisely because the usefulness of the useful is so dubious a matter, it is doubly important that this apparatus demonstrate its usefulness through its function solely for the sake of the consumer. For this reason the line of demarcation between the useful and the useless is drawn so strictly in ideology. The enthronement of culture as an entity unto itself, independent of all material conditions – indeed, as something which makes these conditions matters of total indifference – is a fitting correlation of the faith in the pure usefulness of the useful. Culture is looked upon as thoroughly useless and for that reason as something beyond the planning and administrative methods of material production; this results in a much sharper definition of the profile upon which the claim to validity of both the useful and the useless is based. One factor of actuality has manifested itself within this ideology: the separation of culture from the material processes of life and – finally – the social hiatus between physical and intellectual work. The heritage of this situation is to be observed in the antinomy of culture and administration. The scent of philistinism which clings to administration is of the same type – and not only philologically – as the odium attached to low, useful, and, in the final analysis, physical labour by antiquity. The rigid opposition of culture and administration in thought, the product of a social and spiritual situation which attempts at the same time to force the two together, has nonetheless always been a questionable matter. In art history it is well known that wherever the artifacts of the past manifest the demand for collective labour – and this extends deep into the individual production of significant architects, sculptors and painters – administration spoke with a decisive voice. For that reason even in the past administration by no means lived in happy harmony with those who today unhesitatingly call themselves the creators of culture – a romantic desire fondly projected backward into history. The church and later the regents of the Italian city states, followed by the princes of absolutism, represented administrative instances from the perspective of their relation to the sphere of culture. Their relation to cultural production was probably far more substantial than that between present-day administration and administrated culture. The undisputed dominance of religion reduced the contrast between culture and practical life; the powerful lords of that day – often enough, to be sure, *condottieri* – were probably closer to culture than many of the administrative specialists of a society marked by the radical division of labour. This, however, made their control of culture all the more immediate and rigorous, for it was unchecked by any regulations or rational rules of procedure. The relation of the immanent truth of cultural configurations to that which has today been given the dubious name of 'commission' was at that time, at any rate, hardly less odious than today. Great artists even of a type which seems by and large to have agreed with the objectively valid spirit of their time – such as Bach – lived in permanent conflict with their administrations. Less is known about such conflicts during the High Middle Ages only because at that time they were pre-decided in favour of the administrative power simply as a matter of principle. In relation to this power, demands which have achieved full consciousness of themselves only in the modern concept of individualism scarcely had a chance.

Despite all this there has been an essential change in the relation between culture and organized power. Culture – as that which goes beyond the system of self-preservation of the species – involves an irrevocably critical impulse towards the status quo and all institutions thereof. This is by no means merely a tendency embodied in many cultural structures, but rather a protest against integration which always violently opposes that which is qualitatively different; in a certain sense this criticism is directed against the idea of levelling unification itself. The fact that anything at all thrives which is different and which is not to be turned into cash illuminates the prevailing praxis in all its dubiousness. It is not only through its manifest practical intentions, but rather through its mere existence – indeed, precisely through its impractical nature – that art manifests a polemic, secretly practical character. This, however, cannot be reconciled through the insertion of culture as a category – 'cultural activities' – into the totality of prevailing practice as has been done under current conditions with total smoothness. At one time the line of demarcation between reality and culture was neither so sharp nor so deep as it now is. Works of art did not, for example, reflect upon their own autonomy and upon the formal law unique to each of them; rather they had their place within given contexts, within which they fulfilled a function, no matter how immediate it was. They did not yet assert their existence as works of art to the degree which was later to seem almost a matter of course; it was precisely this factor from which the fullness and comprehensiveness of their success – indeed their very artistic power – benefited. Paul Valéry enlarged upon this topic without falling victim to the balsam-like cliché regarding the human being for whom all things supposedly exist; the human being has become fashionable only since he became fungible. If one reads Vasari's biographies of the painters, one is astonished to note the stress which he places upon the ability of the painters of the Renaissance to imitate nature, that is, to create portraits of great similarity to their models, as something particularly worthy of praise. Since the invention of photography this ability – not easily separated from practical purposes in painting – has become a matter of increasing indifference, an attitude which extends to older painting as well. But even Valéry suspected that such painting owed its aesthetic authenticity to the fact that it had not yet taken an oath to a chemically pure concept of the aesthetic, implying that, in the final analysis, art might exist as art only where it no longer expressed any ambition as art. This attitude involved the full awareness on the part of art that its previous innocence was not to be reestablished through an imagined communal will.

At any rate, the concept of culture has been neutralized to a great extent through its emancipation from the actual processes of life experienced with the rise of the bourgeoisie and the Enlightenment. The opposition of culture to the status quo has been deadened to a large degree. Hegel's late and resigned theory which reserves the concept of absolute spirit – in contrast to his views in the *Phenomenology* – only for cultural spheres in the narrower sense is the first and up until now still the most significant theoretical imprint of this state of affairs. The process of neutralization – the transformation of culture into something independent and external, removed from any possible relation to praxis – makes it possible to integrate it into the organization from which it untiringly cleanses itself; furthermore, this is accomplished neither with contradiction nor with danger. Today manifestations of extreme artistry can be fostered, produced and presented by official institutions; indeed art is dependent upon such support if it is to be produced at all and find its way to an audience. Yet, at the same time, art denounces everything institutional and official. This gives some evidence of the neutralization of culture and of the irreconcilability with administration of that which has been neutralized. Through the sacrifice of its possible relation to praxis, the cultural concept itself becomes an instance of organization; that which is so provokingly useless in culture is transformed into tolerated negativity or even into something negatively useful – into a lubricant for the system, into something which exists for something else, into untruth, or into goods of the culture industry calculated for the consumer. All this is registered today in the uncomfortable relation between culture and administration.

Nothing escapes the attention of radically socialized society, which further effects the culture of which it seizes control. This can be illustrated in simple fashion. Sometime ago a small publication appeared, a pamphlet, apparently written for the needs of those who undertake cultural trips through Europe – of whatever use such a brochure could possibly be. It offered a concise catalogue of artistic festivals during this particular summer and the autumn as well. The reason for such a scheme is obvious: it permits the cultural traveller to divide his time and to seek out that which he thinks will be of interest to him – in short, he can plan his trip according to the same principle which lies behind the organization of these festivals: they are all embraced and controlled by a single comprehensive organization. Inherent in the idea of the festival, however, and of the artistic festival as well, no matter how secularized and weakened it might be, is the claim to something unique, to the emphatic event which is not fungible. Festivals are to be celebrated as they come; they are not to be organized only from the perspective of avoiding overlapping. Administrative reason which takes control of them and rationalizes them banishes festivity from them. This results in an intensification into the grotesque which cannot escape the notice of the more sensitive nerves present at these so-called cultural offerings – even at those of the avant-garde. In an effort to preserve a feeling of contrast to contemporary streamlining, culture is still permitted to drive about in a type of gypsy wagon; the gypsy wagons, however, roll about secretly in a monstrous hall, a fact which they do not themselves notice.

This might well explain to no small degree the loss of inner tension which is to be observed today at various points even in progressive cultural productions – to say nothing of the less progressive

efforts. Whatever raises from within itself a claim to being autonomous, critical and antithetical – while at the same time never being
able to assert this claim with total legitimacy – must necessarily come
to naught; this is particularly true when its impulses are integrated
into something heteronomous to them, which has been worked out
previously from above, that is to say, when it is granted the space in
which to draw breath immediately by that power against which it
rebels. At the same time, this is not a result of the easily criticized
excesses of managerism gone wild. In the administrated world
managers are used as scapegoats almost as frequently as the bureau-
crats; the assignment of objective guilt relationships to people is
itself a product of prevailing ideology. Paradoxical developments are
unavoidable. The total social and economic tendency consumes the
material basis of traditional culture, either liberal or individualistic
in style. The appeal to the creators of culture to withdraw from the
process of administration and keep distant from it has a hollow ring.
Not only would this deprive them of the possibility of earning a
living, but also of every effect, every contact between work of art and
society, something which the work of greatest integrity cannot do
without, if it is not to perish. Those who praise the purity of their
withdrawal from organization – those quiet voices in the nation –
arouse the suspicion that they are provincial and petit bourgeois re-
actionaries. The popular argument that the material basis for the
productive spirit – and this always has meant the non-conforming
spirit – has always been precarious and that this spirit has preserved
its power in defiant self-assertion is threadbare. The fact that an un-
desirable condition is nothing which has set in just today is no reason
for perpetuating it if this condition is no longer necessary; that better
things will make their way by virtue of their own power is nothing but
an edifying gingerbread slogan. 'Much is lost in the night.' From time
to time coincidental discoveries, such as that of Georg Büchner by
Karl Emil Franzos, give an idea of the senseless destruction which
has taken place in the history of mankind, even in the sphere of spiritual production. Furthermore, there has been a qualitative change
in this region. There no longer are any hiding-places – not even in
Europe which in this respect, as in so many others, involuntarily imitates America; there is no longer dignity in poverty – not even any
longer the possibility of modestly surviving the winter for a person
who loses his position in the administrated world. It is sufficient to
call to mind an existence such as that of Paul Verlaine at the end of
the nineteenth century: the lift of the fallen alcoholic who, even when
he was down and out, found friendly and understanding doctors in
Paris hospitals who supported him in the midst of the most extreme
of situations. Anything similar would be unthinkable today. Not that

there is any lack of such doctors or of friendly people in general – in a certain sense the administrated world has witnessed in many areas an increase in humanitarianism from the perspective of concern on the part of everyone for everyone. It is just that such doctors – with an eye towards their administrations – would probably no longer have the right to give shelter to the vagabond genius, to honour him and to protect him from humiliation. Instead, he would become the object of public welfare, attended and fed and treated with great care, to be sure, but torn from his way of life and therewith presumably from the possibility of expressing that which he had once felt to be the purpose of his life in the world – no matter how dubious the attitude towards the production of the definitely degraded and rejected Verlaine was. The concept of socially useful work cannot be separated from the process of integral socialization; it would necessarily also be held up to the person whose usefulness can be defined only in terms of the negation of this process and salvation would hardly turn out to be a blessing to the man saved today.

To become aware of such situations, it is by no means necessary to concentrate upon that customarily defined following the second war by the fatally neutralizing word 'border situation' – 'Grenz-Situation' – although it is clear that such situations – extreme situations – are in themselves inseparable from the substantiality of everything cultural down to the present day: in this region the concept of 'the average' has no place. The changes in the basic social stratum of culture, which is the matter of central concern here, extend into more harmless regions. In Vienna of the 1920s within the Schoenberg circle the strength of tradition among the anti-traditionalists, both in terms of art and of general personal conduct, was surprising. The spirit which attracted people to this circle was decidedly artistic, selective and sensitive; it bore within itself the markings of discriminatory competence and a sense of history. These artists, prepared for the dissolution of established ideas and norms, existed with a certain naiveté and matter-of-factness within Austrian society, which remained half-closed and half-feudal even after the fall of the monarchy. It is precisely to this society that they owe that sensuous culture and impatient subtlety which brought them into conflict with Viennese conformism. The boldness of artistic renewal joined hands with proud negligence. In spite of all irony and scepticism, numerous categories of a still firmly integrated social and spiritual order were accepted. These categories provided a not inconsiderable prerequisite for the insubordinate tenderness of this generation. It was necessary, as it were, to be satiated with tradition in order really to be able to negate it and to be able to turn the unique vital force of tradition against ossification and self-satisfaction. It is only where that which was is still strong enough to form the forces within the subject and at the same time to oppose them that the production of that which has not yet been seems possible. Constructivism and green houses can be conceived only under conditions of warmth and within psychologically protected dwellings – and this is not to be understood only in literal terms.

However, the equalization of the tensions felt today between culture and its objective conditions threatens culture with spiritual death by freezing. In its relation to reality there is a dialectic of non-simultaneity. Only where the development towards the administrated world and social modernity had not yet asserted itself so successfully – in France and Austria, for example – did the aesthetically modern, the avant-garde, thrive. When reality, however, dwells upon the current standard, a tendentious levelling of consciousness takes place. The more easily consciousness adjusts to integral reality, the more it is discouraged from going beyond that which is there once and for all.

Naturally, by no means all cultural spheres are subject to this dialectic of non-simultaneity; many of them are actually in need of the newest administrative standards. This is true of the whole community of natural sciences which probably both absorb and also produce the strongest productive forces today. They could not do justice to their present-day assignments in any other way than through the aid in planning offered by administration; the rationality of the sciences is itself similar to that of administration. The same situation exists wherever team work, collective effort, and wide-range investigation are necessary, such as in empirical social research. This field has not only modelled its own training after the example of administrative categories; without administration, it would sink into chaos – above all, into that which is coincidentally particular and irresponsible. Even art could not possibly oppose all this *en bloc*. A field such as architecture, which, by virtue of its foundation in practical needs, is today better off than the autonomous artistic genres, was never conceivable without administration. The film, above all, because of the scope of costs which can be met only through investment, is dependent upon a type of planning analogous to that of public administration. In the film, to be sure, the contradiction between inescapably calculating and the truth of matters is defined with horrifying clarity: the foolishness of the film is not so much the product of individual failure as of this contradiction. Its principle is the planning intention which includes the cinema-goer in its calculation; this results in lack of harmony.

Administration, however, is not simply imposed upon the supposedly productive human being from without. It multiplies within this person himself. That a particular situation in time brings forth those subjects intended for it is to be taken very literally. Nor are those who produce culture secure before the 'increasingly organic composition of mankind'. (Cf. Adorno, *Minima Moralia*, p. 442, Section 147.) Their security terminates in the situation before them in opposition to spontaneity in much the same way in which it manifests itself within material production. Whoever possesses a flair for such tendencies can expect to encounter disguised administrative categories even in the most advanced avant-garde artistic products – indeed, even in the most finely-nuanced emotions of the individual, in his voice and gestures. Attention must be directed toward aesthetic tendencies in the direction of integral construction; this can be verified at many junctures. Such tendencies envision a type of planning from above, the analogy of which to administration is not to be ignored. Such structures might well be totally predetermined. According to Max Weber's thesis administration, by its very nature, by and large excludes individual arbitrariness in favour of an objectively regulated process; in the same manner the individual action of the idea in art of this type is frowned upon. At the same time, the applied methods of procedures are not arbitrarily thought out – and this is what gives the phenomenon its weight – but rather developed with an immanently artistic consequence. These methods can be traced back very far into history. (Cf. Adorno, *Klangfiguren*, p. 95.) But it is precisely art which gives voice to the seemingly individual and coincidental which is now to be the subject of total aesthetic prohibition and which in turn must pay the price for progressive integration presenting a totally different situation than that found in actual administration. Within certain boundaries, administration – through rational ordering processes – actually prevents negative coincidence, blind control over others, nepotism and favouritism. Ever since Aristotle's *Politics*, it has been well-known that the shadow of injustice falls upon the just rational law within the order of reality so that the rationality of administrative acts stands in need of that corrective which Aristotle included as 'equity'. The work of art is limited by this residue to the same degree. To the work of art clings an impulse of that which is ordered and produced from without – secretly of that subjectivism which is indeed anathema. Today the field of tension within all advanced art is actually defined by the poles of radical construction and equally radical resistance against it; often both factors merge. Furthermore, it is from this perspective that tachism is to be understood. The negation of the concept of the cultural is itself under preparation. The major factor therein is the dismissal of such concepts as autonomy, spontaneity and criticism: autonomy, because the subject, rather than making conscious decisions, both has and wishes to subjugate itself to whatever has been pre-ordained. The reason for this is that the spirit, which according to traditional cultural concepts should be its own law-giver, at every instant now experiences its own impotence in relation to the overwhelming demands of mere being. Spontaneity diminishes because total planning takes precedence over the individual impulse, predetermining this impulse in turn, reducing it to the level of illusion, and no longer tolerating that play of forces which was expected to give rise to a free totality. And finally, criticism is dying out because the critical spirit is as disturbing as sand in a machine to that smoothly-running operation which is becoming more and more the model of the cultural. This critical spirit now seems antiquated, irresponsible and unworthy, much like 'armchair' thinking. The relationship between generations has been reversed ludicrously; youth seeks its validation in the principle of reality while the older generation digresses into the intelligible world. The National Socialists, who anticipated all this in brutal fashion – thereby unmasking it paradisically – were in relation to the category of the critical precisely the heralds of a coming development; this was manifested in their replacement of criticism with their own observations upon art, which in actuality offered only information on factual matters. This same tendency is to be noted in the increasing suppression of the critical spirit today; a journal of the avant-garde proudly displays the sub-title 'Information'.

In many sectors the accounts have not yet been balanced; this is particularly true of those regions isolated or distant from the most powerful social tendencies, although they hardly benefit from their isolation. In official culture, on the other hand, the accounts balance all the more perfectly. UNESCO poets actually come into being who are, for example, capable of enthusiasm because the humane blossoms in the midst of inhuman situations; in the wake of a humanitarianism which steers clear of any controversial issue they inscribe the international slogans of high administration with their very hearts' blood. Nothing need be said about the infantile trash to which the authorities of government and party obligate artists. No one would be astonished if in the West projects were financed involving research on generally valid, absolute values, conducted, however, with the underdeveloped countries in the back of the mind. There is no lack of obliging intellectuals ready to cast suspicions upon the critical spirit of true intellectuals through an affirmation of life borrowed from want-ad marriage offers. This official picture of humanism is completed by accusing everything truly human and in no way official of inhumanity. For criticism takes from man his meagre spiritual possessions, removing the veil which he himself looks upon as benevolent. The anger aroused in him by the unveiled image is diverted to those who tear this veil, in keeping with the hypothesis of Helvetius that truth never damages anyone except him who utters it. My by no means new observation (cf. *Minima Moralia*, p. 395ff., Section 132) that even that which deviates is by no means secure from standardization has recently been used to discredit the polemic application of the concept of conformism – as if the fact that there is a second-rate conformism, preceded at least by an act of resistance, somehow makes more palatable that first spineless conformism, that swimming along with the current and simultaneous adjustment to stronger batallions. In truth – to borrow a word from Heinrich Regius – one attacks the word conformism, because one is in total agreement with the process defined by it.

A further particularly clear phenomenon to which the label of the Muses is attached has its place in administrated culture; this is the attempt – effective in terms of mass psychology – to save the spontaneity which is threatened by administration or, as they refer to it in those circles, through 'correct understanding': every attempt of pedagogy to lay claim to the spiritual is an expression of this desire. The visible result is regression, blind complacency on the part of the subject encouraged to be spontaneous. It is no accident that the jargon of authenticity is spoken everywhere in these spheres, the language of which Karl Lorn has offered such penetrant examples in his recent book on language in the administrated word. Particularly outstanding in this regard is the chapter on pretence. This jargon is not identical with the administrative language of older vintage, as it can be encountered still today in old filing cabinets haunted by the tone of its touchingly subaltern notes. The old administrative language – dust-covered and antiquated – bears significant witness to the relative separation of administration and culture, whereby – against its will – it pays homage to culture. The jargon of authenticity, however, united the heterogeneous under one roof. Linguistic components from an individual sphere – from theological tradition, existential philosophy, the youth movement, the military or from Expressionism – are institutionally absorbed and then, to a certain extent, returned to the private sphere, placed back in the possession of the individual person, who can then speak with ease, freedom and joy about mission and encounter, about authentic pronouncement and concern, as though he himself were pleased. In truth, he is only putting on airs, as though each individual were his own announcer on FM radio. If, for example, a letter contains the phrase 'in approximately', the reader can assume that a few lines later the writer of the letter will announce his intention of approaching the person addressed in the near future. The personal contact stipulated in this way is nothing but the mask of an administrative process which draws the person thus addressed into its function: humanity which can be turned on and off should inspire the person addressed to unpaid achievements.

Nonetheless, what is demonstrated by such models is to be attributed to administration, in regard to which one might console oneself by means of a philosophically disreputable concept of inwardness or with pure culture which is guaranteed genuine. Those who use such words are the first to attack everything unregimented in a rage. In truth, culture itself is expected to pay the bill. Even when culture is viewed as something removed from reality, it is in no way isolated from reality, but rather involved instructions for actual realization, no matter how distant and mediated this might be. If culture is totally deprived of this impulse, it becomes invalid. Within culture administration only repeats the offences committed by culture itself in that it ever degraded itself to an element of representation, to a field of activity, and, finally, to a sector of mass action, of propaganda and of tourism. If culture is defined as the de-barbarization of man, elevating him beyond the state of simple nature, without actually perpetuating this state through violent suppression, then culture is a total failure. It has not been able to take root in man as long as he has lacked the prerequisites for an existence marked by human dignity. It is no coincidence that he is still capable of barbarous outbursts because of suppressed rancour about his fate, about his deeply-felt lack of freedom. The fact that he welcomes the trash of the culture industry with outstretched arms – half aware that it is trash – is another aspect of the same state of affairs, the seeming harmlessness of which is probably restricted to the surface. Culture long ago evolved into its own contradiction, the congealed content of educational privilege; for that reason it now takes its place within the material production process as an administrated supplement to it.

Furthermore, whoever resisted being convinced that it is necessary to bring on something ominously positive immediately is not going to be content to step aside shaking his head once he has taken stock of all these difficulties, simply because the objective possibility of anything better is blocked. The radicalism which promises itself everything by virtue of total change is abstract; for even within the changed totality the problems of the individual obstinately return again. Such radicalism loses ground as soon as its idea volatilizes into a chimera, dispensing every further effort toward improvement. Within itself, it then becomes an agent to sabotage something better. Excessive demand is a sublime form of sabotage. On the other hand, it is not to be overlooked that in the question regarding what is to be done here and now, a type of total social subject is imagined, a community of *hommes de bonne volonté* who need only take their places around a gigantic round table in order to bring order into this chaos of failure. But the difficulties of the cultural, for which the commonplace concept of crisis is no longer in any way sufficient, are so deeply rooted that individual goodwill is severely restricted. There is no point in imagining a unanimous will where objective and subjective antagonism provokes disaster. Finally, the threat experienced by the spirit in the fact of rationalization is an indication that the irrationality of the entire situation continues unchanged and that every particular rationalization benefits this irrationality in that it strengthens the pressures of a blind and unreconciled generality upon the particular.

The antinomy of planning and culture results in the dialectical idea of absorbing that which is spontaneous and not planned into planning, of creative space for these factors and of a strengthening of their possibilities. This idea does not dispense with the basis of social justice. The possibility of decentralization, particularly in view of the state of the forces of technical production as they now approach Utopian dimensions, is favourable to it. Planning of the non-planned within a specific sector – that of education – was emphatically advocated by Helmut Becker; there are other fields which offer analogous situations.

In spite of this seeming plausibility, however, the feeling of untruth cannot be overcome totally: namely, the feeling that the non-planned is degraded to a costume of itself and, consequently, that the freedom involved becomes a fiction. One need only compare the synthetic artists' quarter of New York, Greenwich Village, with the Parisian Rive Gauche of pre-Hitler days. In the New York district licence continues to exist as an officially tolerated institution; for this reason it has become what the Americans call 'phoney'. Furthermore, in the tendency to reserve for artists a particular life style – a tendency which dominated the entire nineteenth century – and to permit them to give form to that which is repulsive to the bourgeois society from which they live has concealed the deception exploited perhaps for the first time by Murger's *bohème* novel.

Planning of the non-planned would have to establish at the outset the degree to which it is compatible with the specific content of the non-planned, that is, to what degree planning from this perspective is 'rational'. Beyond this lies the question regarding the impersonal 'one' – the person, that is, who represents the instance which makes decisions on the greatest difficulties. In the beginning nothing more can be demanded than a cultural policy, thought out within itself and aware of these difficulties – a policy which does not conceive of the concept of culture as a reified fixed configuration of values, but rather a policy which absorbs critical considerations in order to develop them further. Such a cultural policy would not misunderstand itself as god-willed; it would not blindly endorse faith in culture, blind to its entanglement with the social totality – and for that very reason truly entangled – it would find a parallel in the negative naiveté involved in accepting administration as faith, that is, whoever receives an office from god, receives ratio from him as well. Administration which wishes to do its part must renounce itself; it needs the ignominious figure of the expert. No city administration, for example, can decide from which painter it should buy paintings, unless it can rely on people who have a serious, objective and progressive understanding of painting. In establishing the necessity of the expert, one immediately exposes himself again to every imaginable reproach – to the notorious accusation, for example, that the judgement of an expert remains a judgement for experts and as such ignores the community from which, according to popular phraseology, public institutions receive their mandate, or that the expert – necessarily an administrator himself – makes his decision from on high, thus extinguishing spontaneity; furthermore, his authority is not always secure and, among other things, it is a difficult matter to distinguish him from the apparatchik. Although one might be willing to concede the correctness of some of the aspects mentioned here, distrust toward the argument of the man on the street that culture does after all have something to contribute to the life of man will remain: the state of consciousness according to which one is to orient himself from the perspective of this argumentation is in truth the very state of consciousness which would have to be overcome by any culture sufficient to its own concept. All too much pleasure is found in attacks upon exposed modern art, coupled with attacks against administrations which supposedly wasted the pennies of the tax-payer on experiments which the latter viewed either with indifference or rejection. This argumentation is of an illusory democracy; an offshoot of that totalitarian technique tries to gain life through the exploitation of plebicite forms of democracy. What such voices of the popular soul hate most is anything of free spirit; they sympathize with stale reaction. While the total social constitution formally guarantees equal rights, it nonetheless continues to conserve the educational privilege, granting the possibility of differentiated and progressive spiritual experience to only a few. The platitude the progress of spiritual things, particularly of art, proceeds in the beginning against the will of the majority, makes it possible for the mortal enemies of all progress to entrench themselves behind those who, without any guilt of their own, to be sure, are excluded from the vital expression of their own concern. A cultural policy which has rid itself of social naiveté must see through this complex without fear of the mass of majorities. Through cultural policy alone it is hardly possible to eradicate the contradiction between democratic order and the actual consciousness of those who are kept in a continuing state of minority by social conditions. But democracy through representation, to which even the experts in the administration of cultural matters owe their legitimation, nonetheless permits a certain balance; it makes possible the hindrance of manœuvres which serve barbarism through the corruption of the idea of objective quality by means of callous appeal to the common will. Walter Benjamin's thought on critics whose task it is to uphold the interest of the public against the public itself can be applied to cultural policy as well. To serve this purpose is the duty of the expert. The longing for individuals who might work beyond the realm of expertise usually characterizes only regression or the desire for technicians of communication, with whom – simply because they are lacking any real understanding of matters – one can get along better and who dwell all the more comformingly within their own policy. There is no pure immediacy of culture: wherever it permits itself to be consumed arbitrarily by a public as consumer goods, it manipulates people. The subject becomes the subject of culture only through the mediation of objective discipline; the advocate thereof – in the administrated world, at any rate – is the expert. To be sure, it might be possible to find experts whose authority really is founded upon the authority of the thing itself, rather than in the power of suggestion or personal prestige. It would take an expert to decide who the experts are – and this leads into a vicious circle. The relation between administration and expert is not only a matter of necessity, but it is a virtue as well. It opens a perspective for the protection of cultural matters from the realm of control by the market, which today unhesitatingly mutilates culture. The spirit in its autonomous form is no less alienated from the manipulated and by now firmly-fixed needs of consumers than it is from administration. The authoritarian establishment of the independence of the latter allows it – through the co-optation of those to whom these matters are not alien – to make certain corrections in the dictates of these needs. This would scarcely be possible if the sphere of culture were left totally at the mercy of the mechanics of supply and demand, to say nothing of the power of direct command by totalitarian rulers. The most questionable aspect of the administrated world – this very independence of the executive instances – conceals the potential of something better; the institutions are strengthened to such a degree that they – even if they and their function is transparent to themselves – are able to break through the principle of merely existing for something else – of adjustment to the deceptive wishes of a plebicite. These wishes, were they to be fulfilled, would irrevocably repress everything cultural by bringing it forth from its presumed state of isolation. If the administrated world is to be understood as one from which all hiding places are fast disappearing, it should still be possible for this world to compensate for this and, by virtue of the powers of men of insight, to create centres of freedom as they are eradicated by the blind and unconscious process of mere social selection. That irrationality expressed in the independence of administration in its relation to society is the refuge of the inhibited development of culture itself. It is only through deviation from prevalent rationality that culture displays its ratio. Such hopes, however, are rooted in a state of consciousness on the part of administrators which is by no means simply to be taken for granted: it would depend upon their critical independence from the power and the spirit of a consumer society identical with the administrated world itself.

All the suggestions heard thus far would amount to ideas with broken wings, were it not for a bit of false logic encountered in them. One adjusts all too readily to the prevailing conviction that the categories of culture and administration must simply be accepted as that into which they actually have developed to a large degree in historical terms: as static blocks which discretely oppose each other – as mere actualities. In so doing, one remains under the spell of that reification, the criticism of which is inherent in all the more cogent reflections upon culture and administration. No matter how reified both categories are in reality, neither is totally reified; both refer back to living subjects – just as does the most adventurous cybernetic machine. Therefore, the spontaneous consciousness, not yet totally in the grips of reification, is still in a position to alter the function of the institution within which this consciousness expresses itself. For the present, within liberal-democratic order, the individual still has sufficient freedom within the institution and with its help to make a modest contribution to its correction. Whoever makes critically and unflinchingly conscious use of the means of administration and its institutions is still in a position to realize something which would be different from merely administrated culture. The minimal differences from the ever-constant which are open to him define for him – no matter how hopelessly – the difference concerning the totality; it is, however, in the difference itself – in divergence – that hope is concentrated.

Notes

1 *Wirtschaft und Gesellschaft*, Tübingen, 1922. Page references in the text cue to this edition.

Chapter five

Freudian theory and the pattern of fascist propaganda[1]

During the past decade, the nature and content of the speeches and pamphlets of American fascist agitators have been subjected to intensive research by social scientists. Some of these studies, undertaken along the lines of content analysis, have finally led to a comprehensive presentation in the book, *Prophets of Deceit*, by L. Lowenthal and N. Guterman.[2] The overall picture obtained is characterized by two main features. First, with the exception of some bizarre and completely negative recommendations: to put aliens into concentration camps or to expatriate Zionists, fascist propaganda material in this country is little concerned with concrete and tangible political issues. The overwhelming majority of all agitators' statements are directed *ad hominen*. They are obviously based on psychological calculations rather than on the intention to gain followers through the rational statement of rational aims. The term 'rabble-rouser', though objectionable because of its inherent contempt of the masses as such, is adequate in so far as it expresses the atmosphere of irrational emotional aggressiveness purposely promoted by our would-be Hitlers. If it is an impudence to call people 'rabble', it is precisely the aim of the agitator to transform the very same people into 'rabble', that is, crowds bent on violent action without any sensible political aim, and to create the atmosphere of the pogrom. The universal purpose of these agitators is to instigate methodically what, since Gustave Le Bon's famous book, *Psychologie des Foules* (1895), is commonly known as 'the psychology of the masses'.

Second, the agitators' approach is truly systematical and follows a rigidly set pattern of clear-cut 'devices'. This does not merely pertain to the ultimate unity of the political purpose: the abolition of democracy through mass support against the democratic principle, but even more so to the intrinsic nature of the content and presentation of propaganda itself. The similarity of the utterances of various agitators, from much publicized figures such as Coughlin and Gerald Smith to provincial small-time hate-mongers, is so great that it suffices in principle to analyse the statements of one of them in order to know them all.[3] Moreover, the speeches themselves are so monotonous that one meets with endless repetitions as soon as one is acquainted with the very limited number of stock devices. As a matter of fact, constant reiteration and scarcity of ideas are indispensable ingredients of the entire technique.

While the mechanical rigidity of the pattern is obvious and itself the expression of certain psychological aspects of fascist mentality, one cannot help feeling that propaganda material of the fascist brand forms a structural unit with a total common conception, be it conscious or unconscious, which determines every word that is said. This structural unit seems to refer to the implicit political conception as well as to the psychological essence. So far, only the detached and in a way isolated nature of each device has been given scientific attention; the psychoanalytic connotations of the devices have been stressed and elaborated. Now that the elements have been cleared up sufficiently, the time has come to focus attention on the psychological system as such – and it may not be entirely accidental that the term summons the association of paranoia – which comprises and begets these elements. This seems to be the more appropriate since otherwise the psychoanalytical interpretation of the individual devices will remain somewhat haphazard and arbitrary. A kind of theoretical frame of reference will have to be evolved. Inasmuch as the individual devices call almost irresistably for psychoanalytic interpretation, it is but logical to postulate that this frame of reference should consist of the application of a more comprehensive, basic psychoanalytic theory to the agitators' overall approach.

Such a frame of reference has been provided by Freud himself in his book *Group Psychology and the Analysis of the Ego*, published in English as early as 1922, and long before the danger of German fascism appeared to be acute.[4] It is not an overstatement if we say that Freud, though he was hardly interested in the political phase of the problem, clearly foresaw the rise and nature of fascist mass movements in purely psychological categories. If it is true that the analyst's unconscious perceives the unconscious of the patient, one may also presume that his theoretical intuitions are capable of anticipating tendencies still latent on a rational level but manifesting themselves on a deeper one. It may not have been perchance that after the First World War Freud turned his attention to narcissism and ego problems in the specific sense. The mechanisms and instinctual conflicts involved evidently play an increasingly important role in the present epoch, whereas, according to the testimony of practising analysts, the 'classical' neuroses such as conversion hysteria, which served as models for the method, now occur less frequently than at the time of

Freud's own development when Charcot dealt with hysteria clinically and Ibsen made it the subject matter of some of his plays. According to Freud, the problem of mass psychology is closely related to the new type of psychological affliction so characteristic of the era which for socio-economic reasons witnesses the decline of the individual and his subsequent weakness. While Freud did not concern himself with the social changes, it may be said that he developed within the monadological confines of the individual the traces of its profound crisis and willingness to yield unquestioningly to powerful outside, collective agencies. Without ever devoting himself to the study of contemporary social developments, Freud has pointed to historical trends through the development of his own work, the choice of his subject matters, and the evolution of guiding concepts.

The method of Freud's book constitutes a dynamic interpretation of Le Bon's description of the mass mind and a critique of a few dogmatic concepts – magic words, as it were – which are employed by Le Bon and other pre-analytic psychologists as though they were keys for some startling phenomena. Foremost among these concepts is that of suggestion which, incidentally, still plays a large role as a stopgap in popular thinking about the spell exercised by Hitler and his like over the masses. Freud does not challenge the accuracy of Le Bon's well-known characterizations of masses as being largely deindividualized, irrational, easily influenced, prone to violent action and altogether of a regressive nature. What distinguishes him from Le Bon is rather the absence of the traditional contempt for the masses which is the *thema probandum* of most of the older psychologists. Instead of inferring from the usual descriptive findings that the masses are inferior per se and likely to remain so, he asks in the spirit of true enlightenment: what makes the masses into masses? He rejects the easy hypothesis of a social or herd instinct, which for him denotes the problem and not its solution. In addition to the purely psychological reasons he gives for this rejection, one might say that he is on safe ground also from the sociological point of view. The straightforward comparison of modern mass formations with biological phenomena can hardly be regarded as valid since the members of contemporary masses are at least *prima facie* individuals, the children of a liberal, competitive and individualistic society, and conditioned to maintain themselves as independent, self-sustaining units; they are continuously admonished to be 'rugged' and warned against surrender. Even if one were to assume that archaic, pre-individual instincts survive, one could not simply point to this inheritance but would have to explain why modern men revert to patterns of behaviour which flagrantly contradict their own rational level and the present stage of enlightened technological civilization. This is precisely what Freud wants to do. He tries to find out which psychological forces result in the transformation of individuals into a mass. 'If the individuals in the group are combined into a unity, there must surely be something to unite them, and this bond might be precisely the thing that is characteristic of a group.'[5] This quest, however, is tantamount to an exposition of the fundamental issue of fascist manipulation. For the fascist demagogue, who has to win the support of millions of people for aims largely incompatible with their own rational self-interest, can do so only by artificially creating the *bond* Freud is looking for. If the demagogues' approach is at all realistic – and their popular success leaves no doubt that it is – it might be hypothesized that the bond in question is the very same the demagogue tries to produce synthetically; in fact, that it is the unifying principle behind his various devices.

In accordance with general psychoanalytic theory, Freud believes that the bond which integrates individuals into a mass, is of a *libidinal* nature. Earlier psychologists have occasionally hit upon this aspect of mass psychology. 'In McDougall's opinion, men's emotions are stirred in a group to a pitch that they seldom or never attain under other conditions; and it is a pleasurable experience for those who are concerned to surrender themselves so unreservedly to their passions and thus to become merged in the group and to lose the sense of the limits of their individuality.'[6] Freud goes beyond such observations by explaining the coherence of masses altogether in terms of the pleasure principle, that is to say, the actual or vicarious gratifications individuals obtain from surrendering to a mass. Hitler, by the way, was well aware of the libidinal source of mass formation through surrender when he attributed specifically female, passive features to the participants of his meetings, and thus also hinted at the role of unconscious homosexuality in mass psychology.[7] The most important consequence of Freud's introduction of libido into group psychology is that the traits generally ascribed to masses lose the deceptively primordial and irreducible character reflected by the arbitrary construct of specific mass or herd instincts. The latter are effects rather than causes. What is peculiar to the masses is, according to Freud, not so much a new quality as the manifestation of old ones usually hidden. 'From our point of view we need not attribute so much importance to the appearance of new characteristics. For us it would be enough to say that in a group the individual is brought under conditions which allow him to throw off the repressions of his unconscious instincts.'[8] This does not only dispense with auxiliary hypotheses *ad hoc* but also does justice to the simple fact that those who become submerged in masses are not primitive men but display primitive attitudes contradictory to their *normal* rational behaviour. Yet, even the most trivial descriptions leave no doubt about the affinity of certain peculiarities of masses to archaic traits. Particular mention should be made here of the potential short-cut from violent emotions to violent actions stressed by all authors on mass psychology, a phenomenon which in Freud's writings on primitive cultures leads to the assumption that the murder of the father of the primary horde is not imaginary but corresponds to prehistoric reality. In terms of dynamic theory, the revival of such traits has to be understood as the result of a *conflict*. It may also help to explain some of the manifestations of fascist mentality which could hardly be grasped without the assumption of an antagonism between varied psychological forces. One has to think here above all of the psychological category of destructiveness with which Freud dealt in his *Civilization and its Discontents*. As a rebellion against civilization, fascism is not simply the reoccurrence of the archaic but its reproduction in and by civilization itself. It is hardly adequate to define the forces of fascist rebellion simply as powerful id energies which throw off the pressure of the existing social order. Rather, this rebellion borrows its energies partly from other psychological agencies which are pressed into the service of the unconscious.

Since the libidinal bond between members of masses is obviously not of an uninhibited sexual nature, the problem arises as to which psychological mechanisms transform primary sexual energy into feelings which hold masses together. Freud copes with the problem by analysing the phenomena covered by the terms suggestion and suggestibility. He recognises suggestion as the 'shelter' or 'screen' concealing 'love relationships'. It is essential that the 'love relationship' behind suggestion remains unconscious.[9] Freud dwells on the fact that in organized groups such as the Army or the Church there is either no mention of love whatsoever between the members, or it is expressed only in a sublimated and indirect way, through the mediation of some religious image in the love of whom the members unite and whose all-embracing love they are supposed to imitate in their attitude towards each other. It seems significant that in today's society with its artificially integrated fascist masses, reference to love is almost completely excluded.[10] Hitler shunned the traditional role of the loving father and replaced it entirely by the negative one of threatening authority. The concept of love was relegated to the abstract notion of *Germany* and seldom mentioned without the epithet of 'fanatical' through which even this love obtained a ring of hostility and aggressiveness against those not encompassed by it. It is one of the basic tenets of fascist leadership to keep primary libidinal energy on an unconscious level so as to divert its manifestations in a way suitable to political ends. The less an objective idea such as religious salvation plays a role in mass formation, and the more mass manipulation becomes the sole aim, the more thoroughly uninhibited love has to be repressed and moulded into obedience. There is too little in the content of fascist ideology that *could* be loved.

The libidinal pattern of fascism and the entire technique of fascist demagogues are authoritarian. This is where the techniques of the demagogue and the hypnotist coincide with the psychological mechanism by which individuals are made to undergo the regressions which reduce them to mere members of a group.

By the measures that he takes, the hypnotist awakens in the subject a portion of his archaic inheritance which had also made him compliant towards his parents and which had experienced an individual re-animation in his relation to his father: what is thus awakened is the idea of a paramount and dangerous personality, towards whom only a passive-masochistic attitude is possible, to whom one's will has to be surrendered, while to be alone with him, 'to look him in the face', appears a hazardous enterprise. It is only in some such way as this that we can picture the relation of the individual member of the primal horde to the primal father ... The uncanny and coercive characteristics of group formations, which are shown in their suggestion phenomena, may therefore with justice be traced back to the fact of their origin from the primal horde. The leader of the group is still the dreaded primal father; the group still wishes to be governed by unrestricted force; it has an extreme passion for authority; in Le Bon's phrase, it has a thirst for obedience. The primal father is the group ideal, which governs the ego in the place of the ego ideal. Hypnosis has a good claim to being described as a group of two; there remains as a definition for suggestion – a conviction which is not based upon perception and reasoning but upon an erotic tie.[11]

This actually defines the nature and content of fascist propaganda. It is psychological because of its irrational authoritarian aims which cannot be attained by means of rational convictions but only through the skilful awakening of 'a portion of the subject's archaic inheritance'. Fascist agitation is centred in the idea of the leader, no matter whether he actually leads or is only the mandatory of group interests, because only the psychological image of the leader is apt to reanimate the idea of the all-powerful and threatening primal father. This is the ultimate root of the otherwise enigmatic *personalization* of fascist propaganda, its incessant plugging of names and supposedly great men, instead of discussing objective causes. The formation of the imagery of an omnipotent and unbridled father figure, by far transcending the individual father and therewith apt to be enlarged into a 'group ego', is the only way to promulgate the 'passive-masochistic attitude...to whom one's will has to be surrendered', an attitude required of the fascist follower the more his political behaviour becomes irreconcilable with his own rational interests as a private person as well as those of the group or class to which he actually belongs.[12] The follower's reawakened irrationality is, therefore, quite rational from the leader's viewpoint: it necessarily has to be 'a conviction which is not based upon perception and reasoning but upon an erotic tie'.

The mechanism which transforms libido into the bond between leader and followers, and between the followers themselves, is that of *identification*. A great part of Freud's book is devoted to its analysis.[13] It is impossible to discuss here the very subtle theoretical differentiation, particularly the one between identification and introjection. It should be noted, however, that the late Ernst Simmel, to whom we owe valuable contributions to the psychology of fascism, took up Freud's concept of the ambivalent nature of identification as a derivative of the oral phase of the organization of the libido,[14] and expanded it into an analytic theory of anti-Semitism.

We content ourselves with a few observations on the relevancy of the doctrine of identification to fascist propaganda and fascist mentality. It has been observed by several authors and by Erik Homburger Erikson in particular, that the specifically fascist leader type does not seem to be a father figure such as for instance the king of former times. The inconsistency of this observation with Freud's theory of the leader as the primal father, however, is only superficial. His discussion of identification may well help us to understand, in terms of subjective dynamics, certain changes which are actually due to objective historical conditions. Identification is 'the *earliest* expression of an emotional tie with another person, "playing" a part in the early history of the Oedipus complex'.[15] It may well be that this pre-oedipal component of identification helps to bring about the separation of the leader image as that of an all-powerful primal father, from the actual father image. Since the child's identification with his father as an answer to the Oedipus complex is only a secondary phenomenon, infantile regression may go beyond this father image and through an 'anaclitic' process reach a more archaic one. Moreover, the primitively narcissistic aspect of identification as an act of *devouring*, of making the beloved object part of oneself, may provide us with a clue to the fact that the modern leader image sometimes seems to be the enlargement of the subject's own personality, a collective projection of himself, rather than the image of the father whose role during the later phases of the subject's infancy may well have decreased in present day society.[16] All these facets call for further clarification.

The essential role of narcissism in regard to the identifications which are at play in the formation of fascist groups, is recognised in Freud's theory of *idealization*. 'We see that the object is being treated in the same way as our own ego, so that when we are in love a considerable amount of narcissistic libido overflows on the object. It is even obvious, in many forms of love choice, that the object serves as a substitute for some unattained ego ideal of our own. We love it on account of the perfections which we have striven to reach for our own ego, and which we should now like to procure in this roundabout way as a means of satisfying our narcissism.'[17] It is precisely this idealization of himself which the fascist leader tries to promote in his followers, and which is helped by the *Führer* ideology. The people he has to reckon with generally undergo the characteristic modern conflict between a strongly developed rational, self-preserving ego agency[18] and the continuous failure to satisfy their own ego demands. This conflict results in strong narcissistic impulses which can be absorbed and satisfied only through idealization as the partial transfer of the narcissistic libido to the object. This, again, falls in line with the semblance of the leader image to an enlargement of the subject: by making the leader his ideal he loves himself, as it were, but gets rid of the stains of frustration and discontent which mar his picture of his own empirical self. This pattern of identification through idealization, the caricature of true conscious solidarity, is, however, a collective one. It is effective in vast numbers of people with similar characterological dispositions and libidinal leanings. The fascist *community of the people* corresponds exactly to Freud's definition of a group as being 'a number of individuals who have substituted one and the same object for their ego ideal and have consequently identified themselves with one another in their ego'.[19] The leader image, in turn, borrows as it were its primal father-like omnipotence from collective strength.

Freud's psychological construction of the leader imagery is corroborated by its striking coincidence with the fascist leader type, at least as far as its public build-up is concerned. His descriptions fit the picture of Hitler no less than idealizations into which the American demagogues try to style themselves. In order to allow narcissistic identification, the leader has to appear himself as absolutely narcissistic, and it is from this insight that Freud derives the portrait of the 'primal father of the horde' which might as well be Hitler's.

He, at the very beginning of the history of mankind, was the *Superman*[20] whom Nietzsche only expected from the future. Even today, the members of a group stand in need of the illusion that they are equally and justly loved by their leader; but the leader himself need love no one else, he may be of a masterly nature, absolutely narcissistic, but self-confident and independent. We know that love puts a check upon narcissism, and it would be possible to show how, by operating in this way, it became a factor of civilization.[21]

One of the most conspicuous features of the agitator's speeches, namely the absence of a positive programme and of anything they might 'give', as well as the paradoxical prevalence of threat and denial, is thus being accounted for; the leader can be loved only if he himself does not love. Yet Freud is aware of another aspect of the leader image which apparently contradicts the first one. While appearing as a superman, the leader must at the same time work the miracle of appearing as an average person, just as Hitler posed as a composite of King Kong and the suburban barber. This too, Freud explains through his theory of narcissism. According to him,

> the individual gives up his ego ideal and substitutes for it the group ideal as embodied in the leader. [However,] in many individuals the separation between the ego and the ego ideal is not very far advanced; the two still coincide readily; the ego has often preserved its earlier self-complacency. The selection of the leader is very much facilitated by this circumstance. He need only possess the typical qualities of the individuals concerned in a particularly clearly marked and pure form, and need only give an impression of greater force and of more freedom of libido; and in that case the need for a strong chief will often meet him half-way and invest him with a predominance to which he would otherwise perhaps have had no claim. The other members of the group, whose ego ideal would not, apart from this, have become embodied in his person without some correction, are then carried away with the rest by 'suggestion', that is to say, by means of identification.[22]

Even the fascist leader's startling symptoms of inferiority, his resemblance to ham actors and asocial psychopaths, is thus anticipated in Freud's theory. For the sake of those parts of the follower's narcissistic libido which have not been thrown into the leader image but remain attached to the follower's own ego, the superman must still resemble the follower and appear as his 'enlargement'. Accordingly, one of the basic devices of personalized fascist propaganda is the concept of the 'great little man', a person who suggests both omnipotence and the idea that he is just one of the folks, a plain, red-blooded American, untainted by material or spiritual wealth. Psychological ambivalence helps to work a social miracle. The leader image gratifies the follower's twofold wish to submit to authority and to be the authority himself. This fits into a world in which irrational control is exercised though it has lost its inner conviction through universal enlightenment. The people who obey the dictators also sense the latter are superfluous. They reconcile this contradiction through the assumption that they are themselves the ruthless oppressor.

All the agitators' standard devices are designed along the line of Freud's exposé of what became later the basic structure of fascist demagoguery, the technique of personalization,[23] and the idea of the great little man. We limit ourselves to a few examples picked at random.

Freud gives an exhaustive account of the hierarchical element in irrational groups. 'It is obvious that a soldier takes his superior, that is, really, the leader of the army, as his ideal, while he identifies himself with his equals, and derives from this community of their egos the obligations for giving mutual help and for sharing possessions which comradeship implies. But he becomes ridiculous if he tries to identify himself with the general',[24] to wit, consciously and directly. The fascists, down to the last small-time demagogue, continuously emphasize ritualistic ceremonies and hierarchical differentiations. The less hierarchy within the set-up of a highly rationalized and quantified industrial society is warranted, the more artificial hierarchies with no objective *raison d'être* are built up and rigidly imposed by fascists for purely psycho-technical reasons. It may be added, however, that this is not the only libidinous source involved. Thus, hierarchical structures are in complete keeping with the wishes of the sado-masochistic character. Hitler's famous formula, *Verantwortung nach oben, Autorität nach unten*, (responsibility towards above, authority towards below) nicely rationalizes this character's ambivalence.[25]

The tendency to tread on those below, which manifests itself so disastrously in the persecution of weak and helpless minorities, is as outspoken as the hatred against those outside. In practice, both tendencies quite frequently fall together. Freud's theory sheds light on the all-pervasive, rigid distinction between the beloved in-group and the rejected out-group. Throughout our culture, this way of thinking and behaving has come to be regarded as self-evident to such a degree that the question of why people love what is like themselves and hate what is different is rarely asked seriously enough. Here as in many other instances, the productivity of Freud's approach lies in his questioning that which is generally accepted. Le Bon had noticed that the irrational crowd 'goes directly to extremes'.[26] Freud expands this observation and points out that the dichotomy between in- and out-groups is of so deep-rooted a nature that it affects even those groups whose 'ideas' apparently exclude such reactions. By 1921, he was therefore able to dispense with the liberalistic illusion that the progress of civilization would automatically bring about an increase of tolerance and a lessening of violence against out-groups.

> Even during the kingdom of Christ, those people who do not belong to the community of believers, who do not love him, and whom he does not love, stand outside this tie. Therefore, so religion, even if it calls itself the religion of love, must be hard and unloving to those who do not belong to it. Fundamentally, indeed, every religion is in this same way a religion of love for all those whom it embraces; while cruelty and intolerance towards those who do not belong to it are natural to every religion. However difficult we may find it personally, we ought not to reproach believers too severely on this account: people who are unbelieving or indifferent are so much better off psychologically in this respect. If today that intolerance no longer shows itself so violent and cruel as in former centuries, we can scarcely conclude that there has been a softening in human manners. The cause is rather to be found in the undeniable weakening of religious feelings and the libidinal ties which depend upon them. If another group tie takes the place of the religious one – and the socialistic tie seems to be succeeding in doing so – then there will be the same intolerance towards outsiders as in the age of the Wars of Religion.[27]

Freud's error in political prognosis, his blaming the 'socialists' for what their German arch-enemies did, is as striking as his prophecy of fascist destructiveness, the drive to eliminate the out-group.[28] As a matter of fact, neutralization of religion seems to have led to just the opposite of what the enlightener Freud anticipated: the division between the believers and the non-believers has been maintained and reified. However, it has become a structure in itself, independent of any ideational content, and is even more stubbornly defended since it lost its inner conviction. At the same time, the mitigating impact of the religious doctrine of love vanished. This is the essence of the 'sheep and goat' device employed by all fascist demagogues. Since they do not recognize any spiritual criterion in regard to who is chosen and who is rejected, they substitute a pseudo-natural criterion such as the race,[29] which seems to be inescapable and can therefore be applied even more mercilessly than was the concept of heresy during the Middle Ages. Freud has succeeded in identifying the libidinal function of this device. It acts as a negatively integrating force. Since the positive libido is completely invested in the image of the primal father, the leader, and since few positive contents are available, a negative one has to be found. 'The leader or the leading idea might also, so to speak, be negative; hatred against a particular person or institution might operate in just the same unifying way, and might call up the same kind of emotional ties as positive attachment.'[30] It goes without saying that this negative integration feeds on the instinct of destructiveness to which Freud does not explicitly refer in his *Group Psychology*, the decisive role of which he has, however, recognized in his *Civilization and Its Discontents*. In the present context, Freud explains the hostility against the out-group with narcissism:

> In the undisguised antipathies and aversions which people feel towards strangers with whom they have to do, we may recognize the expression of self-love – of narcissism. This self-love works for the self-assertion of the individual, and behaves as though the occurrence of any divergence from his own particular lines of development involved a criticism of them and a demand for their alteration.[31]

The narcissistic *gain* provided by fascist propaganda is obvious. It suggests continuously and sometimes in rather devious ways, that the follower, simply through belonging to the in-group, is better, higher and purer than those who are excluded. At the same time, any kind of critique or self-awareness is resented as a narcissistic loss and elicits rage. It accounts for the violent reaction of all fascists against what they deem *zersetzend*, that which debunks their own stubbornly maintained values, and it also explains the hostility of prejudiced persons against any kind of introspection. Concomitantly, the concentration of hostility upon the out-group does away with intolerance in one's own group to which one's relation would otherwise be highly ambivalent.

> But the whole of this intolerance vanishes, temporarily or permanently, as the result of the formation of a group, and in a group. So long as a group formation persists or so far as it extends, individuals behave as though they were uniform, tolerate other people's peculiarities, put themselves on an equal level with them, and have no feeling of aversion towards them. Such a limitation of narcissism can, according to our theoretical views, only be produced by one factor, a libidinal tie with other people.[32]

This is the line pursued by the agitators' standard 'unity trick'. They emphasize their being different from the outsider but play down such differences within their own group and tend to level out distinctive qualities among themselves with the exception of the hierarchical one. 'We are all in the same boat'; nobody should be better off – the snob, the intellectual, the pleasure seeker are always attacked. The undercurrent of malicious egalitarianism, of the brotherhood of all-compromising humiliation, is a component of fascist propaganda and fascism itself. It found its symbol in Hitler's notorious command of the *Eintopfgericht*. The less they want the inherent social structure changed, the more they prate about social justice, meaning that no member of the 'community of the people' should indulge in individual pleasures. Repressive egalitarianism instead of realization of true equality through the abolition of repression is part and parcel of the fascist mentality and reflected in the agitators' 'if-you-only-knew' device which promises the vindictive revelation of all sorts of forbidden pleasures enjoyed by others. Freud interprets this phenomenon in terms of the transformation of individuals into members of a psychological 'brother horde'. Their coherence is a reaction formation against their primary jealousy of each other, pressed into the service of group coherence.

> What appears later on in society in the shape of *Gemeingeist, esprit de corps*, 'group spirit', etc. does not belie its derivation from what was originally envy. No one must want to put himself forward, every one must be the same and have the same. Social justice means that we deny ourselves many things so that others may have to do without them as well, or, what is the same thing, may not be able to ask for them.[33]

It may be added that the ambivalence towards the brother has found a rather striking, ever-recurring expression in the agitators' technique. Freud and Rank have pointed out that in fairy tales, small animals such as bees and ants 'would be the brothers in the primal horde, just as in the same way in dream symbolism insects or vermin signify brothers and sisters (contemptuously, considered as babies)'.[34] Since the members of the in-group have supposedly 'succeeded in identifying themselves with one another by means of similar love for the same object',[35] they cannot admit this contempt for each other. Thus, it is expressed by completely negative cathexis of these low animals, fused with hatred against the out-group, and projected upon the latter. Actually it is one of the favourite devices of fascist agitators – examined in great detail by Leo Lowenthal[36] – to compare out-groups, all foreigners and particularly refugees and Jews, with low animals and vermin.

If we are entitled to assume a correspondence of fascist propagandist stimuli to the mechanisms elaborated in Freud's *Group Psychology*, we have to ask ourselves the almost inevitable question how did the fascist agitators, crude and semi-educated as they were, obtain knowledge of these mechanisms? Reference to the influence exercised by Hitler's *Mein Kampf* upon the American demagogues would not lead very far, since it seems impossible that Hitler's theoretical knowledge of group psychology went beyond the most trivial observations derived from a popularized Le Bon. Neither can it be maintained that Goebbels was a mastermind of propaganda and fully aware of the most advanced findings of modern depth-psychology. Perusal of his speeches and selections from his recently published diaries give the impression of a person shrewd enough to play the game of power politics but utterly naive and superficial in regard to all social or psychological issues below the surface of his own catchwords and newspaper editorials. The idea of the sophisticated and 'radical' intellectual Goebbels is part of the devil's legend associated with his name and fostered by eager journalism; a legend, incidentally, which itself calls for psychoanalytic explanation. Goebbels himself thought in stereotypes and was completely under the spell of personalization. Thus, we have to seek for sources other than erudition for the much advertised fascist command of psychological techniques of mass manipulation. The foremost source seems to be the already mentioned basic identity of leader and follower which circumscribes one of the aspects of identification. The leader can guess the psychological wants and needs of those susceptible to his propaganda because he resembles them psychologically, and is distinguished from them by a capacity to express without inhibitions what is latent in them, rather than by any intrinsic superiority. The leaders are generally oral character types, with a compulsion to speak incessantly and to befool the others. The famous spell they exercise over their followers seems largely to depend on their orality: language itself, devoid of its rational significance, functions in a magical way and furthers those archaic regressions which reduce individuals to members of crowds. Since this very quality of uninhibited but largely associative speech presupposes at least a temporary lack of ego control, it may well indicate weakness rather than strength. The fascist agitators' boasting of strength is indeed frequently accompanied by hints at such weakness, particularly when begging for monetary contributions – hints which, to be sure, are skilfully merged with the idea of strength itself. In order successfully to meet the unconscious dispositions of his audience, the agitator so to speak simply turns his own unconscious outward. His particular character syndrome makes it possible for him to do exactly this, and experience has taught him consciously to exploit this faculty, to make rational use of his irrationality, similarly to the actor, or a certain type of journalist who knows how to sell their innervations and sensitivity.

127

Without knowing it, he is thus able to speak and act in accord with the psychological theory for the simple reason that the psychological theory is true. All he has to do in order to make the psychology of his audience click, is shrewdly to exploit his own psychology.

The adequacy of the agitators' devices to the psychological basis of their aim is further enhanced by another factor. As we know, fascist agitation has by now come to be a profession, as it were, a livelihood. It had plenty of time to test the effectiveness of its various appeals and, through what might be called natural selection, only the most catchy ones have survived. Their effectiveness is itself a function of the psychology of the consumers. Through a process of 'freezing', which can be observed throughout the techniques employed in modern mass culture, the surviving appeals have been standardized, similarly to the advertising slogans which proved to be most valuable in the promotion of business. This standardization, in turn, falls in line with the stereotypical thinking, that is to say, with the 'stereo-pathy' of those susceptible to this propaganda and their infantile wish for endless, unaltered repetition. It is hard to predict whether the latter psychological disposition will prevent the agitators' standard devices from becoming blunt through excessive application. In National Socialist Germany, everybody used to make fun of certain propagandistic phrases such as 'blood and soil' (*Blut und Boden*), jokingly called *Blubo*, or the concept of the nordic race from which the verb *aufnorden* (to 'northernize') was derived. Nevertheless, these appeals do not seem to have lost their attractiveness. Rather, their very 'phoniness' may have been relished cynically and sadistically as an index for the fact that power alone decided one's fate in the Third Reich, that is, power unhampered by rational objectivity.

Furthermore, one may ask: why is the applied group psychology discussed here peculiar to fascism rather than to most other movements that seek mass support? Even the most casual comparison of fascist propaganda with that of liberal, progressive parties will show this to be so. Yet, neither Freud nor Le Bon envisaged such a distinction. They spoke of crowds 'as such', similar to the conceptualizations used by formal sociology, without differentiating between the political aims of the groups involved. As a matter of fact, both thought of traditional socialistic movements rather than of their opposite, though it should be noted that the Church and the Army – the examples chosen by Freud for the demonstration of this theory – are essentially conservative and hierarchical. Le Bon, on the other hand, is mainly concerned with non-organized, spontaneous, ephemeral crowds. Only an explicit theory of society, by far transcending the range of psychology, can fully answer the question raised here. We content ourselves with a few suggestions. First, the objective aims of fascism are largely irrational in so far as they contradict the material interest of great numbers of those whom they try to embrace, notwithstanding the pre-war boom of the first years of the Hitler regime. The continuous danger of war inherent in fascism spells destruction and the masses are at least preconsciously aware of it. Thus, fascism does not altogether speak the untruth when it refers to its own irrational powers, however faked the mythology which ideologically rationalizes the irrational may be. Since it would be impossible for fascism to win the masses through rational arguments, its propaganda must necessarily be deflected from discursive thinking; it must be oriented psychologically, and has to mobilize irrational, unconscious, regressive processes. This task is facilitated by the frame of mind of all those strata of the population who suffer from senseless frustrations and therefore develop a stunted, irrational mentality. It may well be the secret of fascist propaganda that it simply takes men for what they are: the true children of today's standardized mass culture, largely robbed of autonomy and spontaneity, instead of setting goals the realization of which would transcend the psychological *status quo* no less than the social one. Fascist propaganda has only to *reproduce* the existent mentality for its own purposes; it need not induce a change – and the compulsive repetition which is one of its foremost characteristics will be at one with the necessity for this continuous reproduction. It relies absolutely on the total structure as well as on each particular trait of the authoritarian character which is itself the product of an internalization of the irrational aspects of modern society. Under the prevailing conditions, the irrationality of fascist propaganda becomes rational in the sense of instinctual economy. For if the status quo is taken for granted and petrified, a much greater effort is needed to see through it than to adjust to it and to obtain at least some gratification through identification with the existent – the focal point of fascist propaganda. This may explain why ultra-reactionary mass movements use the 'psychology of the masses' to a much greater extent than do movements which show more faith in the masses. However, there is no doubt that even the most progressive political movement can deteriorate to the level of the 'psychology of the crowd' and its manipulation, if its own rational content is shattered through the reversion to blind power.

The so-called psychology of fascism is largely engendered by manipulation. Rationally calculated techniques bring about what is naively regarded as the 'natural' irrationality of masses. This insight may help us to solve the problem of whether fascism as a mass phenomenon can be explained at all in psychological terms. While there certainly exists potential susceptibility for fascism among the masses, it is equally certain that the manipulation of the unconscious, the kind of suggestion explained by Freud in genetic terms, is indispensable for actualization of this potential. This, however, corroborates the assumption that fascism as such is *not* a psychological issue and that any attempt to understand its roots and its historical role in psychological terms still remains on the level of ideologies such as the one of 'irrational forces' promoted by fascism itself. Although the fascist agitator doubtlessly takes up certain tendencies within those he addresses, he does so as the mandatory of powerful economic and political interests. Psychological dispositions do not actually cause fascism; rather, fascism defines a psychological area which can be successfully exploited by the forces which promote it for entirely non-psychological reasons of self-interest. What happens when masses are caught by fascist propaganda is not a spontaneous primary expression of instincts and urges but a quasi-scientific revitalization of their psychology – the artificial regression described by Freud in his discussion of organized groups. The psychology of the masses has been taken over by their leaders and transformed into a means for their domination. It does not express itself directly through mass movements. This phenomenon is not entirely new but was foreshadowed throughout the counter-revolutionary movements of history. Far from being the source of fascism, psychology has become one element among others in a superimposed system the very totality of which is necessitated by the potential mass of resistance – the masses' own rationality. The content of Freud's theory, the replacement of individual narcissism by identification with leader images, points in the direction of what might be called the appropriation of mass psychology by the oppressors. To be sure, this process has a psychological dimension, but it also indicates a growing tendency towards the abolition of psychological motivation in the old, liberalistic sense. Such motivation is systematically controlled and absorbed by social mechanisms which are directed from above. When the leaders become conscious of mass psychology and take it into their own hands, it ceases to exist in a certain sense. This potentiality is contained in the basic construct of psychoanalysis inasmuch as for Freud the concept of psychology is essentially a negative one. He defines the realm of psychology by the supremacy of the unconscious and postulates that what is id should become ego. The emancipation of man from the heteronomous rule of his unconscious would be tantamount to the abolition of his 'psychology'. Fascism furthers this abolition in the opposite sense through the perpetuation of dependence instead of the realization of potential freedom, through expropriation of the unconscious by social control instead of making the subjects conscious of their unconscious. For, while psychology always denotes some bondage of the individual, it also presupposes freedom in the sense of a certain self-sufficiency and autonomy of the individual. It is not accidental that the nineteenth century was the great era of psychological thought. In a thoroughly reified society, in which there are virtually no direct relationships between men, and in which each person has been reduced to a social atom, to a mere function of collectivity, the psychological processes, though they still persist in each individual, have ceased to appear as the determining forces of the social process. Thus, the psychology of the individual has lost what Hegel would have called substance. It is perhaps the greatest merit of Freud's book that though he restricted himself to the field of individual psychology and wisely abstained from introducing sociological factors from outside, he nevertheless reached the turning point where psychology abdicates. The psychological 'impoverishment' of the subject that 'surrendered itself to the object' which 'it has substituted for its most important constituent';[37] that is, the super-ego, anticipates almost with clairvoyance the post-psychological de-individualized social atoms which form the fascist collectivities. In these social atoms the psychological dynamic of group formation have overreached themselves and are no longer a reality. The category of 'phoniness' applies to the leaders as well as to the act of identification on the part of the masses and their supposed frenzy and hysteria. Just as little as people believe in the depth of their hearts that the Jews are the devil, do they completely believe in their leader. They do not really identify themselves with him but act this identification, perform their own enthusiasm, and thus participate in their leader's performance. It is through this performance that they strike a balance between their continuously mobilized instinctual urges and the historical stage of enlightenment they have reached, and which cannot be revoked arbitrarily. It is probably the suspicion of this fictitiousness of their own 'group psychology' which makes fascist crowds so merciless and unapproachable. If they would stop to reason for a second, the whole performance would go to pieces, and they would be left to panic. Freud came upon this element of 'phoniness' within an unexpected context, namely, when he discussed hypnosis as a retrogression of individuals to the relation between primal horde and primal father.

> As we know from other reactions, individuals have preserved a variable degree of personal aptitude for reviving old situations of this kind. Some knowledge that in spite of everything hypnosis is only a game, a deceptive renewal of these old impressions, may however remain behind and take care that there is a resistance against any too serious consequences of the suspension of the will in hypnosis.[38]

In the meantime, this game has been socialized, and the consequences have proved to be very serious. Freud made a distinction between hypnosis and group psychology by defining the former as taking place between two people only. However, the leaders' appropriation of mass psychology, the streamlining of their technique, has enabled them to collectivize the hypnotic spell. The Nazi battle cry of 'Germany awake' hides its very opposite. The collectivization and institutionalization of the spell, on the other hand, have made the transference more and more indirect and precarious so that the aspect of performance, the 'phoniness' of enthusiastic identification and of all the traditional dynamics of group psychology, have tremendously increased. This increase may well terminate in sudden awareness of the untruth of the spell, and eventually in its collapse. Socialized hypnosis breeds within itself the forces which will do away with the spook of regression through remote control, and in the end awaken those who keep their eyes shut though they are no longer asleep.

Notes

1 This chapter forms part of the author's continuing collaboration with Max Horkheimer.
2 (1949) New York: Harper Brothers. Cf. also: Leo Lowenthal and Norbert Guterman, (1949) 'Portrait of the American Agitator', *Public Opinion Quarterly*, (Fall), pp. 417ff.
3 This requires some qualification. There is a certain difference between those who, speculating rightly or wrongly on large-scale economic backing, try to maintain an air of respectability and deny that they are anti-Semites before coming down to the business of Jew-baiting – and overt Nazis who want to act on their own, or at least make believe that they do, and indulge in the most violent and obscene language. Moreover, one might distinguish between agitators who play the old-fashioned, homely, Christian conservative and can easily be recognized by their hostility against the 'dole', and those who, playing a more streamlined modern version, appeal mostly to youth and sometimes pretend to be revolutionary. However, such differences should not be overrated. The basic structure of their speeches as well as their supply of devices is identical in spite of carefully fostered differences in overtones. What one has to face is a division of labour rather than genuine divergencies. It may be noted that the National Socialist party shrewdly maintained differentiations of a similar kind, but that they never amounted to anything nor led to any serious clash of political ideas within the party. The belief that the victims of 30 June 1934 were revolutionaries is mythological. The blood purge was a

matter of rivalries between various rackets and had no bearing on social conflicts.

4 The German title, under which the book was published in 1921, is *Massenpsychologie und Ichanalyse*. The translator, James Strachey, rightly stresses that the term group here means the equivalent of Le Bon's *foule* and the German *Masse*. It may be added that in this book the term ego does not denote the specific psychological agency as described in Freud's later writing in contrast to the id and the super-ego; it simply means the individual. It is one of the most important implications of Freud's *Group Psychology* that he does not recognize an independent, hypostastized 'mentality of the crowd,' but reduces the phenomena observed and described by writers such as Le Bon and McDougall to regressions which take place in each one of the individuals who form a crowd and fall under its spell.

5 S. Freud (1922) *Group Psychology and the Analysis of the Ego*, London, p. 7.

6 Ibid., p. 27.

7 Freud's book does not follow up this phase of the problem but a passage in the addendum indicates that he was quite aware of it. 'In the same way, love for women breaks through the group ties of race, of national separation, and of the social class system, and it thus produces important effects as a factor in civilization. It seems certain that homosexual love is far more compatible with group ties, even when it takes the shape of uninhibited sexual tendencies' (p. 123). This was certainly borne out under German fascism where the borderline between overt and repressed homosexuality, just as that betwen overt and repressed sadism, was much more fluent than in liberal middle-class society.

8 Ibid., pp. 9 and 10.

9 "...love relationships...also constitute the essence of the group mind. Let us remember that the authorities make no mention of any such relations." (Ibid., p. 40.)

10 Perhaps one of the reasons for this striking phenomenon is the fact that the masses whom the fascist agitator – prior to seizing power – has to face are primarily not organized ones but the accidental crowds of the big city. The loosely knit character of such motley crowds makes it imperative that discipline and coherence be stressed at the expense of the centrifugal uncanalized urge to love. Part of the agitator's task consists in making the crowd believe that it is organized like the Army or the Church. Hence the tendency towards over-organization. A fetish is made of organization as such; it becomes an end instead of a means and this tendency prevails throughout the agitator's speeches.

11 Ibid., pp. 99–100. This key statement of Freud's theory of group psychology incidentally accounts for one of the most decisive observations about the fascist personality: the externalization of the super-ego. The term 'ego ideal' is Freud's earlier expression for what he later called the super-ego. Its replacement through a 'group ego' is exactly what happens to fascist personalities. They fail to develop an

independent autonomous conscience and substitute for it an identification with collective authority which is irrational as Freud described it, heteronomous, rigidly oppressive, largely alien to the individuals' own thinking and, therefore, easily exchangeable in spite of its structural rigidity. The phenomenon is adequately expressed in the Nazi formula that what serves the German people is good. The pattern reoccurs in the speeches of American fascist demagogues who never appeal to their prospective followers' own conscience but incessantly invoke external, conventional and stereotyped values which are taken for granted and treated as authoritatively valid without ever being subject to a process of living experience or discursive examination. As pointed out in detail in the book, *The Authoritarian Personality*, by T.W. Adorno, Else Frenkel-Brunswik, Daniel L. Levinson and R. Nevitt Sanford (1950), Harper Brothers, New York, prejudiced persons generally display belief in conventional values instead of making moral decisions of their own and regard as right 'what is being done'. Through identification, they too tend to submit to a group ego at the expense of their own ego ideal which becomes virtually merged with external values.

12 The fact that the fascist follower's masochism is inevitably accompanied by sadistic impulses is in harmony with Freud's general theory of ambivalence, originally developed in connection with the Oedipus complex. Since the fascist integration of individuals into masses satisfied them only vicariously, their resentment against the frustrations of civilization survives but is canalized to become compatible with the leader's aims; it is psychologically fused with authoritarian submissiveness. Though Freud does not pose the problem of what was later called 'sado-masochism', he was nevertheless well aware of it, as evidenced by his acceptance of Le Bon's idea that 'since a group is in no doubt as to what constitutes truth or error, and is conscious, moreover, of its own great strength, it is as intolerant as it is obedient to authority. It respects force and can only be slightly influenced by kindness, which it regards merely as a form of weakness. What it demands of its heroes is strength, or even violence. It wants to be ruled and oppressed and to fear its masters.' (Freud, 1922, p. 17).

13 Ibid., pp. 58ff.

14 Ibid., p. 61.

15 Ibid., p. 60.

16 Cf. Max Horkheimer (1949) 'Authoritarianism and the Family Today', in R.N. Anshen (ed.) *The Family: Its Function and Destiny*, Harper Brothers, New York.

17 Freud (1922) p. 74.

18 The translation of Freud's book renders his term '*Instantz*' by 'faculty', a word which, however, does not carry the hierarchical connotation of the German original. 'Agency' seems to be more appropriate.

19 Ibid., p. 80.

20 It may not be superfluous to stress that Nietzsche's concept of the

Superman has as little in common with this archaic imagery as his vision of the future with fascism. Freud's allusion is obviously valid only for the 'Superman' as he became popularized in cheap slogans.

21 Ibid., p. 93.
22 Ibid., p. 102.
23 For further details on personalization compare Freud (1922) p. 44, footnote, where he discusses the relation between ideas and leader personalities, and p. 53, where he defines as 'secondary leaders' those essentially irrational ideas which hold groups together. In technological civilization, no *immediate* transference to the leader, unknown and distant as he actually is, is possible. What happens is rather a regressive repersonalization of impersonal, detached social powers. This possibility was clearly envisaged by Freud. '...A common tendency, a wish in which a number of people can have a share, may...serve as a substitute. This abstraction, again, might be more or less completely embodied in the figure of what we might call a secondary leader.'
24 Ibid., p. 110.
25 German folklore has a drastic symbol for this trait. It speaks of *Radfahrernaturen*, bicyclist's characters. Above they bow, they kick below.
26 Freud, Ibid., p. 16.
27 Ibid., pp. 50–1.
28 With regard to the role of 'neutralized', diluted religion in the make-up of the fascist mentality, compare *The Authoritarian Personality*. Important psycholanalytic contributions to this whole area of problems are contained in Theodor Reik's *Der eigene und der fremde Gott*, and in Paul Federn's *Die vaterlose Gesellschaft*.
29 It may be noted that the ideology of race distinctly reflects the idea of primitive brotherhood revived, according to Freud, through the specific regression involved in mass formation. The notion of race shares two properties with brotherhood: it is supposedly 'natural', a bond of 'blood', and it is de-sexualized. In fascism this similarity is kept unconscious. It mentions brotherhood comparatively rarely, and usually only in regard to Germans living *outside* the borders of the Reich ('Our Sudeten brothers'). This, of course, is partly due to recollections of the ideal of *fraternité* of the French Revolution, taboo to the Nazis.
30 Ibid., p. 53.
31 Ibid., pp. 55–6.
32 Ibid., p. 56.
33 Ibid., pp. 87–8.
34 Ibid., p. 114.
35 Ibid., p. 87.
36 Cf. *Prophets of Deceit*.
37 Freud, Ibid., p. 76.
38 Ibid., p. 99.

Chapter six

How to look at television

The effect of television cannot be adequately expressed in terms of success or failure, likes or dislikes, approval or disapproval. Rather, an attempt should be made, with the aid of depth-psychological categories and previous knowledge of mass media, to crystallize a number of theoretical concepts by which the potential effect of television – its impact upon various layers of the spectator's personality – could be studied. It seems timely to investigate systematically socio-psychological stimuli typical of televised material both on a descriptive and psychodynamic level, to analyse their presuppositions as well as their total pattern, and to evaluate the effect they are likely to produce. This procedure may ultimately bring forth a number of recommendations on how to deal with these stimuli to produce the most desirable effect of television. By exposing the socio-psychological implications and mechanisms of television, which often operate under the guise of false realism, not only may the shows be improved, but, more important possibly, the public at large may be sensitized to the nefarious effect of some of these mechanisms.

We are not concerned with the effectiveness of any particular show or programme; but we are concerned with the nature of present-day television and its imagery. Yet, our approach is practical. The findings should be so close to the material, should rest on such a solid foundation of experience, that they can be translated into precise recommendations and be made convincingly clear to large audiences.

Improvement of television is not conceived primarily on an artistic, purely aesthetic level, extraneous to present customs. This does not mean that we naively take for granted the dichotomy between autonomous art and mass media. We all know that their relationship is highly complex. Today's rigid division between what is called 'long-haired' and 'short-haired' art is the product of a long historical development. It would be romanticizing to assume that formerly art was entirely pure, that the creative artist thought only in terms of the inner consistency of the artifact and not also of its effect upon the spectators. Theatrical art, in particular, cannot be separated from audience reaction. Conversely, vestiges of the aesthetic claim to be something autonomous, a world unto itself, remain even within the most trivial product of mass culture. In fact, the present rigid division of art into autonomous and commercial aspects is itself largely a function of commercialization. It was hardly accidental that the slogan *l'art pour l'art* was coined polemically in the Paris of the first half of the nineteenth century, when literature really became large-scale business for the first time. Many of the cultural products bearing the anti-commercial trademark 'art for art's sake' show traces of commercialism in their appeal to the sensational or in the conspicuous display of material wealth and sensuous stimuli at the expense of the meaningfulness of the work. This trend was pronounced in the Neo-Romantic theatre of the first decades of our century.

Older and recent popular culture

In order to do justice to all such complexities, much closer scrutiny of the background and development of modern mass media is required than communications research, generally limited to present conditions, is aware of. One would have to establish what the output of contemporary cultural industry has in common with older 'low' or popular forms of art as well as with autonomous art, and where the differences lie. Suffice it here to state that the archetypes of present popular culture were set comparatively early in the development of middle-class society – at about the turn of the seventeenth and the beginning of the eighteenth centuries in England. According to the studies of the English sociologist Ian Watt, the English novels of that period, particularly the works of Defoe and Richardson, marked the beginning of an approach to literary production that consciously created, served, and finally controlled a 'market'. Today the commercial production of cultural goods has become streamlined, and the impact of popular culture upon the individual has concomitantly increased. This process has not been confined to quantity, but has resulted in new qualities. While recent popular culture has absorbed all the elements and particularly all the 'don'ts' of its predecessor, it differs decisively inasmuch as it has developed into a system. Thus, popular culture is no longer confined to certain forms such as novels or dance music, but has seized all media of artistic expression. The structure and meaning of these forms show an amazing parallelism, even when they appear to have little in common on the surface (such as jazz and the detective novel). Their output has increased to such an extent that it is almost impossible for anyone to dodge them; and even those formerly aloof from popular culture – the rural population on one hand and the highly educated on the other – are somehow affected. The more the system of 'merchandising' culture is expanded, the more it tends also to assimilate the 'serious' art of the past by adapting this art to the system's own requirements. The control is so extensive that any infraction of its rules is *a priori* stigmatized as 'highbrow' and has but little chance to reach the population at large. The system's concerted effort results in what might be called the prevailing ideology of our time.

Certainly, there are many typical changes within today's pattern; for example, men were formerly presented as erotically aggressive and women on the defensive, whereas this has been largely reversed in modern mass culture, as pointed out particularly by Wolfenstein and Leites. More important, however, is that the pattern itself, dimly perceptible in the early novels and basically preserved today, has by now become congealed and standardized. Above all, this rigid institutionalization transforms modern mass culture into a medium of undreamed of psychological control. The repetitiveness, the selfsameness, and the ubiquity of modern mass culture tend to make for automatized reactions and to weaken the forces of individual resistance.

When the journalist Defoe and the printer Richardson calculated the effect of their wares upon the audience, they had to speculate, to follow hunches; and therewith, a certain latitude to develop deviations remained. Such deviations have nowadays been reduced to a kind of multiple choice between very few alternatives. The following may serve as an illustration. The popular or semi-popular novels of the first half of the nineteenth century, published in large quantities and serving mass consumption, were supposed to arouse tension in the reader. Although the victory of the good over the bad was generally provided for, the meandering and endless plots and subplots hardly allowed the readers of Sue and Dumas to be continuously aware of the moral. Readers could expect anything to happen. This no longer holds true. Every spectator of a television mystery knows with absolute certainty how it is going to end. Tension is but superficially maintained and is unlikely to have a serious effect any more. On the contrary, the spectator feels on safe ground all the time. This longing for 'feeling on safe ground' – reflecting an infantile need for protection, rather than the desire for a thrill – is catered to. The element of excitement is preserved only with tongue in cheek. Such changes fall in line with the potential change from a freely competitive to a virtually 'closed' society into which one wants to be admitted or from which one fears to be rejected. Everything somehow appears 'predestined'.

The increasing strength of modern mass culture is further enhanced by changes in the sociological structure of the audience. The old cultured elite does not exist any more; the modern intelligentsia only partially corresponds to it. At the same time, huge strata of the population formerly unacquainted with art have become cultural 'consumers'. Modern audiences, although less capable of the artistic sublimation bred by tradition, have become shrewder in their demands for perfection of technique and for reliability of information, as well as in their desire for 'services'; and they have become more convinced of the consumers' potential power over the producer, no matter whether this power is actually wielded.

How changes within the audience have affected the meaning of popular culture may also be illustrated. The element of internalization played a decisive role in early Puritan novels of the Richardson type. This element no longer prevails, for it was based on the essential role of 'inwardness' in both original Protestantism and earlier middle-class society. As the profound influence of the basic tenets of Protestantism has gradually receded, the cultural pattern has become more and more opposed to the 'introvert.' As Riesman puts it,

> ...the conformity of earlier generations of Americans of the type I term 'inner-directed' was mainly assured by their internalization of adult authority. The middle-class urban American of today, the 'other-directed', is, by contrast, in a characterological sense more the product of his peers – that is in sociological terms, his 'peer-groups', the other kids at school or in the block.[1]

This is reflected by popular culture. The accents on inwardness, inner conflicts, and psychological ambivalence (which plays so large a role in earlier popular novels and on which their originality rests) have given way to unproblematic, cliché-like characterization. Yet the code of decency that governed the inner conflicts of the Pamelas, Clarissas and Lovelaces remains almost literally intact.[2] The middle-class 'ontology' is preserved in an almost fossilized way, but is severed from the mentality of the middle classes. By being superimposed on people with whose living conditions and mental make-up it is no longer in accord, this middle-class 'ontology' assumes an increasingly authoritarian and at the same time hollow character.

The overt 'naiveté' of older popular culture is avoided. Mass culture, if not sophisticated, must at least be up to date – that is to say, 'realistic', or posing as realistic – in order to meet the expectations of a supposedly disillusioned, alert, and hard-boiled audience. Middle-class requirements bound up with internalization – such as concentration, intellectual effort, and erudition – have to be continuously lowered. This does not hold only for the United States, where historical memories are scarcer than in Europe, but it is universal, applying to England and Continental Europe as well.[3]

However, this apparent progress of enlightenment is more than counterbalanced by retrogressive traits. The earlier popular culture maintained a certain equilibrium between its social ideology and the actual social conditions under which its consumers lived. This probably helped to keep the border line between popular and serious art during the eighteenth century more fluid than it is today. Abbé Prévost was one of the founding fathers of French popular literature; but his *Manon Lescaut* is completely free from clichés, artistic vulgarisms, and calculated effects. Similarly, later in the eighteenth century, Mozart's *Zauberflöte* struck a balance between the 'high' and the popular style which is almost unthinkable today.

The curse of modern mass culture seems to be its adherence to the almost unchanged ideology of early middle-class society, whereas the lives of its consumers are completely out of phase with this ideology. This is probably the reason for the gap between the overt and the hidden 'message' of modern popular art. Although on an overt level the traditional values of English Puritan middle-class society are promulgated, the hidden message aims at a frame of mind which is no longer bound by these values. Rather, today's frame of mind transforms the traditional values into the norms of an increasingly hierarchical and authoritarian social structure. Even here it has to be admitted that authoritarian elements were also present in the older ideology which, of course, never fully expressed the truth. But the 'message' of adjustment and unreflecting obedience seems to be dominant and all-pervasive today. Whether maintained values derived from religious ideas obtain a different meaning when severed from their root should be carefully examined. For example, the concept of the 'purity' of women is one of the invariables of popular culture. In the earlier phase this concept is treated in terms of an inner conflict between concupiscence and the internalized Christian ideal of chastity, whereas in today's popular culture it is dogmatically posited as a value per se. Again, even the rudiments of this pattern are visible in productions such as *Pamela*. There, however, it seems a by-product; whereas in today's popular culture the idea that only the 'nice girl' gets married and that she must get married at any price has come to be accepted before Richardson's conflicts even start.[4]

The more inarticulate and diffuse the audience of modern mass media seems to be, the more mass media tend to achieve their 'integration'. The ideals of conformity and conventionalism were inherent in popular novels from the very beginning. Now, however, these ideals have been translated into rather clear-cut prescriptions of what to do and what not to do. The outcome of conflicts is pre-established, and all conflicts are mere sham. Society is always the winner, and the individual is only a puppet manipulated through social rules. True, conflicts of the nineteenth-century type – such as women running away from their husbands, the drabness of provincial life, and daily chores – occur frequently in today's magazine stories. However, with a regularity which challenges quantitative treatment, these conflicts are decided in favour of the very same conditions from which these women want to break away. The stories teach their readers that one has to be 'realistic', that one has to give up romantic ideas, that one has to adjust oneself at any price, and that nothing more can be expected of any individual. The perennial middle-class conflict between individuality and society has been reduced to a dim memory, and the message is invariably that of identification with the status quo. This theme too is not new, but its unfailing universality invests it with an entirely different meaning. The constant plugging of conventional values seems to mean that these values have lost their substance, and that it is feared that people would really follow their instinctual urges and conscious insights unless continuously re-assured from outside that they must not do so. The less the message is really believed and the less it is in harmony with the actual exist-ence of the spectators, the more categorically it is maintained in modern culture. One may speculate whether its inevitable hypocrisy is concomitant with punitiveness and sadistic sternness.

Multilayered structure

A depth-psychological approach to television has to be focused on its multilayered structure. Mass media are not simply the sum total of the actions they portray or of the messages that radiate from these actions. Mass media also consist of various layers of meanings super-imposed on one another, all of which contribute to the effect. True, due to their calculative nature, these rationalized products seem to be more clear-cut in their meaning than authentic works of art, which can never be boiled down to some unmistakeable 'message'. But the heritage of polymorphic meaning has been taken over by cultural in-dustry inasmuch as what it conveys becomes itself organized in order to enthral the spectators on various psychological levels simulta-neously. As a matter of fact, the hidden message may be more important than the overt, since this hidden message will escape the controls of consciousness, will not be 'looked through', will not be warded off by sales resistance, but is likely to sink into the spectator's mind.

Probably all the various levels in mass media involve *all* the mechanisms of consciousness and unconsciousness stressed by psychoanalysis. The difference between the surface content, the overt message of televised material, and its hidden meaning is generally marked and rather clear-cut. The rigid superimposition of various layers probably is one of the features by which mass media are distinguishable from the integrated products of autonomous art, where the various layers are much more thoroughly fused. The full effect of the material on the spectator cannot be studied without consideration of the hidden meaning in conjunction with the overt one, and it is precisely this interplay of various layers which has hitherto been neglected and which will be our focus. This is in accordance with the assumption shared by numerous social scientists that certain political and social trends of our time, particularly those of a totalitarian nature, feed to a considerable extent on irrational and frequently unconscious motivations. Whether the conscious or the unconscious message of our material is more important is hard to predict and can be evaluated only after careful analysis. We do appreciate, however, that the overt message can be interpreted much more adequately in the light of psychodynamics – that is, in its relation to instinctual urges as well as control – than by looking at the overt in a naive way and by ignoring its implications and presuppositions.

The relation between overt and hidden message will prove highly complex in practice. Thus, the hidden message frequently aims at reinforcing conventionally rigid and 'pseudo-realistic' attitudes similar to the accepted ideas more rationalistically propagated by the surface message. Conversely, a number of repressed gratifications which play a large role on the hidden level are somehow allowed to manifest themselves on the surface in jests, off-colour remarks, suggestive situations, and similar devices. All this interaction of various levels, however, points in some definite direction: the tendency to channelize audience reaction. This falls in line with the suspicion widely shared, though hard to corroborate by exact data, that the majority of television shows today aim at producing, or at least reproducing, the very smugness, intellectual passivity and gullibility that seem to fit in with totalitarian creeds even if the explicit surface message of the shows may be anti-totalitarian.

With the means of modern psychology, we will try to determine the primary prerequisites of shows eliciting mature, adult, and responsible reactions – implying not only in content but in the very way things are being looked at, the idea of autonomous individuals in a free democratic society. We perfectly realize that any definition of such an individual will be hazardous; but we know quite well what a human being deserving of the appellation 'autonomous individual' should *not* be, and this 'not' is actually the focal point of our consideration.

When we speak of the multilayered structure of television shows, we are thinking of various superimposed layers of different degrees of manifestness or hiddenness that are utilized by mass culture as a technological means of 'handling' the audience. This was expressed felicitously by Leo Lowenthal when he coined the term 'psychoanalysis in reverse'. The implication is that somehow the psychoanalytic concept of a multilayered personality has been taken up by cultural industry, and that the concept is used in order to ensnare the consumer as completely as possible and in order to engage him psychodynamically in the service of premeditated effects. A clear-cut division into allowed gratifications, forbidden gratifications, and recurrence of the forbidden gratifications in a somewhat modified and deflected form is carried through.

To illustrate the concept of the multilayered structure: the heroine of an extremely light comedy of pranks is a young schoolteacher who is not only underpaid but is incessantly fined by the caricature of a pompous and authoritarian school principal. Thus, she has no money for her meals and is actually starving. The supposedly funny situations consist mostly of her trying to hustle a meal from various acquaintances, but regularly without success. The mention of food and eating seems to induce laughter – an observation that can frequently be made and invites a study of its own.[5] Overtly, the play is just slight amusement mainly provided by the painful situations into which the heroine and her arch-opponent constantly run. The script does not try to 'sell' any idea. The 'hidden meaning' emerges simply by the way the story looks at human beings; thus the audience is invited to look at the characters in the same way without being made aware that indoctrination is present. The character of the underpaid, maltreated schoolteacher is an attempt to reach a compromise between prevailing scorn for the intellectual and the equally conventionalized respect for 'culture'. The heroine shows such an intellectual superiority and high-spiritedness that identification with her is invited, and compensation is offered for the inferiority of her position and that of her ilk in the social set-up. Not only is the central character supposed to be very charming, but she wisecracks constantly. In terms of a set pattern of identification, the script implies: 'If you are as humorous, good-natured, quick-witted, and charming as she is, do not worry about being paid a starvation wage. You can cope with your frustration in a humorous way; and your superior wit and cleverness put you not only above material privations, but also above the rest of mankind'. In other words, the script is a shrewd method of promoting adjustment to humiliating conditions by presenting them as objectively comical and by giving a picture of a person who experiences even her own inadequate position as an object of fun apparently free of any resentment.

Of course, this latent message cannot be considered as unconscious in the strict psychological sense, but rather as 'inobtrusive'; this message is hidden only by a style which does not pretend to touch anything serious and expects to be regarded as featherweight. Nevertheless, even such amusement tends to set patterns for the members of the audience without their being aware of it.

Another comedy of the same thesis is reminiscent of the funnies. A cranky old woman sets up the will of her cat (Mr Casey) and makes as heirs some of the schoolteachers in the permanent cast. Later the actual inheritance is found to consist of the cat's valueless toys. The plot is so constructed that each heir, at the reading of the will, is tempted to act as if he had known this person (Mr Casey). The ultimate point is that the cat's owner had placed a hundred-dollar bill inside each of the toys; and the heirs run to the incinerator to recover their inheritance. The audience is given to understand: 'Don't expect the impossible, don't daydream, but be realistic'. The denunciation of that archetypal daydream is enhanced by the association of the wish for unexpected and irrational blessings with dishonesty, hypocrisy, and a generally undignified attitude. The spectator is given to understand: 'Those who dare daydream, who expect that money will fall to them from heaven, and who forget any caution about accepting an absurd will are at the same time those whom you might expect to be capable of cheating'.

Here, an objection may be raised: is such a sinister effect of the hidden message of television known to those who control, plan, write and direct shows? Or it may even be asked: are those traits possible projections of the unconscious of the decision-makers' own minds according to the widespread assumption that works of art can be properly understood in terms of psychological projections of their authors? As a matter of fact, it is this kind of reasoning that has led to the suggestion that a special socio-psychological study of decision-makers in the field of television be made. We do not think that such a study would lead us very far. Even in the sphere of autonomous art, the idea of projection has been largely overrated. Although the authors' motivations certainly enter the artifact, they are by no means so all-determining as is often assumed. As soon as an artist has set himself his problem, it obtains some kind of impact of its own; and, in most cases, he has to follow the objective requirements of his product much more than his own urges of expression when he translates his primary conception into reality. To be sure, these objective requirements do not play a decisive role in mass media, which stress the effect on the spectator far beyond any artistic problem. However, the total set-up here tends to limit the chances of the artists' projections utterly. Those who produce the material follow, often grumblingly, innumerable requirements, rules of thumb, set patterns, and mechanisms of control which by necessity reduce to a minimum the range of any kind of artistic self-expression. The fact that most products of mass media are not produced by one individual but by collective collaboration – as happens to be true with most of the illustrations so far discussed – is only one contributing factor to this generally prevailing condition. To study television shows in terms of the psychology of the authors would almost be tantamount to studying Ford cars in terms of the psychoanalysis of the late Mr Ford.

Presumptuousness

The typical psychological mechanisms utilized by television shows and the devices by which they are automatized function only within a small number of given frames of reference operative in television communication, and the socio-psychological effect largely depends on them. We are all familiar with the division of television content into various classes, such as light comedy, westerns, mysteries, so-called sophisticated plays, and others. These types have developed into formulas which, to a certain degree, pre-established the attitudinal pattern of the spectator before he is confronted with any specific content and which largely determine the way in which any specific content is being perceived.

In order to understand television, it is, therefore, not enough to bring out the implications of various shows and types of shows; but an examination must be made of the presuppositions within which the implications function before a single word is spoken. Most important is that the typing of shows has gone so far that the spectator approaches each one with a set pattern of expectations before he faces the show itself – just as the radio listener who catches the beginning of Tschaikowsky's Piano Concerto as a theme song, knows automatically, 'aha, serious music!' or, when he hears organ music, responds equally automatically, 'aha, religion!' These halo effects of previous experiences may be psychologically as important as the implications of the phenomena themselves for which they have set the stage, and these presuppositions should, therefore, be treated with equal care.

When a television show bears the title 'Dante's Inferno', when the first shot is that of a night club by the same name, and when we find sitting at the bar a man with his hat on and at some distance from him a sad-looking, heavily made-up woman ordering another drink, we are almost certain that some murder will shortly be committed. The apparently individualized situation actually works only as a signal that moves our expectations into a definite direction. If we had never seen anything but 'Dante's Inferno', we probably would not be sure about what was going to happen; but, as it is, we are actually given to understand by both subtle and not so subtle devices that this is a crime play, that we are entitled to expect some sinister and probably hideous and sadistic deeds of violence, that the hero will be saved from a situation from which he can hardly be expected to be saved, that the woman on the bar-stool is probably not the main criminal but is likely to lose her life as a gangster's moll, and so on. This conditioning to such universal patterns, however, scarcely stops at the television set.

The way the spectator is made to look at apparently everyday items, such as a night-club, and to take as hints of possible crime common settings of his daily life, induces him to look at life itself as though it and its conflicts could generally be understood in such terms.[6] This, convincingly enough, may be the nucleus of truth in the old-fashioned arguments against all kinds of mass media for inciting criminality in the audience. The decisive thing is that this atmosphere of the normality of crime, its presentation in terms of an average expectation based on life situations, is never expressed in so many words but is established by the overwhelming wealth of material. It may affect certain spectator groups more deeply than the overt moral of crime and punishment regularly derived from such shows. What matters is not the importance of crime as a symbolic expression of otherwise uncontrolled sexual or aggressive impulses, but the confusion of this symbolism with a pedantically maintained realism in all matters of direct sense perception. Thus, empirical life becomes infused with a kind of meaning that virtually excludes adequate experience no matter how obstinately the veneer of such 'realism' is built up. This affects the social and psychological function of drama.

It is hard to establish whether the spectators of Greek tragedy really experienced the catharsis Aristotle described – in fact this theory, evolved after the age of tragedy was over, seems to have been a rationalization itself, an attempt to state the purpose of tragedy in pragmatic, quasi-scientific terms. Whatever the case, it seems pretty certain that those who saw the *Oresteia* of Aeschylus or Sophocles' *Oedipus* were not likely to translate these tragedies (the subject matter of which was known to everyone, and the interest in which was centred in artistic treatment) directly into everyday terms. This audience did not expect that on the next corner of Athens similar things would go on. Actually, pseudo-realism allows for the direct and extremely primitive identification achieved by popular culture, and it presents a façade of trivial buildings, rooms, dresses and faces as though they were the promise of something thrilling and exciting taking place at any moment.

In order to establish this socio-psychological frame of reference, one would have to follow up systematically categories – such as the normality of crime or pseudo-realism and many others – to determine their structural unity and to interpret the specific devices, symbols, and stereotypes in relation to this frame of reference. We hypothesize at this phase that the frames of reference and the individual devices will tend in the same direction.

Only against psychological backdrops such as pseudo-realism and against implicit assumptions such as the normality of crime can the specific stereotypes of television plays be interpreted. The very standardization indicated by set frames of reference automatically produces a number of stereotypes. Also, the technology of television production makes stereotyping almost inevitable. The short time available for the preparation of scripts and the vast material continuously to be produced call for certain formulas. Moreover, in plays lasting only a quarter to half an hour each, it appears inevitable that the kind of person the audience faces each time should be indicated drastically through red and green lights. We are not dealing with the problem of the existence of stereotypes as such. Since stereotypes are an indispensable element of the organization and anticipation of experience, preventing us from falling into mental disorganization and chaos, no art can entirely dispense with them. Again, the functional change is what concerns us. The more stereotypes become reified and rigid in the present set-up of cultural industry, the more people are tempted to cling desperately to clichés which seem to bring some order into the otherwise ununderstandable. Thus, people may not only lose true insight into reality, but ultimately their very capacity for life experience may be dulled by the constant wearing of blue and pink spectacles.

Stereotyping

In coping with this danger, we may not do full justice to the meaning of some of the stereotypes which are to be dealt with. We should never forget that there are two sides to every psychodynamic phenomenon, the unconscious or id element and the rationalization. Although the latter is psychologically defined as a defence mechanism, it may very well contain some non-psychological, objective truth which cannot simply be pushed aside on account of the psychological function of the rationalization. Thus some of the stereotypical messages, directed toward particularly weak spots in the mentality of large sectors of the population, may prove to be quite legitimate. However, it may be said with fairness that the questionable blessings of morals, such as 'one should not chase after rainbows', are largely overshadowed by the threat of inducing people to mechanical simplifications by distorting the world in such a way that it seems to fit into pre-established pigeonholes.

The example here selected, however, should indicate rather drastically the danger of stereotyping. A television play concerning a fascist dictator, a kind of hybrid between Mussolini and Peron, shows the dictator in a moment of crisis; and the content of the play is his inner and outer collapse. Whether the cause of his collapse is a popular upheaval or a military revolt is never made clear. But neither this issue nor any other of a social or political nature enters the plot itself. The course of events takes place exclusively on a private level. The dictator is just a heel who treats sadistically both his secretary and his 'lovely and warmhearted' wife. His antagonist, a general, was formerly in love with the wife; and they both still love each other, although the wife sticks loyally to her husband. Forced by her husband's brutality, she attempts flight, and is intercepted by the general who wants to save her. The turning point occurs when the guards surround the palace to defend the dictator's popular wife. As soon as they learn that she has departed, the guards quit; and the dictator, whose 'inflated ego' explodes at the same time, gives up. The dictator is nothing but a bad, pompous and cowardly man. He seems to act with extreme stupidity; nothing of the objective dynamics of dictatorship comes out. The impression is created that totalitarianism grows out of character disorders of ambitious politicians, and is overthrown by the honesty, courage, and warmth of those figures with whom the audience is supposed to identify. The standard device employed is that of the spurious personalization of objective issues. The representatives of ideas under attack, as in the case of the fascists here, are presented as villains in a ludicrous cloak-and-dagger fashion, whereas those who fight for the 'right cause' are personally idealized. This not only distracts from any real social issues but also enforces the psychologically extremely dangerous division of the world into black (the out-group) and white (we, the in-group). Certainly, no artistic production can deal with ideas or political creeds *in abstracto* but has to present them in terms of their concrete impact upon human beings; yet it would be utterly futile to present individuals as mere specimens of an abstraction, as puppets expressive of an idea. In order to deal with the concrete impact of totalitarian systems, it would be more commendable to show how the life of ordinary people is affected by terror and impotence than to cope with the phoney psychology of the big-shots, whose heroic role is silently endorsed by such a treatment even if they are pictured as villains. There seems to be hardly any question of the importance of an analysis of pseudo-personalization and its effect, by no means limited to television.

Although pseudo-personalization denotes the stereotyped way of 'looking at things' in television, we should also point out certain stereotypes in the narrower sense. Many television plays could be characterized by the soubriquet 'a pretty girl can do no wrong'. The heroine of a light comedy is, to use George Legman's term, 'a bitch heroine.' She behaves toward her father in an incredibly inhuman and cruel manner only slightly rationalized as 'merry pranks'. But she is punished very slightly, if at all. True, in real life bad deeds are rarely punished at all, but this cannot be applied to television. Here, those who have developed the production code for the movies seem right: what matters in mass media is not what happens in real life, but rather the positive and negative 'messages', prescriptions, and taboos that the spectator absorbs by means of identification with the material he is looking at. The punishment given to the pretty heroine only nominally fulfils the conventional requirements of the conscience for a second. But the spectator is given to understand that the pretty heroine really gets away with everything just because she is pretty.

The attitude in question seems to be indicative of a universal penchant. In another sketch that belongs to a series dealing with the confidence racket, the attractive girl who is an active participant in the racket not only is paroled after having been sentenced to a long term, but also seems to have a good chance of marrying her victim. Her sex morality, of course, is unimpeachable. The spectator is supposed to like her at first sight as a modest and self-effacing character, and he must not be disappointed. Although it is discovered that she is a crook, the original identification must be restored, or rather maintained. The stereotype of the nice girl is so strong that not even the proof of her delinquency can destroy it; and, by hook or by crook, she must be what she appears to be. It goes without saying that such psychological models tend to confirm exploitative, demanding, and aggressive attitudes on the part of young girls – a character structure which has come to be known in psychoanalysis under the name of oral aggressiveness.

Sometimes such stereotypes are disguised as national American traits, a part of the American scene where the image of the haughty, egoistic, yet irresistible girl who plays havoc with poor dad has come to be a public institution. This way of reasoning is an insult to the American spirit. High-pressure publicity and continuous plugging to institutionalize some obnoxious type does not make the type a sacred

symbol of folklore. Many considerations of an apparently anthropological nature today tend only to veil objectionable trends, as though
they were of an ethnological, quasi-natural character. Incidentally, it
is amazing to what degree television material even on superficial
examination brings to mind psychoanalytic concepts with the qualification of being a psychoanalysis in reverse. Psychoanalysis has
described the oral syndrome combining the antagonistic trends of
aggressive and dependent traits. This character syndrome is closely
indicated by the pretty girl that can do no wrong, who, while being
aggressive against her father exploits him at the same time, depend-
ing on him as much as, on the surface level, she is set against him. The
difference between the sketch and psychoanalysis is simply that the
sketch exalts the very same syndrome which is treated by psychoanalysis as a reversion to infantile developmental phases and which
the psychoanalyst tries to dissolve. It remains to be seen whether
something similar applies as well to some types of male heroes,
particularly the super-he-man. It may well be that he too can do
no wrong.

Finally, we should deal with a rather widespread stereotype which,
inasmuch as it is taken for granted by television, is further enhanced.
At the same time, the example may serve to show that certain psychoanalytic interpretations of cultural stereotypes are not really too far-
fetched; the latent ideas that psychoanalysis attributes to certain
stereotypes come to the surface. There is the extremely popular idea
that the artist is not only maladjusted, introverted and *a priori* somewhat funny; but that he is really an 'aesthete', a weakling, and a 'sissy'.
In other words, modern synthetic folklore tends to identify the artist
with the homosexual and to respect only the 'man of action' as a real,
strong man. This idea is expressed in a surprisingly direct manner in
one of the comedy scripts at our disposal. It portrays a young man
who is not only the 'dope' who appears so often on television but is
also a shy, retiring, and accordingly untalented poet, whose moronic
poems are ridiculed.[7] He is in love with a girl but is too weak and in-
secure to indulge in the necking practices she rather crudely suggests;
the girl, on her part, is caricatured as a boy-chaser. As happens frequently in mass culture, the roles of the sexes are reversed – the girl
is utterly aggressive and the boy, utterly afraid of her, describes himself as 'woman-handled' when she manages to kiss him. There are
vulgar innuendoes of homosexuality of which one may be quoted: the
heroine tells her boy-friend that another boy is in love with someone,
and the boy friend asks, 'What's he in love with?' She answers, 'A girl,
of course', and her boy-friend replies, 'Why, of course? Once before
it was a neighbour's turtle, and what's more its name was Sam'. This
interpretation of the artist as innately incompetent and a social

outcast (by the innuendo of sexual inversion) is worthy of examination.

We do not pretend that the individual illustrations and examples, or the theories by which they are interpreted, are basically new. But in view of the cultural and pedagogical problem presented by television, we do not think that the novelty of the specific findings should be a primary concern. We know from psychoanalysis that the reasoning, 'But we know all this!' is often a defence. This defence is made in order to dismiss insights as irrelevant because they are actually uncomfortable and make life more difficult for us than it already is by shaking our conscience when we are supposed to enjoy the 'simple pleasures of life'. The investigation of the television problems we have here indicated and illustrated by a few examples selected at random demands, most of all, taking seriously notions dimly familiar to most of us by putting them into their proper context and perspective and by checking them by pertinent material. We propose to concentrate on issues of which we are vaguely but uncomfortably aware, even at the expense of our discomfort's mounting, the further and the more systematically our studies proceed. The effort here required is of a moral nature itself: knowingly to face psychological mechanisms operating on various levels in order not to become blind and passive victims. We can change this medium of far-reaching potentialities only if we look at it in the same spirit which we hope will one day be expressed by its imagery.

Notes

1 David Riesman (1950) *The Lonely Crowd*, New Haven, p. v.
2 The evolution of the ideology of the extrovert has probably also its long history, particularly in the lower types of popular literature during the nineteenth century when the code of decency became divorced from its religious roots and therewith attained more and more the character of an opaque taboo. It seems likely, however,that in this respect the triumph of the films marked the decisive step. Reading as an act of perception and apperception probably carries with it a certain kind of internalization; the act of reading a novel is fairly close to a *monologue interieur*. Visualization in modern mass media makes for externalization. The idea of inwardness, still maintained in older portrait painting through the expressiveness of the face, gives way to unmistakable optical signals that can be grasped at a glance. Even if a character in a movie or television show is not what he appears to be, his appearance is treated in such a way as to leave no doubt about his true nature. Thus a villain who is not presented as a brute must at least be 'suave,' and his repulsive slickness and mild manner unambiguously indicate what we are to think of him.

3   It should be noted that the tendency against 'erudition' was already present at the very beginning of popular culture, particularly in Defoe who was consciously opposed to the learned literature of his day, and has become famous for having scorned every refinement of style and artistic construction in favor of an apparent faithfulness to 'life'.

4   One of the significant differences seems to be that in the eighteenth century the concept of popular culture itself moving toward an emancipation from the absolutistic and semi-feudal tradition had a progressive meaning, stressing autonomy of the individual as being capable of making his own decisions. This means, among other things, that the early popular literature left space for authors who violently disagreed with the pattern set by Richardson and, nevertheless, obtained popularity of their own. The most prominent case in question is that of Fielding, whose first novel started as a parody of Richardson. It would be interesting to compare the popularity of Richardson and Fielding at that time. Fielding hardly achieved the same success as Richardson. Yet it would be absurd to assume that today's popular culture would allow the equivalent of a *Tom Jones*. This may illustrate the contention of the 'rigidity' of today's popular culture. A crucial experiment would be to make an attempt to base a movie on a novel such as Evelyn Waugh's *The Loved One*. It is almost certain that the script would be rewritten and edited so often that nothing remotely similar to the idea of the original would be left.

5   The more rationality (the reality principle) is carried to extremes, the more its ultimate aim (actual gratification) tends, paradoxically, to appear as 'immature' and ridiculous. Not only eating, but also uncontrolled manifestations of sexual impulses tend to provoke laughter in audiences – kisses in motion pictures have generally to be led up to, the stage has to be set for them, in order to avoid laughter. Yet mass culture never completely succeeds in wiping out potential laughter. Induced, of course, by the supposed infantilism of sensual pleasures, laughter can largely be accounted for by the mechanism of repression. Laughter is a defence against the forbidden fruit.

6   This relationship again should not be oversimplified. No matter to what extent modern mass media tend to blur the difference between reality and the aesthetic, our realistic spectators are still aware that all is 'in fun'. It cannot be assumed that the direct primary perception of reality takes place within the television frame of reference, although many movie-goers recall the alienation of familiar sights when leaving the theatre: everything still has the appearance of being part of the movie plot. What is more important is the interpretation of reality in terms of psychological carry-overs, the preparedness to see ordinary objects as though some threatening mystery were hidden behind them. Such an attitude seems to be syntonic with mass delusions such as suspicion of omnipresent graft, corruption, and conspiracy.

7   It could be argued that this very ridicule expresses that this boy is not meant to represent the artist but just the 'dope'. But this is probably too rationalistic. Again, as in the case of the schoolteacher, official

respect for culture prevents caricaturing the artist as such. However, by characterizing the boy, among other things by his writing poetry, it is indirectly achieved that the artistic activities and silliness are associated with each other. In many respects mass culture is organized much more by way of such associations than in strictly logical terms. It may be added that quite frequently attacks on any social type seek protection by apparently presenting the object of the attack as an exception, while it is understood by innuendo that he is considered as a specimen of the whole concept.

Chapter seven

Transparencies on film

Children when teasing each other in their squabbles, follow the rule: no fair copycat. Their wisdom seems to be lost on the all too thoroughly grown-up adults. The Oberhauseners attacked the nearly sixty-year-old trash production of the film industry with the epithet 'Daddy's Cinema'. Representatives of the latter in turn could come up with no better retort than 'Kiddy's Cinema'. This cat, as once again the saying goes among children, does not copy. How pathetic to pit experience acquired during the adolescence of the medium. What is repulsive about Daddy's Cinema is its infantile character, regression manufactured on an industrial scale. The sophistry of the defenders insists on the very type of achievement the concept of which is challenged by the opposition. However, even if there were something to that reproach – if films that did not play along with business really were in some ways clumsier than the latter's smoothly polished wares – then the triumph would be pitiful. It would only demonstrate that those supported by the power of capital, technological routine and highly trained specialists could do better in some respects than those who rebel against the colossus and thus must necessarily forego the advantages of its accumulated potential. In this comparatively awkward and unprofessional cinema, uncertain of its effects, is inscribed the hope that the so-called mass media might eventually become something qualitatively different. While in autonomous art anything lagging behind the already established technical standard does not rate, *vis-à-vis* the culture industry – whose standard excludes everything but the predigested and the already integrated, just as the cosmetic trade eliminates facial wrinkles – works which have not completely mastered their technique, conveying as a result something consolingly uncontrolled and accidental, have a liberating quality. In them the flaws of a pretty girl's complexion become the corrective to the immaculate face of the professional star.

It is known that in the Torless film[1] large segments of Musil's early novel were incorporated into the dialogue almost unchanged. They are considered superior to the lines by the scriptwriters, which no living person would ever utter, and which in the meantime have been ridiculed by American critics. In their own way, however, Musil's sentences also tend to sound artificial as soon as they are heard, not read. This may be to some extent the fault of the novel which incorporates a type of rationalistic casuistry into the internal movement of its text under the guise of a psychology that the more progressive Freudian psychology of the period exposed as a rationalization. Nevertheless, this is hardly the whole point. The artistic difference between the media is obviously still greater than expected by those who feel able to avoid bad prose by adapting good prose. Even when dialogue is used in a novel, the spoken word is not directly spoken but is rather distanced by the act of narration – perhaps even by the typography – and thereby abstracted from the physical presence of living persons. Thus, fictional characters never resemble their empirical counterparts no matter how minutely they are described. In fact, it may be due to the very precision of their presentation that they are removed even further from empirical reality; they become aesthetically autonomous. Such distance is abolished in film: to the extent that a film is realistic, the semblance of immediacy cannot be avoided. As a result, phrases justified by the diction of narrative which distinguishes them from the false everydayness of mere reportage, sound pompous and inauthentic in film. Film, therefore, must search for other means of conveying immediacy: improvization which systematically surrenders itself to unguided chance should rank high among possible alternatives.

The late emergence of film makes it difficult to distinguish between technique and technology as clearly as is possible in music. In music up to the electronic period, the intrinsic technique – the sound structure of the work – was distinct from its performance, the means of reproduction. Film suggests the equation of technique and technology since, as Benjamin observed, the cinema has no original which is then reproduced on a mass scale: the mass product is the thing itself. This equation, however, is problematic, in film as well as in music. Experts in cinematographic techniques refer to the fact that Chaplin was either unaware of or purposely ignored these techniques, being content with the photographic rendering of sketches, slapstick routines or other performances. This in no way lowers Chaplin's status and one can hardly doubt that he was 'filmic'. Nowhere but on the screen could this enigmatic figure – reminiscent of old-fashioned photographs right from the start – have developed its concept. As a consequence, it appears impossible to derive norms of criticism from cinematographic technique as such. The most plausible theory of film technique, that which focuses on the movement of objects,[2] is both provocatively denied and yet preserved, in negative form, in the static character of films like Antonioni's *La Notte*. Whatever is 'uncinematic' in this film gives it the power to express, as if with hollow eyes, the emptiness of time. Irrespective of the technological origins of the cinema, the aesthetics of film will do better to base itself on a subjective mode of experience which film resembles and which constitutes its artistic character. A person who, after a year in the city, spends a few weeks in the mountains abstaining from all work, may unexpectedly experience colourful images of landscapes consolingly coming over him or her in dreams or daydreams. These images do not merge into one another in a continuous flow, but are rather set off against each other in the course of their appearance, much like the magic lantern slides of our childhood. It is in the discontinuity of that movement that the images of the interior monologue resemble the phenomenon of writing: the latter similarly moving before our eyes while fixed in its discrete signs. Such movement of interior images may be to film what the visible world is to painting or the acoustic world to music. As the objectifying recreation of this type of experience, film may become art. The technological medium par excellence is thus intimately related to the beauty of nature (*tief verwandt dem Naturschönen*).

   If one decides to take the self-censors more or less literally and confront films with the context of their reception, one will have to proceed more subtly than those traditional content analyses which, by necessity, relied primarily on the intentions of a film and neglected the potential gap between such intentions and their actual effect. This gap, however, is inherent in the medium. If according to the analysis of 'television as ideology' film accommodates various layers of behavioural response patterns, this would imply that the ideology provided by the industry, its officially intended models, may by no means automatically correspond to those that affect the spectators. If empirical communications research were finally to look for problems which could lead to some results, this one would merit priority. Overlapping the official models are a number of unofficial ones which supply the attraction yet are intended to be neutralized by the former. In order to capture the consumers and provide them with substitute satisfaction, the unofficial, if you will, heterodox ideology must be depicted in a much broader and juicier fashion than suits the moral of the story; the tabloid newspapers furnish weekly examples of such excess. One would expect the public's libido, repressed by a variety of taboos, to respond all the more promptly since these behavioural patterns, by the very fact that they are allowed to pass, reflect an element of collective approval. While intention is always directed against the playboy, the *dolce vita* and wild parties, the opportunity to behold them seems to be relished more than the hasty verdict. If today you can see in Germany, in Prague, even in conservative Switzerland and in Catholic Rome, everywhere, boys and girls crossing the streets locked in each others arms and kissing each other unembarrassed, then they have learned this, and probably more, from the films which peddle Parisian libertinage as folklore. In its attempts to manipulate the masses the ideology of the culture industry itself becomes as internally antagonistic as the very society which it aims to control. The ideology of the culture industry contains the antidote to its own lie. No other plea could be made for its defence.

The photographic process of film, primarily representational, places a higher intrinsic significance on the object, as foreign to subjectivity, than aesthetically autonomous techniques; this is the retarding aspect of film in the historical process of art. Even where film dissolves and modifies its objects as much as it can, the disintegration is never complete. Consequently, it does not permit absolute construction: its elements, however abstract, always retain something representational; they are never purely aesthetic values. Due to this difference, society projects into film quite differently – far more directly on account of the objects – than into advanced painting or literature. That which is irreducible about the objects in film is itself a mark of society, prior to the aesthetic realization of an intention. By virtue of this relationship to the object, the aesthetics of film is thus inherently concerned with society. There can be no aesthetics of the cinema, not even a purely technological one, which would not include the sociology of the cinema. Kracauer's theory of film which practises sociological abstention compels us to consider that which is left out in his book; otherwise anti-formalism turns into formalism. Kracauer ironically plays with the resolve of his earliest youth to celebrate film as the discoverer of the beauties of daily life: such a programme, however, was a programme of *Jugendstil* just as all those films which attempt to let wandering clouds and murky ponds speak for themselves are relics of *Jugendstil*. By choosing objects presumably cleansed of subjective meaning, these films infuse the object with exactly that meaning which they are trying to resist.

Benjamin did not elaborate on how deeply some of the categories he postulated for film – exhibition, test – are imbricated with the commodity character which his theory opposes. The reactionary nature of any realist aesthetic today is inseparable from this commodity character. Tending to reinforce, affirmatively, the phenomenal surface of society, realism dismisses any attempt to penetrate that surface as a romantic endeavour. Every meaning, including critical meaning, which the camera eye imparts to the film would already invalidate the law of the camera and thus violate Benjamin's taboo, conceived as it was with the explicit purpose of outdoing the provocative Brecht and thereby – this may have been its secret purpose – gaining freedom from him. Film is faced with the dilemma of finding a procedure which neither lapses into arts-and-crafts nor slips into a mere documentary mode. The obvious answer today, as forty years ago, is that of montage which does not interfere with things but rather arranges them in a constellation akin to that of writing. The viability of a procedure based on the principle of shock, however, raises doubts. Pure montage, without the addition of intentionality in its elements, does not derive intention merely from the principle itself. It seems illusory to claim that through the renunciation of all meaning, especially the cinematically inherent renunciation of psychology, meaning will emerge from the reproduced material itself. It may be, however, that the entire issue is rendered obsolete by the insight that the refusal to interpret, to add subjective ingredients, is in itself a subjective act and as such *a priori* significant. The individual subject who remains silent speaks not less but more through silence than when speaking aloud. Those film-makers ostracized for being too intellectual should, by way of revision, absorb this insight into their working methods. Nonetheless, the gap between the most progressive tendencies in the visual arts and those of film continues to exist, compromising the latter's most radical intentions. For the time being, evidently, film's most promising potential lies in its interaction with other media, themselves merging into film, such as certain kinds of music. One of the most powerful examples of such interaction is the television film *Antithese*[3] by composer Mauricio Kagel.

That, among its functions, film provides models for collective behaviour is not just an additional imposition of ideology. Such collectivity, rather, inheres in the innermost elements of film. The movements which the film presents are mimetic impulses which, prior to all content and meaning, incite the viewers and listeners to fall into step as if in a parade. In this respect, film resembles music just as, in the early days of radio, music resembled film strips. It would not be incorrect to describe the constitutive subject of film as a 'we' in which the aesthetic and sociological aspects of the medium converge. *Anything Goes*[4] was the title of a film from the 1930s with a popular English actress Gracie Fields; this 'anything' captures the very substance of film's formal movement, prior to all content. As the eye is carried along, it joins the current of all those who are responding to the same appeal. The indeterminate nature of this collective 'anything' (*Es*), however, which is linked to the formal character of film facilitates the ideological misuse of the medium: the pseudo-revolutionary blurring in which the phrase 'things must change' is conveyed by the gesture of banging one's fist on the table. The liberated film would have to wrest its *a priori* collectivity from the mechanisms of unconscious and irrational influence and enlist this collectivity in the service of emancipatory intentions.

Film technology has developed a series of techniques which work against the realism inherent in the photographic process. Among these are soft-focus shots – a long outdated arty custom in photography – superimpositions, and also, frequently, flashbacks. It is about time to recognize the ludicrousness of such effects and get rid of them because these techniques are not grounded in the necessities of individual works but in mere convention; they inform the viewer as to what is being signified or what needs to be added in order to comprehend whatever escapes basic cinematic realism. Since these techniques almost always contain some expressive – even if commonplace – values of their own, a discrepancy arises between expression and conventional sign. This is what gives these inserts the appearance of *kitsch*. Whether it creates the same effect in the context of montage and extradiegetic associations has yet to be examined. In any case, such cinematographic divagations require particular tact on the part of the film-maker. The lesson to be learned from this phenomenon is dialectical: technology in isolation, which disregards the nature of film as language, may end up in contradiction to its own internal logic. Emancipated film production should no longer depend uncritically upon technology (that is, the mere equipment of its profession) in the manner of a by no means still 'new objectivity' (*einer keineswegs mehr neuen Sachlichkeit*). In commercial film production, however, the aesthetic logic inherent in the material is caught in a stage of crisis even before it is given a chance to really unfold. The demand for a meaningful relationship between technique, material and content does not mix well with the fetishism of means.

It is undeniable that Daddy's Cinema indeed corresponds to what the consumers want, or, perhaps, rather that it provides them with an unconscious canon of what they do not want, that is, something different from what they are presently being fed. Otherwise, the culture industry could not have become a mass culture. The identity of these two phenomena, however, is not so beyond doubt as critical thought assumes as long as it focuses on the aspect of production and refrains from empirical analyses of reception. Nevertheless, the favourite argument of the whole- and half-hearted apologists, that culture industry is the art of the consumer, is untrue; it is the ideology of ideology. Even the reductive equation of the culture industry with the low art of all ages does not hold up. The culture industry contains an element of rationality – the calculated reproduction of the low – which, while certainly not missing in the low art of the past, was not its rationale. Moreover, the venerable roughness and idiocy of such hybrids of *circenses* and burlesque so popular during the late Roman empire do not justify the revival of such phenomena after they have become aesthetically and socially transparent. Even if considered apart from its historical perspective, the validity of the argument for consumer-oriented art can be attacked in the very present. Its proponents depict the relationship between art and its reception as static and harmonious, according to the principle of supply and demand, in itself a dubious model. Art unrelated to the objective spirit of its time is equally unimaginable as art without the moment which transcends it. The separation from empirical reality which pertains to the constitution of art from the outset requires precisely that moment. The conformity to the consumer, on the contrary, which likes to masquerade as humanitarianism, is nothing but the economic technique of consumer exploitation. Artistically, it means the renunciation of all interference with the syrupy substance of the current idiom and, as a result, with the reified consciousness of the audience. By reproducing the latter with hypocritical subservience, the culture industry changes this reified consciousness all the more, that is, for its own purposes: it actually prevents that consciousness from changing on its own, as it secretly and, deep down, unadmittedly desires. The consumers are made to remain what they are: consumers. That is why the culture industry is not the art of the consumer but rather the projection of the will of those in control onto their victims. The automatic self-reproduction of the status quo in its established forms is itself an expression of domination.

One will have observed that it is difficult, initially, to distinguish the preview of a 'coming attraction' from the main film for which one is waiting. This may tell us something about the main attractions. Like the previews and like the pop hits, they are advertisements for themselves, bearing the commodity character like a mark of Cain on their foreheads. Every commercial film is actually only the preview of that which it promises and will never deliver.

How nice it would be if, under the present circumstances, one could claim that the less films appear to be works of art, the more they would be just that. One is especially drawn to this conclusion in reaction to those snobbish psychological class A pictures which the culture industry forces itself to make for the sake of cultural legitimation. Even so, one must guard against taking such optimism too far: the standardized Westerns and thrillers – to say nothing of the products of German humour and the patriotic tear-jerkers (*Heimatschnulze*) – are even worse than the official hits. In integrated culture one cannot even depend on the dregs.

Notes

1 *Der junge Torless* (1965/66), a film by Volker Schlöndorff, based on Robert Musil, *Die Verwirrungen des Zöglings Torless* (translator's footnote).
2 Cf. Siegfried Kracauer (1960) *Theory of Film: The Redemption of Physical Reality*, New York: Oxford University Press, pp. 41ff.
3 *Antithese: Film for one performer with electronic and everyday sounds* (1965); first broadcast April 1, 1966 by NDR III, Hamburg (translator's footnote).
4 *Anything Goes* (1936; Paramount), directed by Lewis Milestone, with Bing Crosby, Ethel Merman, Grace Bradley (sic!) and others; songs by Cole Porter (translator's footnote).

Chapter eight

Free time

The question concerning free time, what people do with it and what opportunities could eventually evolve from it, must not be posed as an abstract generalisation. Incidentally the expression 'free time' or 'spare time' originated only recently – its precursor, the term 'leisure' (*Muße*) denoted the privilege of an unconstrained, comfortable lifestyle, hence something qualitatively different and far more auspicious – and it indicates a specific difference, that of time which is neither free nor spare, which is occupied by work, and which moreover one could designate as heteronomous. Free time is shackled to its opposite. Indeed the oppositional relation in which it stands imbues free time with certain essential characteristics. What is more, and far more importantly, free time depends on the totality of social conditions, which continues to hold people under its spell. Neither in their work nor in their consciousness do people dispose of genuine freedom over themselves. Even those conciliatory sociologies which use the term 'role' as a key recognize this fact, in so far as the term itself, borrowed from the domain of the theatre, suggests that the existence foisted upon people by society is identical neither with people as they are in themselves nor with all that they could be. Of course one should not attempt to make a simple distinction between people as they are in themselves and their so-called social roles. These roles affect the innermost articulation of human characteristics, to such an extent that in the age of truly unparalleled social integration, it is hard to ascertain anything in human beings which is not functionally determined. This is an important consideration for the question of free time. It means to say that even where the hold of the spell is relaxed, and people are at least subjectively convinced that they are acting of their own free will, this will itself is shaped by the very same forces which they are seeking to escape in their hours without work. The question which today would really do justice to the phenomenon of free time would be following: what becomes of

162

free time, where productivity of labour continues to rise, under persisting conditions of unfreedom, that is, under relations of production into which people are born, and which prescribe the rules of human existence today just as they always have done? Free time has already expanded enormously in our day and age. And this expansion should increase still further, due to inventions in the fields of automation and atomic power, which have not yet been anywhere like fully exploited. If one were to try and answer the question without ideological preconceptions, one could not avoid the suspicion that 'free time' is tending toward its own opposite, and is becoming a parody of itself. Thus unfreedom is gradually annexing 'free time', and the majority of unfree people are as unaware of this process as they are of the unfreedom itself.

I should like to elucidate the problem with the help of a trivial experience of my own. Time and time again, when questioned or interviewed, one is asked about one's hobbies. When the illustrated weeklies report on the life of one of those giants of the culture industry, they rarely forego the opportunity to report, with varying degrees of intimacy, on the hobbies of the person in question. I am shocked by the question when I come up against it. I have no hobby. Not that I am the kind of workaholic, who is incapable of doing anything with his time but applying himself industriously to the required task. But, as far as my activities beyond the bounds of my recognised profession are concerned, I take them all, without exception, very seriously. So much so, that I should be horrified by the very idea that they had anything to do with hobbies – preoccupations with which I had become mindlessly infatuated merely in order to kill the time – had I not become hardened by experience to such examples of this now widespread, barbarous mentality. Making music, listening to music, reading with all my attention, these activities are part and parcel of my life; to call them hobbies would make a mockery of them. On the other hand I have been fortunate enough that my job, the production of philosophical and sociological works and university teaching, cannot be defined in terms of that strict opposition to free time, which is demanded by the current razor-sharp division of the two. I am however well aware that in this I enjoy a privilege, with both the element of fortune and of guilt which this involves: I speak as one who has had the rare opportunity to follow the path of his own intentions and to fashion his work accordingly. This is certainly one good reason why there is no hard and fast opposition between my work itself and what I do apart form it. If free time really was to become just that state of affairs in which everyone could enjoy what was once the prerogative of a few – and compared to feudal society bourgeois society has taken some steps in this direction – then I would picture it after my own experience of life outside work, although given different conditions, this model would in its turn necessarily alter.

If we suppose with Marx that in bourgeois society labour power has become a commodity in which labour is consequently reified, then the expression 'hobby' amounts to a paradox: that human condition which sees itself as the opposite of reification, the oasis of unmediated life within a completely mediated total system, has itself been reified just like the rigid distinction between labour and free time. The latter is a continuation of the forms of profit-oriented social life. Just as the term 'show business' is today taken utterly seriously, the irony in the expression 'leisure industry' has now been quite forgotten. It is widely known but no less true therefore that specific leisure activities like tourism and camping revolve around and are organised for the sake of profit. At the same time the difference between work and free time has been branded as a norm in the minds of people, at both the conscious and the unconscious level. Because, in accordance with the predominant work ethic, time free of work should be utilized for the recreation of expended labour power, then work-less time, precisely because it is a mere appendage of work, is severed from the latter with puritanical zeal. And here we come across a behavioural norm of the bourgeois character. On the one hand one should pay attention at work and not be distracted or lark about; wage labour is predicated on this assumption and its laws have been internalized. On the other hand free time must not resemble work in any way whatsoever, in order, presumably, that one can work all the more effectively afterwards. Hence the inanity of many leisure activities. And yet, in secret as it were, the contraband of modes of behaviour proper to the domain of work, which will not let people out of its power, is being smuggled into the realm of free time. In earlier times children were allotted marks for attentiveness in their school reports. This had its corollary in the subjective, perhaps even well-meaning worries of adults that the children should not overstrain themselves in their free time; not read too much and not stay awake too late in the evening. Secretly parents sensed a certain unruliness of mind which was incompatible with the efficient division of human life. Besides, the prevalent ethos is suspicious of anything which is miscellaneous, or heterogeneous, of anything which has not clearly and unambiguously been assigned to its place. The rigorous bifurcation of life enjoins the same reification, which has now almost completely subjugated free time.

This subjugation can be clearly seen at work in the hobby ideology. The naturalness of the question of what hobby you have, harbours the assumption that you must have one, or better still, that you should have a range of different hobbies, in accordance with what the 'leisure industry' can supply. Organized freedom is compulsory. Woe betide you if you have no hobby, no pastime; then you are a swot or an old-timer, an eccentric, and you will fall prey to ridicule in a society which foists upon you what your free time should be. Such compulsion is by no means merely external in character. It is linked to the inner needs of people in the functional system. Camping – an activity so popular amongst the old youth movements – was a protest against the tedium and convention of bourgeois life. People had to 'get out', in both senses of the phrase. Sleeping out beneath the stars meant that one had escaped from the house and from the family. After the youth movements had died out this need was then harnessed and institutionalized by the camping industry. The industry alone could not have forced people to purchase its tents and dormobiles, plus huge quantities of extra equipment, if there had not already been some longing in people themselves; but their own need for freedom gets functionalized, extended and reproduced by business; what they want is forced upon them once again. Hence the ease with which the free time is integrated; people are unaware of how utterly unfree they are, even where they feel most at liberty, because the rule of such unfreedom has been abstracted from them.

Taken in its strict sense, in contradistinction to work, as it at least used to apply in what would today be considered an out-dated ideology, there is something vacuous (Hegel would have said abstract) about the notion of free time. An archetypal instance is the behaviour of those who grill themselves brown in the sun merely for the sake of a sun-tan, although dozing in the blazing sunshine is not at all enjoyable, might very possibly be physically unpleasant, and certainly impoverishes the mind. In the sun-tan, which can be quite fetching, the fetish character of the commodity lays claim to actual people; they themselves become fetishes. The idea that a girl is more erotically attractive because of her brown skin is probably only another rationalization. The sun-tan is an end in itself, of more importance than the boy-friend it was perhaps supposed to entice. If employees return from their holidays without having acquired the mandatory skin tone, they can be quite sure their colleagues will ask them the pointed question, 'Haven't you been on holiday then?' The fetishism which thrives in free time, is subject to further social controls. It is obvious that the cosmetics industry with its overwhelming and ineluctable advertisements, is a contributory factor here, but people's willingness to ignore the obvious is just as great.

The act of dozing in the sun marks the culmination of a crucial element of free time under present conditions – boredom. The miracles which people expect from their holidays or from other special treats in their free time, are subject to endless spiteful ridicule, since even

165

here they never get beyond the threshold of the eversame: distant places are no longer – as they still were for Baudelaire's *ennui* – different places. The victim's ridicule is automatically connected to the very mechanisms which victimize. At an early age Schopenhauer formulated a theory of boredom. True to his metaphysical pessimism he teaches that people either suffer from the unfulfilled desires of their blind will, or become bored as soon as these desires are satisfied. The theory well describes what becomes of people's free time under the sort of conditions of heteronomy, and which in new German tends to be termed *Fremdbestimmtheit* (external determination). In its cynicism Schopenhauer's arrogant remark that mankind is the factory product of nature also captures something of what the totality of the commodity character actually makes man into. Angry cynicism still does more honour to human beings than solemn protestations about man's irreducible essence. However, one should not hypostatize Schopenhauer's doctrine as something of universal validity or even as an insight into the primal character of the human species. Boredom is a function of life which is lived under the compulsion to work, and under the strict division of labour. It need not be so. Whenever behaviour in spare time is truly autonomous, determined by free people for themselves, boredom rarely figures; it need not figure in activities which cater merely for the desire for pleasure, any more than it does in those free time activities which are reasonable and meaningful in themselves. Even fooling about need not be crass, and can be enjoyed as a blessed release from the throes of self-control. If people were able to make their own decisions about themselves and their lives, if they were not caught up in the realm of the eversame, they would not have to be bored. Boredom is the reflection of objective dullness. As such it is in a similar position to political apathy. The most compelling reason for apathy is the by no means unjustified feeling of the masses that political participation within the sphere society grants them, and this holds true for all political systems in the world today, can alter their actual existence only minimally. Failing to discern the relevance of politics to their own interests, they retreat from all political activity. The well-founded or indeed neurotic feeling of powerlessness is intimately bound up with boredom: boredom is objective desperation. It is also, however, symptomatic of the deformations perpetrated upon man by the social totality, the most important of which is surely the defamation and atrophy of the imagination (*Phantasie*). Imagination is suspected of being only sexual curiosity and longing for the forbidden by the spirit (*Geist*) of a science which is no longer spirit. Those who want to adapt must learn increasingly to curb their imagination. For the most part the very development of the imagination is crippled by the experience of early childhood. The lack of imagination which is cultivated and inculcated by society renders people helpless in their free time. The impertinent question of what people should do with the vast amount of free time now at their disposal – as if it was a question of alms and not human rights – is based upon this very unimaginativeness. The reason why people can actually do so little with their free time is that the truncation of their imagination deprives them of the faculty which made the state of freedom pleasurable in the first place. People have been refused freedom, and its value belittled, for such a long time that now people no longer like it. They need the shallow entertainment, by means of which cultural conservatism patronizes and humiliates them, in order to summon up the strength for work, which is required of them under the arrangement of society which cultural conservatism defends. This is one good reason why people have remained chained to their work, and to a system which trains them for work, long after that system has ceased to require their labour.

Under prevailing conditions it would erroneous and foolish to expect or to demand that people should be genuinely productive in their free time; for productivity – the ability to bring forth something that was not already there – is the very thing which has been eradicated from them. At best what they then produce in free time is scarcely better than the ominous hobby – the imitation of poems or pictures which, given the almost irrevocable division of labour, others could do better than these amateurs (*Freizeitler*). What they create has something superfluous about it. This superfluousness makes known the inferior quality of the product, which in turn vitiates any pleasure taken in its production.

Even the most superfluous and senseless activity undertaken in people's free time is integrated in society. Once again a social need is at work. Certain forms of service, in particular domestic servants, are dying out; demand is disproportionate to supply. In America only the really wealthy can afford to keep servants, and Europe is following close behind. This means that many people carry out activities which were formerly delegated. The slogan 'do it yourself' latches onto this as practical advice. However, it also latches on to the resentment which people feel towards mechanization, which unburdens people, without – and not the fact itself but only its current interpretation is a matter of dispute – their having any use for the newly acquired time. Thus, once again in the interests of certain specialized industries, people are encouraged to perform tasks, which others could do more simply and more proficiently for them, and which for this very reason, deep down, they must despise. Actually, the idea that one can save the money one spends on services, in a society based upon the division of labour, belongs to a very old level of bourgeois consciousness;

it is an economy made from stubborn self-interest, an economy which flies in the face of the fact that it is only the exchange of specialized skills which keeps the whole mechanism going in the first place. William Tell, the obnoxious paradigm of absolute individuality, proclaimed that the household axe spared the need for the carpenter – indeed a whole ontology of bourgeois consciousness could be compiled from Schiller's maxims.

'Do it yourself', this contemporary type of spare time behaviour fits however into a much more far-reaching context. More than thirty years ago I described such behaviour as 'pseudo-activity'. Since then pseudo-activity has spread alarmingly, even (and especially) amongst those people who regard themselves as anti-establishment. Generally speaking there is good reason to assume that all forms of pseudo-activity contain a pent-up need to change the petrified relations of society. Pseudo-activity is misguided spontaneity. Misguided, but not accidentally so; because people do have a dim suspicion of how hard it would be to throw off the yoke that weighs upon them. They prefer to be distracted by spurious and illusory activities, by institutionalized vicarious satisfactions, than to face up to the awareness of how little access they have to the possibility of change today. Pseudo-activities are fictions and parodies of the same productivity which society on the one hand incessantly calls for, but on the other holds in check and, as far as the individual is concerned, does not really desire at all. Productive free time is only possible for people who have outgrown their tutelage, not for those who under conditions of heteronomy, have become heteronomous for themselves.

Free time then does not merely stand in opposition to labour. In a system where full employment itself has become the ideal, free time is nothing more than a shadowy continuation of labour. As yet we still lack an incisive sociology of sport, and particularly of the spectator. Nevertheless one hypothesis, amongst others, springs to mind; namely that, by dint of the physical exertion exacted by sport, by dint of the functionalization of the body in team-activity, which interestingly enough occurs in the most popular sports, people are unwittingly trained into modes of behaviour which, sublimated to a greater or lesser degree, are required of them by the work process. The accepted reason for playing sport is that it makes believe that fitness itself is the sole, independent end of sport: whereas fitness for work is certainly one of the covert ends of sport. Frequently it is in sport that people first inflict upon themselves (and celebrate as a triumph of their own freedom) precisely what society inflicts upon them and what they must learn to enjoy.

Let me say a little more on the relation of free time and the culture industry. Since Horkheimer and I coined the term more than thirty years ago, so much has been written about this means of domination and integration, that I should like to pick out a particular problem, which at the time we were not able to gain a proper perspective on. The ideology critic, dealing with the culture industry, and working on the premise that the standards of the culture industry are the ossified standards of what was formerly entertainment and low art, has the tendency to believe that the culture industry totally and utterly dominates and controls both the conscious and the unconscious of those people at whom it is directed – the same people out of whose taste during the liberal era the culture industry grew. Nevertheless there is reason to believe that production regulates consumption in the process of mental life, just as it does in that of material life, especially where the former has so closely approximated the latter, as it has in the culture industry. One would have thought the culture industry was perfectly adapted to its consumers. But since the culture industry has meanwhile become total – itself a phenomenon of the eversame, from which it promises temporarily to divert people – it is doubtful whether the culture industry and consumer-consciousness can be simply equated with one another. A few years ago at the Frankfurt Institute for Social Research we conducted a study devoted to this problem. Unfortunately, the full analysis of this material was postponed in favour of more pressing tasks. Nevertheless a passing inspection of it does reveal something which might well be relevant to the so-called problem of free time. The study concerned the wedding of Princess Beatrix of Holland with the junior German diplomat Claus von Amsberg. The objective was to assess the reactions of the German public to the wedding, which was broadcast by all the mass media, dwelt on incessantly by the illustrated weeklies, and so consumed by the public in their free time. Since the way in which the event was presented, like the articles written about it, accorded it an unusual degree of importance, we expected the spectators and readers to treat it just as seriously. In particular we expected to observe the operation of the characteristic contemporary ideology of personalization; through which, as a clear compensation for the functionalization of reality, the value of individual people and private relationships is immeasurably overestimated in comparison to actual social determinants. I should now like to say with due caution, that these expectations were too simplistic. In fact the study offers a virtually text book example of how critical-theoretical thought can both learn from and be corrected by empirical social research. It was possible to detect symptoms of a split consciousness. On the one hand people enjoyed it as a concrete event in the here and now quite unlike anything else in their everyday life: it was to be a 'unique experience' (*einmalig*) to use a cliché beloved of modern German. To

169

this extent the reaction of the audience corresponded to the familiar pattern, according to which even the relevant, possibly political news was transformed into a consumer item by the way in which the information was transmitted. The format of our interview, however, was devised in such a way that the questions concerned with determining the immediate reactions of the viewers, were supplemented by control questions about the political significance that the interviewees ascribed to the grand event. Here it turned out that many of the people interviewed – we shall ignore the exact proportion – suddenly showed themselves to be thoroughly realistic, and proceeded to evaluate critically the political and social importance of the same event, the well publicized once-in-a-lifetime nature of which they had drooled over breathlessly in front of their television sets. What the culture industry presents people with in their free time, if my conclusions are not too hasty, is indeed consumed and accepted, but with a kind of reservation, in the same way that even the most naive theatre or filmgoers do not simply take what they behold there for real. Perhaps one can go even further and say that it is not quite believed in. It is obvious that the integration of consciousness and free time has not yet completely succeeded. The real interests of individuals are still strong enough to resist, within certain limits, total inclusion. That would concur with the social prediction that a society, whose inherent contradictions persist undiminished, cannot be totally integrated even in consciousness. Society cannot have it all its own way, especially not in free time, which does indeed lay claim to people, but by its very nature still cannot totally claim them without pushing them over the edge. I shall refrain from spelling out the consequences; but I think that we can here glimpse a chance of maturity (*Mündigkeit*), which might just eventually help to turn free time into freedom proper.

Chapter nine

Resignation

We older representatives of that for which the name Frankfurt School has established itself have recently had the reproach of resignation levelled against us. We had, it is stated, developed elements of a critical theory of society, but we were not prepared to draw the practical consequences from this theory. We neither designed programmes for action nor did we support the actions of those who felt themselves inspired by critical theory. I shall sidestep the question whether this demand can be made at all upon theoretical thinkers who always remain to a certain degree sensitive and by no means unshakable instruments. The task assigned such individuals within a society characterized by the division of labour might indeed be questionable; they themselves might well be deformed by it. But they have also been formed by it. And there is no way in which they can repeal that which they have become merely through an act of their own will. I should not want to deny the impulse of subjective weakness inherent in the confinement to theory. The objection raised against us can be stated approximately in these words; a person who in the present hour doubts the possibility of radical change in society and who for that reason neither takes part in nor recommends spectacular, violent action is guilty of resignation. He does not consider the vision of change which he once held capable of realization; indeed, he actually had no true desire to see it realized in the first place. In leaving conditions as they are, he offers his tacit approval of them.

Distance from praxis is disreputable in the eyes of everyone. Anyone who does not take immediate action and who is not willing to get his hands dirty is the subject of suspicion; it is felt that his antipathy toward such action was not legitimate, and further that his view has even been distorted by the privileges he enjoys. Distrust of those who distrust praxis extends from those on the opposite side, who repeat the old slogan, 'We've had enough of talking' all the way to the objective spirit of advertising, which propagates the picture – it's called *Leitbild* or 'image as motif' – of the actively involved human being, no matter whether his activity lies in the realm of economics or athletics. One should take part. Whoever restricts himself to thinking but does not get involved is weak, cowardly and virtually a traitor. This hostile cliché on the intellectual is to be encountered with deep roots within that branch of the opposition that is in turn reviled as intellectual without any awareness thereof on their part. Thinking activists answer; among the things to be changed is that very separation of theory and praxis. Praxis is essential if we are ever to be liberated from the domination of practical people and practical ideals. The trouble with this view is that it results in the prohibition of thinking. Very little is needed to turn the resistance against re-pression repressively against those who – little as they might wish to glorify their state of being – do not desert the standpoint that they have come to occupy. The often-evoked unity of theory and praxis has a tendency to give way to the predominance of praxis. Numerous views define theory itself as a form of repression – as though praxis did not stand in a far more direct relationship to repression. For Marx, the dogma of this unity was animated by the immanent possi-bility of action which even then was not to be realized. Today it is rather the opposite situation that prevails. One clings to action be-cause of the impossibility of action. But Marx himself reveals a con-cealed wound in this regard. He no doubt delivered the eleventh thesis on Feuerbach in such an authoritarian fashion because he was not at all sure of it himself. In his youth he had demanded the 'ruth-less criticism of everything that exists'. Now he mocked criticism. But his famous joke about the Young Hegelians, his coinage 'critical criticism', was a dud and went up in smoke as nothing but a tautology. The forced precedence of praxis brought the criticism which Marx himself practised to an irrational halt. In Russia and in the orthodoxy of other countries, the malicious mockery of critical criticism became the instrument that permitted the status quo to establish itself in such horrifying fashion. The only meaning that praxis retained was this: increased production of the means of production. The only criti-cism still tolerated was that people still were not working hard enough. This demonstrates how easily the subordination of theory to praxis results in the support of renewed repression.

Repressive intolerance toward a thought not immediately accom-panied by instructions for action is founded in fear. Unmanipulated thought and the position that allows nothing to be deduced from this thought must be feared because that which cannot be admitted is per-fectly clear: this thought is right. An aged bourgeois mechanism with which the men of the Enlightenment of the eighteenth century were very familiar displays itself anew but unchanged: suffering caused by a negative condition – in this case by obstructed reality – turns into anger toward the person who expresses it. Thought, enlightenment conscious of itself, threatens to disenchant pseudo-reality within which, according to Habermas' formulation, activism moves. This activism is tolerated only because it is viewed as pseudo-activity. Pseudo-activity is allied with pseudo-reality in the design of a subjective position; an activity that overplays itself and fires itself up for the sake of its own publicity without admitting to what degree it serves as a substitute for satisfaction, thus elevating itself to an end in itself. All those behind bars are despondent in their desire to be released. In such situations one no longer thinks or thinks only in fictive postulates. Within absolutized praxis, only reaction is possible and for this reason the reaction is false. Only thinking could offer an escape, and then only that thinking, the results of which are not pre-scribed – as is so frequently the case in those discussions in which it is predetermined who is right and which therefore do not advance the cause – but rather degenerate without fail into tactics. When the doors are barricaded, it is doubly important that thought not be interrupted. It is rather the task of thought to analyse the reasons behind this situation and to draw the consequences from these reasons. It is the responsibility of thought not to accept the situation as finite. If there is any chance of changing the situation, it is only through undiminished insight. The leap into praxis will not cure thought from resignation as long as it is paid for with the secret knowledge that this course is simply not the right one.

Generally speaking, pseudo-activity is the attempt to preserve en-claves of immediacy in the midst of a thoroughly mediated and ob-durate society. This process is rationalized through the acceptance of any small change as one step on the long way toward total change. The unfortunate model for pseudo-activity is the 'do-it-yourself' syn-drome – activities that do that which has long been done better through the means of industrial production and which arouse in un-free individuals, hampered in their spontaneity, the confident feeling that they are of central concern. The nonsense of the 'do-it-yourself' approach to the production of material goods and in the making of many repairs is equally obvious. However, it is not total. In view of the reduction of so-called services – sometimes superfluous in terms of technical standards – measures taken by a private person fulfil a semi-rational purpose. In politics, however, the 'do-it-yourself' atti-tude is not of quite the same character. The society that confronts human beings in such an impenetrable manner is these humans themselves. Confidence in the limited action of small groups is remi-niscent of the spontaneity which atrophies beneath the encrusted to-tality and without which this totality cannot be transformed into something different. The administered world has a tendency to strangle all spontaneity or at least to channel it into pseudo-activity. This, however, is not achieved so totally without difficulty as the agents of the administered world would like to imagine. Nonetheless, spontaneity is not to be absolutized – just as little as it is to be separated from the objective situation and idolized in the same manner as is the administered world itself. Otherwise the axe will break down the next door in the house – a process which never spares the carpenter – and the riot squad will appear on the spot. Political acts of violence can also sink to the level of pseudo-activity, resulting in mere theatre. It is hardly a wonder that the ideal of direct action and propaganda glorifying the deed have been resurrected, upon the heels of the willing integration of formerly progressive organizations that, in all lands of the earth, manifest the character of that against which they were once directed. This process, however, has not weakened the criticism of anarchism, the return of which is the return of a ghost. The impatience toward theory manifested in this return does nothing to advance thought beyond itself. Theory falls behind the thought which it forgets.

For the individual, life is made easier through capitulation to the collective with which he identifies. He is spared the cognition of his impotence; within the circle of their own company, the few become many. It is this act – not unconfused thinking – which is resignation. No transparent relation prevails between the interests of the ego and the collective to which it assigns itself. The ego must abrogate itself, if it is to share in the predestination of the collective. Explicitly a remnant of the Kantian categorical imperative manifests itself: your signature is required. The feeling of a new security is purchased with the sacrifice of autonomous thinking. The consolation that thought within the context of collective action is an improvement proves deceptive: thinking, employed only as the instrument of action, is blunted in the same manner as all instrumental reason. At the present moment, no higher form of society is concretely visible: for that reason, anything that seems in easy reach is regressive. According to Freud, however, whoever regresses has not achieved the goal of his drives. Objectively viewed, reformation is renunciation, even if it considers itself the opposite and innocently propagates the pleasure principle.

In contrast, the uncompromisingly critical thinker, who neither superscribes his conscience nor permits himself to be terrorized into action, is in truth the one who does not give up. Furthermore, thinking is not the spiritual reproduction of that which exists. As long as thinking is not interrupted, it has a firm grasp upon possibility. Its insatiable quality, the resistance against petty satiety, rejects the foolish wisdom of resignation. The Utopian impulse in thinking is all the stronger, the less it objectifies itself as Utopia – a further form of regression – whereby it sabotages its own realization. Open thinking points beyond itself. For its part, such thinking takes a position as a figuration of praxis which is more closely related to a praxis truly involved in change than in a position of mere obedience for the sake of praxis. Beyond all specialized and particular content, thinking is actually and above all the force of resistance, alienated from resistance only with great effort. This emphatic concept of thinking is by no means secure; no security is granted it by existing conditions nor by the ends yet to be attained nor by any type of organized force. Whatever was once thought, however, can be suppressed; it can be forgotten and can even vanish. But it cannot be denied that something of it survives. For thinking has the momentum of the general. What has been cogently thought must be thought in some other place and by other people. This confidence accompanies even the loneliest and most impotent thought. Whoever thinks is without anger in all criticism:[1] thinking sublimates anger. Because the thinking person does not have to inflict anger upon himself, he furthermore has no desire to inflict it upon others. The happiness visible to the eye of a thinker is the happiness of mankind. The universal tendency toward suppression goes against thought as such. Such thought is happiness, even where unhappiness prevails; thought achieves happiness in the expression of unhappiness. Whoever refuses to permit this thought to be taken from him has not resigned.

Notes

1 This sentence was recently used in *Der Spiegel* (1977, 43: 214) as the headline for a brief article on the relationship of the Frankfurt School to terror as recently manifested in the German Federal Republic.

Name index

Subject index